Postwar British Literature and Po Studies

Postcolonial Literary Studies

Series Editors: David Johnson, The Open University and Ania Loomba, University of Pennsylvania

Published titles:

Medieval Literature and Postcolonial Studies, Lisa Lampert-Weissig
Renaissance Literature and Postcolonial Studies, Shankar Raman
Eighteenth-century British Literature and Postcolonial Studies,
   Suvir Kaul
Victorian Literature and Postcolonial Studies, Patrick Brantlinger
Postwar British Literature and Postcolonial Studies, Graham MacPhee

Forthcoming titles:

Romantic Literature and Postcolonial Studies, Elizabeth A. Bohls
Modernist Literature and Postcolonial Studies, Rajeev Patke

Visit the Postcolonial Literary Studies website at
www.euppublishing.com/series/epls

Postwar British Literature and Postcolonial Studies

Graham MacPhee

Edinburgh University Press

© Graham MacPhee, 2011

Edinburgh University Press Ltd
22 George Square, Edinburgh

www.euppublishing.com

Typeset in 10.5/13 Sabon
by Servis Filmsetting Ltd, Stockport, Cheshire, and
printed and bound in Great Britain by
CPI Antony Rowe, Chippenham and Eastbourne

A CIP record for this book is available from the British Library

ISBN 978 0 7486 3900 7 (hardback)
ISBN 978 0 7486 3901 4 (paperback)

The right of Graham MacPhee
to be identified as author of this work
has been asserted in accordance with
the Copyright, Designs and Patents Act 1988.

Contents

In Memoriam Ian W. MacPhee
1921–2006

Series Editors' Preface

Postcolonial Literary Studies foregrounds the colonial and neo-colonial contexts of literary and cultural texts, and demonstrates how these texts help to understand past and present histories of empires. The books in the series relate key literary and cultural texts both to their historical and geographical moments, and to contemporary issues of neo-colonialism and global inequality. In addition to introducing the diverse body of postcolonial criticism, theory and scholarship in literary studies, the series engages with relevant debates on postcolonialism in other disciplines – history, geography, critical theory, political studies, economics and philosophy. The books in the series exemplify how post-colonial studies can reconfigure the major periods and areas of literary studies. Each book provides a comprehensive survey of the existing field of scholarship and debate with a time line, a literature survey, discussion of key critical, theoretical, historical and political debates, case studies providing exemplary critical readings of key literary texts and guides to further reading. At the same time, each book is also an original critical intervention in its own right. In much the same way that feminism has redefined how all literary texts are analysed, our ultimate aim is that this series will contribute to all texts in literary studies being read with an awareness of their colonial and neo-colonial resonances.

DJ and AL

Acknowledgements

I owe a debt of thanks to many people over the years who have discussed the issues and ideas raised here with me, including Desmond Bailey, Graham White, Prem Poddar, Conor McCarthy, Paul Maltby, Jed Esty, John Marx, Leili Kashani, Anjali Kamat and Mustafa Gundogdu. I would like to thank all those at the 2007–8 Penn Humanities Forum at the University of Pennsylvania for their responses to and thoughts on my project, especially Warren Breckman, Lisa Mitchell, Llyd Wells and Iliana Pagán Teitelbaum. I would also like to thank Michele Gregory for her kind invitation to the Women and Society Seminar at Columbia University. A special debt of thanks is owed to Susan Alice Fischer for her generous and always insightful discussion. I am also very grateful to all the participants in the National/Transnational/Global Cultures Research Group at West Chester University, and especially Carolyn Sorisio, Hyoejin Yoon and Eleanor Shevlin. And I owe an even wider debt of thanks to all the students at West Chester University who have taken classes with me on British literature and postcolonial studies.

I am grateful to the Faculty Development Committee and the College of Arts and Sciences at West Chester University for their support. An earlier version of part of Chapter 3 appeared in *College Literature* 38.1, and I am grateful for permission to include it here.

I would like to thank Ania Loomba and David Johnson for their invaluable and insightful contribution as series editors, and Jackie Jones at Edinburgh University Press. I am grateful to them all for their patience and good humour in working on the project.

Finally, I would like to thank Sally Eberhardt for everything.

Timeline

Date	Historical Events	Literary and Other Publications
1921	Irish War of Independence ends; Faisal bin Al-Hussein installed as king of Iraq by the British following the military suppression of the Iraqi Revolt	
1922	Irish Civil War and the creation of the Irish Free State	James Joyce, *Ulysses*; T.S. Eliot, *The Waste Land*
1924		E.M. Forster, *A Passage to India*
1925		Virginia Woolf, *Mrs Dalloway*
1928		Leonard Woolf, *Imperialism and Civilisation*
1930	Gandhi begins the Salt March, which leads to the Civil Disobedience Movement	
1931	Statute of Westminster grants effective independence to white settler-colonies, formally establishing the British Commonwealth of Nations	
1934		George Orwell, *Burmese Days*

1935		Mulk Raj Anand, *Untouchable*
1936	Revolt in Palestine against British rule – over 1,000 Palestinians killed	C.L.R. James, *Minty Alley*
1938		C.L.R. James, *The Black Jacobins*; George Orwell, *Homage to Catalonia*
1939	World War II begins; signing of the Hitler–Stalin Pact	
1941	United States enters World War II	Virginia Woolf, *Between the Acts*
1942	'Quit India' Movement launched – Gandhi and majority of the Indian National Congress leadership imprisoned; Japan captures Singapore and Burma	
1943–4	Famine in Bengal results in an estimated 3 million people dying of starvation	
1944	Creation of the International Monetary Fund and World Bank at the Bretton Woods Conference	
1945	War ends in Europe; US drops nuclear bombs on Hiroshima and Nagasaki and Japan surrenders; independence struggle in Vietnam leads to France's attempt to reimpose colonial rule and nine years of war (–1954); Fifth Pan-African Congress held in Manchester	T.S. Eliot, *The Four Quartets*; Evelyn Waugh, *Brideshead Revisited*
1946	The violent right-wing Zionist group, the Irgun, bombs British headquarters at the King David Hotel in Jerusalem; Winston Churchill delivers his 'Iron Curtain' speech	W.E.B. du Bois, *The World and Africa*

1947	Partition and independence of India and Pakistan	
1948	Burma and Ceylon (Sri Lanka) gain independence; Afrikaner Nationalist Party takes power in South Africa and imposes apartheid policy; British withdraw from Palestine as the State of Israel is declared and an estimated 700,000 Palestinians become refugees; docking of *SS Empire Windrush*; guerrilla war against British rule in Malaya begins, leading to twelve years of war (–1960); United Nations General Assembly adopts the Universal Declaration of Human Rights	G.V. Desani, *All About H. Hatterr*; Graham Greene, *The Heart of the Matter*
1949		George Orwell, *1984*
1950	US–Korean War begins	Aimé Césaire, *Discourse on Colonialism* (first English translation 1953); Doris Lessing, *The Grass is Singing*
1951		Hannah Arendt, *The Origins of Totalitarianism*
1952	Anticolonial Mau Mau rebellion in Kenya begins and state of emergency is declared	Frantz Fanon, *Black Skin, White Masks*; Sam Selvon, *A Brighter Sun*
1953		George Lamming, *In the Castle of My Skin*
1954	French defeat at Dien Bien Phu signals end of French military involvement in South East Asia	George Lamming, *The Emigrants*

1955	Bandung Conference of independent African and Asian states creates Non-Aligned Movement; beginning of military campaign for the end of British rule in Cyprus	Graham Greene, *The Quiet American*
1956	Britain, France, and Israel temporarily invade Egypt (the 'Suez Crisis'); Sudan gains independence from Britain and Egypt; USSR topples the independent socialist government of Hungary	Anthony Burgess, *Time for a Tiger* (first volume of *The Malayan Trilogy*); Sam Selvon, *The Lonely Londoners*
1957	Ghana and peninsular Malaya gain independence	Albert Memmi, *The Coloniser and the Colonised*
1958	Riots in Notting Hill and Nottingham	
1959	Anti-British riots in Northern Rhodesia (Zambia) and Nyasaland (Malawi); carnival organised by Claudia Jones in St Pancras Town Hall gives birth to the Notting Hill Carnival	Frantz Fanon, *A Dying Colonialism*; John Arden, *Serjeant Musgrave's Dance*
1960	British Prime Minister Harold Macmillian's 'Wind of Change' speech; Sharpeville Massacre in South Africa	George Lamming, *The Pleasures of Exile*
1961		Frantz Fanon, *The Wretched of the Earth*
1963		C.L.R. James, *Beyond a Boundary*
1964	Nyasaland (Malawi), Northern Rhodesia (Zambia) and Malaya gain independence; African National Congress (ANC) leaders Nelson Mandela and Walter Sisulu receive life sentences and are imprisoned on Robben Island	

1965	Minority white government in Rhodesia (Zimbabwe) signs the Unilateral Declaration of Independence from Britain	
1966	Barbados, Bechuanaland (Botswana), British Guiana (Guyana) and Basutoland (Lesotho) gain independence; armed struggle begins in Zimbabwe	Jean Rhys, *Wide Sargasso Sea*
1967	British withdrawal from Aden	V.S. Naipaul, *The Mimic Men*
1968	Tet Offensive in Vietnam; Enoch Powell's 'Rivers of Blood' speech; USSR suppresses 'Prague Spring' in Czechoslovakia	
1969	British troops sent to Northern Ireland following the Nationalist uprising in Derry	
1970		J.G. Farrell, *Troubles*
1971	Bahrain gains independence; collapse of the Sterling Area; withdrawal of British troops from Trucial States and Muscat and Oman; independent state of Bangladesh established after civil war between East and West Pakistan	
1972	Bloody Sunday – fourteen civilians killed by British troops in Derry	Buchi Emecheta, *In the Ditch*
1973	'Oil crisis' begins as OPEC members raise world oil prices and administer cuts in production; Bretton Woods system breaks down and world gold standard collapses	J.G. Farrell, *The Siege of Krishnapur*
1974		Buchi Emecheta, *Second-Class Citizen*

1975	Vietnam War ends in US defeat	Linton Kwesi Johnson, *Dread Beat and Blood*; Seamus Heaney, *North*
1976	Soweto uprisings begin in South Africa	
1978		Stuart Hall et al. (eds), *Policing the Crisis*; Edward Said, *Orientalism*
1979	Iranian Revolution deposes the Shah and installs Ayatollah Khomeini as supreme leader; Margaret Thatcher elected prime minister; USSR invades Afghanistan	
1980		Brian Friel, *Translations*; Linton Kwesi Johnson, *Inglan is a Bitch*
1981	Belize gains independence; riots in Toxteth, Moss Side and Brixton	Salman Rushdie, *Midnight's Children*; Mulk Raj Anand, *Conversations in Bloomsbury*
1982	Falklands/Malvinas War begins	Salman Rushie, 'The New Empire within Britain'; Center for Contemporary Cultural Studies, *The Empire Strikes Back*
1983		Benedict Anderson, *Imagined Communities*; Sam Selvon, *Moses Migrating*
1984		Harold Pinter, *One for the Road*

1985–6	Miners Strike	David Dabydeen (ed), *The Black Presence in English Literature*; Hanid Kureishi, *My Beautiful Laundrette*; Caryl Phillips, *The Final Passage*; Tony Harrison, *V*
1987		Paul Gilroy, *There Ain't No Black in the Union Jack*
1988	USSR withdraws from Afghanistan	Salman Rushie, *The Satanic Verses*; Harold Pinter, *Mountain Language*; Stuart Hall, *The Hard Road to Renewal*
1989	Fall of the Berlin Wall and collapse of Soviet bloc; Tiananmen Square protests in China	Janet Abu-Lugbod, *Before European Hegemony*; Ashcroft, Griffith and Tiffin (eds), *The Empire Writes Back*; James Kelman, *A Disaffection*; Kazuo Ishiguro, *The Remains of the Day*
1990	Nelson Mandela released from prison; Namibia gains independence	Hanif Kureishi, *The Buddha of Suburbia*; Ambalavaner Sivanandan, *Communities of Resistance*
1991	First Gulf War begins	
1993		Paul Gilroy, *The Black Atlantic*; Moniza Alvi, *The Country at My Shoulder*; Samuel Huntingdon, 'The Clash of Civilisations'

1994	Democratic elections in South Africa result in Nelson Mandela's election to presidency	Abdulrazak Gurnah, *Paradise*; Homi Bhabha, *The Location of Culture*
1995		David Dabydeen, *Turner*; Hanif Kureishi, *The Black Album*
1997	Hong Kong returned to China by Britain; 'New Labour' victory in British General Election	
1998	Good Friday Agreement signed, leading to the end of direct British rule of the Six Counties of the North of Ireland the following year	
2000	Establishment of the Scottish Parliament and the National Assembly of Wales	Zadie Smith, *White Teeth*; Kazuo Ishiguro, *When We Were Orphans*, Bhikhu Parekh, *The Future of Multi-Ethnic Britain*
2001	Attack on World Trade Center (9/11); riots in Oldham, Bradford and other northern towns in response to racial attacks on British-Asian communities, unemployment and de facto racial segregation	Abdulrazak Gurnah, *By the Sea*; James Kelman, *Translated Accounts*
2002		Linton Kwesi Johnson, *Mi Revalueshanary Fren*; Maggie Gee, *The White Family*
2003	US and Britain invade Iraq; an estimated 1 million people march against the war in London	Monica Ali, *Brick Lane*

2004		Andrea Levy, *Small Island*; James Kelman, *You Have to Be Careful in the Land of the Free*; David Peace, *GB84*
2005	July 7th bombings in London underground; last British citizens freed from the US prison at Guantanamo Bay	Leila Aboulela, *Minaret*; Abdulrazak Gurnah, *Desertion*; Ian McEwan, *Saturday*; Harold Pinter, 'Art, Truth, and Politics'; Victoria Brittain and Gillian Slovo, *Guatanamo: Honor Bound to Defend Freedom*
2008		Nadeem Aslan, *The Wasted Vigil*; Amitav Ghosh, *Sea of Poppies*; Caryl Phillips, *In the Falling Snow*
2010	Official end of US combat operations in Iraq, although US military forces and bases remain; British and US military operations continue in Afghanistan	Andrea Levy, *The Long Song*

Introduction

She's illegal, so deport her
Said the Empire that brought her
> (Benjamin Zephaniah, 'The Death of Joy Gardner', 1996)

Early on a summer morning in 1993, six police officers burst into the home of Joy Gardner, a forty-year-old Jamaican woman living in London. Joy Gardner had been refused permission to remain in Britain even though her son had been born there and her mother had resident status. In front of her five-year-old son, the officers forced her to the floor and bound her in a leather body belt and manacles, winding thirteen feet of adhesive tape around her mouth to stop her screaming. She was taken to hospital in a coma but never recovered. Three of the police officers were later acquitted of charges of manslaughter after claiming that Ms Gardner was the most violent woman they had ever dealt with. Benjamin Zephaniah's poem about Joy Gardner's killing communicates not only its brutality and the human reality of her loss, but also the larger paradoxes and contradictions which it brought to light. Joy Gardner, who as the poem notes was a 'Christian', 'was over here' because the 'Bible sent us everywhere / To make Great Britain great'; that is, because of the imperialist ideologies that justified slavery and colonialism in the name of 'civilisation', Christianity and the spread of 'free trade' (Zephaniah 1996: 12). But now that that history has passed, the presence of Joy Gardener and others no longer considered part of that 'us' becomes an inexplicable and threatening presence, such an outrage against decency and the good order of the nation as to become criminal: 'She's illegal, so deport her / Said the Empire that brought her' (Zephaniah 1996: 11). In these two lines Zephaniah encapsulates a paradox that is central to this study: that while the very parameters of postwar British society and culture are the product of its violent and exploitative imperial history, the dominant perspectives that have emerged from and been shaped by that history conceive it as utterly disconnected from the present – as fundamentally past, and so as proof of how imperially innocent that present has become.

The terms of this paradox are complex, multiple and contradictory, and require that we register contrary historical tendencies without resolving them into a single sum or conclusion, and that we understand that any impulse may simultaneously move in a number of different directions. As Paul Gilroy argues, there is a significant dimension of 'conviviality' in contemporary Britain, 'an ordinary, demotic multi-culturalism' which emerges from 'the processes of cohabitation and interaction' and which has 'made multiculture an ordinary feature of social life in Britain's urban areas' (Gilroy 2005: 99, xv). But at the same time he argues that the diffuse and variegated texture of everyday life in Britain – in many ways an achievement to be celebrated – can coalesce into an exclusive national community that excludes others not explicitly on the old grounds of biological race, but on the basis of their perceived cultural alienness, unassimilability or menace: as 'bogus asylum seekers' or 'illegal immigrants', as Islamic 'fundamentalists' and potential 'terrorists', as work-shy 'benefit cheats' and 'scroungers', as insular communities unwilling to integrate and learn the language, or simply under the abstract and impersonal rubric of 'security threat' (2005: 141). For Gilroy, an important element in this unstable and confused condition is the remarkable amnesia about imperial history and the accompanying lack of self-awareness concerning Britain's continuing international role, a lack buttressed by the persistent insistence in popular culture on national 'greatness' (2005: 89–98). Alongside the achievement of 'conviviality' stands what Gilroy refers to as 'post-imperial melancholia', a 'complex' pathology that marks the persistence of aspects of the social, political and cultural logics of imperialism precisely in its disavowal or forgetting.

This broader cultural assessment is important for understanding the approach adopted by this book. While the legacy of empire remains central to British culture in significant ways, the uneven and incomplete process of decolonisation blocks or occludes an adequate recognition of this enduring impact, displacing and scattering such recognition into a range of tropes and affective constructions that permeate the wider culture. Therefore, rather than restricting the relevance of postcolonial studies to a particular body of writing by authors from British colonies and their descendants, this study argues that all postwar British literature needs to be read with a consciousness of the continuing relevance of that imperial legacy. This requires a sensitivity to the displaced and often submerged ways in which this legacy informs conceptions of individual and collective identity and agency, and may continue to set the terms for mapping the social landscape and imagining its future possibilities. This is not to extend the definition 'postcolonial' to all and everything, but to argue that the range of ideas, identities, histories and potentials articulated by what has been recognised as postcolonial literature needs to be understood as much more central to postwar British literature and culture than has previously been understood.

In this spirit, this book offers an accessible overview of how the literature and culture of the period is informed by and responds to colonisation, decolonisation and Britain's subsequent global role. Equally, it introduces and assesses many of the key intellectual frameworks associated with postcolonial studies that have sought to interpret this interplay. At the same time, it also offers an original argument and mode of critique that pursues a holistic approach to literary texts and cultural shifts by insisting on their location within a multilayered nexus of political, social, economic and military histories. This approach was axiomatic to anticolonial intellectuals like Aimé Césaire, Frantz Fanon and C.L.R. James, whose efforts engendered the field we now call postcolonial studies. Thus, while this is indeed a literary and cultural study, it also draws on scholars and thinkers from other disciplines, and will look to place its textual readings within larger social, political and economic frameworks. This is not, however, an encyclopedic history, and nor does it offer an exhaustive survey of all the authors, styles, movements or concerns that might reasonably be gathered under the headings of either postcolonial studies or postwar British literature.

The structure of this book responds to the uneven and contradictory nature of this post-imperial predicament. Chapter 1 seeks to reassess the structural significance of decolonisation, which has in popular consciousness often been reduced to a punctual moment associated with the end of Britain's Indian Empire in 1947 or with the national humiliation of the Suez Crisis in 1956. Instead, the chapter identifies decolonisation as a more dispersed, multidirectional and contradictory process that permeates the period up to 1971. This focus responds to the 'cautionary note' that Dominic Head picks up from James English concerning the recent tendency to focus on literary developments after 1979, and the consequent risk of excluding the social, political and cultural impacts of Britain's changing international role as it unfolded in the preceding decades (Head 2008: 23; see English 2006: 1–15). However, it also suggests that the rubric of 'decolonisation' or 'the end of empire' needs to be understood as enabling Britain's insertion within a new structuring of global hegemony (or world system) under United States leadership, as much as it involves a relinquishing of independent imperial ambitions. In tracing something of the complex continuities and transformations that characterised the modernist literary culture of the interwar period, this chapter establishes how the postwar articulation of 'the nation' and its continuing imbrication in a much wider world is bound up with understandings of English as both a territorially bounded language and the new global *lingua franca*.

Chapter 2 considers some of the key critical debates and theoretical frameworks that inform contemporary approaches to the literature and culture of post-imperial Britain. However, this chapter is also conceived as extending the historical coverage of Chapter 1, since the central theoretical movements and terms now operative largely emerged in the period since the 1970s. This chapter offers an overview of the emergence and institutionalisation of postcolonial studies in Britain, as well as a consideration of its relationship to an earlier moment of cultural criticism associated with the British Cultural Studies of the late 1950s and 1960s. It critically examines some of the different ways in which a number of the concerns central to postcolonial studies – including migrancy, diaspora, subjectivity, race, agency, political orientation and global capitalism – have been articulated in a specifically British context, and explores how the particularities of Britain's postwar historical predicament may themselves offer important insights into such larger theoretical frameworks. The chapter concludes with an interrogation of some of the central terms of this field, including the fundamental concepts of the 'nation' and of 'globalisation', and raises the question of the suitability and relevance of 'national literature' and 'postcolonial studies' as analytical paradigms.

Chapter 3 provides a series of critical readings of selected literary works that concretely dramatise or interrogate the central concerns, historical developments, debates and ideas of the book. This selection is not in any way meant to be representative or comprehensive, nor to imply a kind of alternative canon. Rather, each of the texts has been chosen for its particular capacity to open up critical dialogue with the preceding chapters through its historical location, its aesthetic and formal qualities, and its thematic and political concerns. While Chapter 1 focuses on the ability of literary texts and cultural discourses to encode – perhaps unconsciously – larger historical and political predicaments and to articulate new ideological 'solutions' to them, the final chapter focuses on the potential for literary works to challenge dominant modes of perception and interpretation, and to imagine other possible worlds and different possible futures.

Chapter 1

Rethinking the End of Empire

In 1919 the British Empire was at its greatest extent; by 1970 it had all but disappeared. The question that might reasonably be asked is why such an apparently historically transitory phenomenon should be relevant not only to the decades immediately after World War II, but to us today in the opening decades of the twenty-first century. This very question was posed by Salman Rushdie in 1982 in a prescient but at the time deeply controversial essay, 'The New Empire within Britain', written at a moment when the popular political discourse of Thatcherism claimed to recover the 'greatness' of Victorian Britain, but without recalling the history of imperialism that had attended it. 'After all,' Rushdie writes, 'surely the one thing we can confidently say about that roseate age of England's precedence, when the map of half the world blushed with pleasure as it squirmed beneath Pax Britannica, is that it's over, isn't it?' (Rushdie 1991: 129). But as his closing question suggests, and as the essay goes on convincingly to argue, history does not deal so neatly with the past's 'being over'. Indeed, the perception of it all being 'over', the essay argues, is itself a recent and laboured construction of the ex-imperial metropolis, one replete with its own set of tropes and conventions that present a picture of the finality and punctuality of the end of imperialism, and its redundancy and irrelevance to a world that is thoroughly new and unconnected with this outmoded past.

This sense of the continuing effectivity of European imperialism is central to the critical project of Edward Said, often seen as one of the founding figures of postcolonial studies. Said argues that 'Imperialism did not end, did not suddenly become "past," once decolonization had set in motion the dismantling of the classic empires' (Said 1993: 282). However transitory the European empires may seem in retrospect (and they will increasingly seem so), they supervised an enormous global reorganisation, including the large scale redeployment of global resources, the structural transformation of economic, legal, social and political forms, the redrawing of political and social demarcations, the transfer of peoples on a massive scale, the dissemination of European culture and its educational and technical models across the globe, and the ingestion by Europe and the United States ('the West') of at least versions of a myriad of cultures, practices, ideas and knowledges conceived as 'non-Western'. And whatever disputes there may be about specific benefits or gains associated with European imperialism, it bequeathed a world marked by a massive and enduring imbalance: on the one hand, the extraordinary enrichment of the West and the concentration of political, economic and military power in its hands; on the other, the structural underdevelopment of non-Western economies (now often referred to as the 'global South'), the destabilising and in many cases the liquidation of indigenous societies and cultures (and indeed whole populations), the creation or intensification of ethnic divisions, and environmental degradation on a catastrophic scale (Lazarus 2004: 19–40). We would be wise, then, to be sceptical that such a penetrating period of historical transformation might so easily be 'over', and might instead look for its continuing impacts – what the German philosopher Walter Benjamin would call its 'after lives' – not only 'out there' in the former colonies and semi-colonies, but also 'in here', within the erstwhile imperial metropolitan centres such as Britain (Benjamin 1996).

This chapter takes Said's concern for the after lives of empire seriously, and questions the punctuality and finality of decolonisation in the decades after World War II. Even while recognising the profound importance of Britain's forced exit from South Asia in 1947, we must be cautious in taking this date – or indeed any other punctual moment – as marking the onset of a uniform period of decolonisation (Connor 1996: 86–7). On such a view, the debacle of the Suez Crisis of 1956, when Britain was forced by the Eisenhower administration to withdraw its invasion force from Egypt, is sometimes seen as a final moment of reckoning when Britain was forced to accept what was obvious to all others, namely that imperial thinking was already out of date. This uniform and unidirectional process of decolonisation is seen in cultural terms to provoke a parallel disengagement from the world overseas and to engender a widespread provincialism, which turned its back on the global and focused almost exclusively on the national and the local (Head 2008: 30–1). Where the empire is featured in what was at the time considered 'mainstream' British literature – as in the work of such writers as Graham Greene, Anthony Burgess, George Orwell and Evelyn Waugh – it therefore appears as a self-enclosed and backwards looking trend, the province of ex-colonial officers and bureaucrats whose memories of colonial life dramatise the loss of Britain's global ambitions and underline the rapid contraction of the cultural imaginary to an insular and shrunken world. Where the legacy of empire is seen as more dynamic and forward looking is rather in the writing of colonial and ex-colonial migrants to Britain, whose work was at the time considered as marginal and even external to the national culture, but which has rightly now come to be regarded as creating the basis for the multi-cultural literary culture that we recognise today.

There is certainly some truth in this picture – and especially in the dynamic and long lasting impact of colonial and ex-colonial migrants and of their descendants on British culture and literature both before and after World War II. However, in this chapter I will argue that we need to complicate this history by challenging the homogeneity and completeness of the process of decolonisation, and by questioning the supposed marginality of global involvement and international power in British literature and culture right up to the 1970s. In fact, as economic and political historians point out, the two decades after World War II saw a renewed commitment to empire, although the focus had now shifted away from South Asia and towards the Middle East, South East Asia and Southern and East Africa. But rather than simply being a rerun of earlier modes of imperialism, this 'second colonial occupation' as it is sometimes termed, functioned as a transitional process that integrated British overseas power into the new international order under US hegemony (Cain and Hopkins 1993: 277). In the words of John Springhall, over a period of about two decades, 'the British Empire was internationalized then dismantled', providing a mechanism for integrating strategically important ex-colonies into the new world system dominated by the United States (Springhall 2001: 12). Or understood within the longer perspective provided by Giovanni Arrighi in *The Long Twentieth Century*, British imperialism as one 'world system' – or configuration of globalisation – was superseded by a new world system centred on the United States, which built on the British world system as well as borrowing from earlier forms of globalisation (Arrighi 1994: 58–84). In occluding the complexity of this transition, cultural and literary histories risk ignoring the complex and contradictory ways in which, as Gautam Premnath argues, 'decolonization is an incomplete rather than a superseded project' (Premnath 2000: 59).

As a result, this chapter will focus on the period up to 1970, and will tend to consider the writing of canonical or what were then considered 'mainstream' literary and cultural voices. Although, as Kaplan and Kelly observe, there 'could have been no era of decolonization without the pressure on European empires of sustained anticolonial movements', our discussion will necessarily centre on British responses to that anti-imperialist dynamic, and in particular on how Britain sought to manage and direct the process of decolonisation, rather than on the agency of national liberation struggles themselves (Kaplan and Kelly 2004: 140).[1] Despite this strategic limitation (and assuming that we keep it in mind), our approach is nonetheless valuable in the present context because it complicates straightforward accounts of imperial withdrawal in two ways. First, it shows how decolonisation, while an epochal achievement and a real victory for national liberation movements, was also part of a larger reformulation of Western global hegemony; and second, it identifies how global involvement continued to be a key element in postwar British culture, albeit in transformed and often contradictory ways. But as well as complicating existing literary and cultural histories of the period, we should also complicate the linear thinking implicit in conceptions of decolonisation as punctual and final. To invoke the language of the German philosopher Ernst Bloch, we need to view decolonisation as 'nonsynchronous', as a process that is 'polyphonous', 'multitemporal' and 'multispatial' (Bloch 1977: 37–8).[2] For although we like to think of the 'here and now' as though it were homogeneous, we need to recognise that it harbours elements of other times and places within it, although in new and quite different configurations.

Beyond Bloomsbury

London's status as a global metropolis in the interwar period depended both on the wealth and resources accrued over more than three centuries of colonial expansion, and on its contemporary location within emerging economic and technological networks: this was the city of Barings Bank and *The Times* newspaper, but also of the Anglo-Persian Oil Company and the British Broadcasting Corporation (see North: 1999; Khalidi 2005: 83–4). Interwar London combined the legacy of Victorian imperialism with the incipient dynamism of a new regime of globalisation, a nonsynchronous combination that was the central concern of the Bloomsbury Group, a loose social network of artists, writers and intellectuals – including most famously Virginia and Leonard Woolf, E.M. Forster, Lytton Strachey and the economist J.M. Keynes – who were closely associated with aesthetic modernism and with a liberal, revisionist approach to Victorian culture and ideas. In Virginia Woolf's *Mrs Dalloway*, for example, this complex fusion of past and future defines the new shape of urban experience. While Peter Walsh finds his male ego confirmed by the imperial statuary of Trafalgar Square – 'the spectacular images of great soldiers stood looking ahead of them, as if they too had made the same renunciation' – the novel also records the uncanny ability of a sky-writing aeroplane to reorganise perception, shifting the attention of Londoners of all classes from monarchy, the traditional centre of imperial Victorian spectacle, to the language of mass advertising (Woolf 1981: 51, 21; see Wicke 1988).

If the modernism of Bloomsbury was aware of the entwinement of past and future modes of globalisation at work in the imperial metropolis, the writing of Mulk Raj Anand provides a valuable perspective on Bloomsbury itself by including it within the horizon of globalisation. Anand was to become an important Indian novelist, writing in an English that sought to capture the experience of Indian peasants and *dalits* (people excluded from the caste system); but he came to London in 1925 as an unknown student, having been imprisoned and beaten by the British for his anticolonial activism (Nasta 2002: 27–30; Anand 1983). He soon became familiar with the literary and artistic eminences of Bloomsbury, as well as a broader range of modernist writers who traversed London in the interwar period, including T.S. Eliot, D.H. Lawrence and Aldous Huxley. In his retrospective memoir, *Conversations in Bloomsbury*, Anand remarks on 'the undeclared ban on political talk' in the drawings rooms of Bloomsbury (Anand 1995: ix), and observes an unthinking acceptance of the British Empire by many London intellectuals (24), accompanied by 'lurking prejudices . . . about the East' (18).

These attitudes reflect the dominance of an imperial ideology that had emerged over centuries, but which, with the 'new imperialism' of the late nineteenth century, had come to define Britishness itself in terms of the imperial project (Metcalf 1995: 59–65; Catherine Hall 2000). Early twentieth-century imperial ideology was a syncretic construction, combining a liberal conception of progress with a conservative account of ingrained ethnic and racial differences. Its basis, as Thomas Metcalf explains, lay in the 'civilizing mission' of empire, its vocation to advance what were considered more 'backward' or 'developmentally arrested' cultures, and elevate their position on what the Victorian liberal philosopher John Stuart Mill called the 'ladder of civilization' (Metcalf 1995: 31). In this liberal view, 'contemporary European, and especially British, culture alone represented civilization', and since '[n]o other culture had any intrinsic validity', all were expected to transform themselves in order to progress towards that pinnacle. British culture was therefore cast as radically *universal*: as Metcalf observes, 'There was no such thing as "Western" civilization' because 'there existed only "civilization"', a universal set of ideas, perspectives, values and judgements embodied in British culture but applicable to all (1995: 34). However, against the implicit universality of this progressive view, which suggested that all people might potentially be the same given the right conditions, imperial ideology also stressed inherent differences between cultures that separated non-Europeans as fundamentally more 'primitive' and 'immature' from the achievements of the British, who represented the final, modern end of human development. As John Burrow put it, 'mankind was one not because it was everywhere the same, but because the differences represented different stages in the same process' (quoted in Metcalf 1995: 68). The British thus insisted that their colonial subjects were 'like children', and 'required a long process of tutelage before they could participate in the governance of their country' – although as Metcalf ironically notes, the 'tasks of the school master' were 'so broadly defined, and the level of competence for the pupil set so high' that the prospect of independence and adulthood seemed perpetually to recede into the distance (Metcalf 1995: 199–200).

However, notwithstanding this widespread acceptance of imperial ideology among intellectuals, Anand also identifies a more complex pattern of shifting attitudes that point to an increasing relativisation of Western culture and British identity in the wake of the extended experience of colonialism, an experience radicalised by the shocks of World War I and British defeat in its oldest colony, Ireland, in 1921. This contradictory pattern appears most starkly for Anand in the figure of T.S. Eliot, whose high estimation of Rudyard Kipling's jingoistic and imperialist fiction and poetry is accompanied by a defence of British rule in India and a dismissal of Gandhi as an 'anarchist', patriarchal attitudes towards women, and an aristocratic and anti-democratic politics (Anand 1995: 16, 44, 48). Yet at the same time, Eliot was sensitive to the disintegrative character of European modernity, which shatters collective affiliations and undermines the structures of tradition and belief that lend them a measure of stability, so relativising what had once seemed natural and all-encompassing. This relativised understanding of Western modernity was coupled with his conception of Hinduism and Buddhism as complex, ancient and autochthonous structures of belief. As a result – at least at this point in his career – Eliot could not help regarding European Christianity as just one body of 'myth' among others (Anand 1995: 136). For Anand, Eliot's modernism is rent by the conflict between its unconscious assumption of Western superiority and the relativising impulse that undermines the very basis for this assumption. Ultimately, Eliot 'solves' this contradiction through a familiar orientalising move, conceding exclusive ownership of the ground of culture whilst retaining unchallenged control of politics: responding to an Indian student's indictment of colonial injustice, Eliot recommends that 'the Indians should pursue their culture, and leave government to the British empiricists' (1995: 16).

However, as Anand recounts in his memoir he also met British intellectuals who explicitly rejected imperialism and its outright racism and authoritarianism, most notably Leonard Woolf and E.M. Forster. Woolf and Forster had both spent periods of time in the British Raj and were therefore aware of the violence and racism of colonialism, which they linked to Victorian sexual repression and the institutionalisation of a rigid and brutal masculinity in British elite (or 'Public') schools. Woolf, who had served as a colonial magistrate in Sri Lanka (then Ceylon), tells of a 'coolie woman' who was imprisoned and repeatedly raped by a British 'Planter Sahib', observing that 'I found our boys in the tea plantations . . . running riot . . . [D.H.] Lawrence is right. Their mothers told them they were born of sin – so they run amuck when they get the chance' (Anand 1995: 74). For Woolf, his own colonial experience made clear connections between a hierarchical and repressive society at home, colonial violence abroad, and the literary production that romanticised and justified this violence: he reflects that 'we go and compensate ourselves for our guilts by bossing other people', while in 'our Public schools they breed sadists like Kipling who talks of "lesser breeds without the law"' (1995: 75). In a more summative vein, Forster conjures a vision of Indian social life that sets imperial British culture in relief, delineating its texture and disposition through an act of parallax. The involvement of religious elements in the everyday creates a

> Miscellaneous hotchpotch. Everyone mucks in – gods and men . . . The Greeks lived like that . . . And perhaps the early Christians . . . Not that I believe in mumbo-jumbo, but the Indians have a way of unmasking the various selves. We are literal and stick stubbornly to the facial personality. We have mapped out the world – '
> 'And colored it pink,' added Leonard [Woolf]. (Anand 1995: 79–80)

The pattern of comparison here is certainly not without its orientalising dimension, but it nonetheless figures an alternative set of non-European cultural traditions as something more than intuitive, emotional or purely aesthetic. For Forster, there is both a social and an ontological gain in this heterogeneous vision of the indissolubility of sacred and profane.

Conversely, this expanded perspective renders the empiricist individualism of Western modernity as at once restrictive and exorbitant, locked in a spiritless materialism that reduces the otherness of social experience in an endless desire for conquest – the dream of a world map all 'colored ... pink'.

However, Anand's memoir does more than simply record the opinions of the leading literary intellectuals of the day; it also situates them within a different horizon of experience and understanding. For Forster and Woolf, the 'passage out' – from metropolitan centre to colonial periphery – allowed their own social location to be reconceptualised by relativising it as just one among many. Anand's 'passage back' – from colony to imperial centre – enabled the perception of a more dynamic interrelation, in which the colony does not simply reveal something about the metropolis that was already there, but points to the constitutive role of colonisation in constructing the ostensibly integral 'metropolis'. Anand was fascinated by the social institutionalisation of class differences in Britain – and indeed with racial segregation in the US – which provided a complex set of comparisons and isomorphs (involving both similarity and difference) with his own experience of caste and colonial domination in India (Anand 1995: 35–6). And notwithstanding the roster of eminent intellectuals he met in London, he was also keen to talk to members of the working class. Anand records that in a pub opposite the British Museum he befriended two transport workers, Bill Bland and Harry Tomkins, who had both served in the British Army in India, the latter having become an autodidact, socialist and Irish Republican. What had appeared in India as an integral and unified Britishness is now rendered as just one version among others within a politically divided and conflict-ridden class society (1995: 8); but further, the social and political conflicts within the 'centre' could be understood through reference to the structures of colonial domination. Unlike Eliot, Anand records that Bland and Tomkins are deeply unimpressed by Kipling's mythologising of imperialist soldiering: objecting to the implausible underestimation of indigenous military prowess in *Kim*, Tomkins exclaims 'What cheek – a little English boy commanding a hundred of those Pythons [Pashtuns]!' (1995: 84). But what strikes Anand more profoundly is Tomkins' ability to see the everyday assumptions and verities of British imperialist 'commonsense' as ideology – that is, a structuring of lived experience that remains within the parameters of understanding shaped by the demands of imperial nationalism and the interests of the dominant classes. '[Y]ou are inside the whale,' he says to his friend, referring to Bland's uncritical acceptance of ruling-class justifications of the beneficence of empire and its 'civilizing mission' (1995: 86).[3] In coming to see his own role in India as equivalent to the repressive violence of the Black and Tans, the notorious British militia in Ireland, Tomkins recasts his own affiliation to the social consensus, and makes the connection between the ruthless pursuit of class interest in imperialism and his own location as a worker in Britain (1995: 85).

This unsettling of the domestic in light of Britain's overseas empire forges a connection for Anand between the violent and exploitative relationships inherent in imperialism and the divided nature of class society within Britain: 'here men owned vast factories and planted their feet on the necks of others', he reflects, so that the imperialist model is replicated within the domestic space, with each capitalist becoming 'a John Bull who stood like a colossus on the map of the world' within their own sphere of exploitation (Anand 1995: 43). This image not only maps colonial exploitation onto domestic exploitation, but effects a reversal of the direction in traffic that belies the self-contained and integral nature of the imperial nation. John Bull, as image of imperial domination and aggressive masculine subjectivity, is returned to the shores of the British Isles to provide a model for the 'unity' and 'self-identity' of the nation. As C.L.R. James, the Trinidadian intellectual and activist, wrote in 1936, 'British imperialism does not govern only the colonies in its own interests', but also 'the British people' themselves (James 1992: 66). Such a model of the nation is structured around exploitation and domination, and therefore implies social fracture as its precondition, while its homology with and dependence on the colonial enterprise reveals its involvement in externality. The nation, then, is not homogeneous or identical to itself, but is the scene of political and class conflict which is in turn located within structures of domination that far exceed its borders.

This sense of the fractured and antagonistic nature of British society makes Anand's perceptions of London intellectual life particularly nuanced and sensitive to inconsistency and contradiction, even in the case of anti-imperialist intellectuals whom he admired, like Forster and Woolf. While both could grasp the injustice of colonialism, their sense of outrage was grounded in an ideal of a harmonious, organic national community whose values were being travestied. As Anand speculates, 'They probably still had, in spite of the industrial revolution, a nostalgia for "Merry Old England", of the days of beef-eating, drinking beer, and dancing around the Maypole' (Anand 1995: 46). Despite their real opposition to Eliot's conservative defence of empire and to Kipling's brutal masculinity, at least in this respect they had something in common with them (see Boehmer 2002: 169–214; Said 1993: 200–6).

Little England and Global Englishes

Anand's assessment of the canonical figures of London literary life before World War II helps to resituate accounts of postwar British cultural and literary history. If this history has previously been mapped as a series of responses to these canonical figures, securely located on the *terra firma* of the metropolis as centre of the known world, Anand's perspective helps to decentre that metropolis as self-contained source and engine of intellectual innovation and cultural change prior to the period of decolonisation (see Boehmer 2002: 1–33; Connor 1996: 83–5). A crucial dimension of recent literary scholarship has been to extend literary and cultural inquiry beyond the canon – to include non-canonical writers who hail from former colonies or are the descendants of colonial subjects – and indeed beyond the literary – to include writing regarded as 'non-literary', as well as other forms of popular culture. But as Anand's reflections suggest, we must avoid granting an integrity and autonomy to the canon itself; instead, we need to reframe and relocate the canon, depriving it of a secure location within a discrete and self-contained national culture and polity. From Anand's point of view, the innovations of metropolitan modernism were as much a response to the sense of vertiginous relativisation in the face of dynamics engendered elsewhere, as they were an expression of an 'autonomous' aesthetic, cultural or political dynamic. While a central concern of this study is to range beyond the established canon, we need also to relocate our sense of that canon within a different conception of political and social history, and to register a range of different literary and cultural dynamics that reach beyond them.

Anand was of course by no means the only intellectual to note the retroactive impact of colonialism upon the imperial metropolis, or what the Martinican anticolonial writer Aimé Césaire called in 1950 its 'boomerang effect' (Césaire 2000: 41). Nor, of course, was he the first colonial subject to live in Britain and contribute to its intellectual and cultural life. Since at least the eighteenth century non-European intellectuals, like the Africans Ignatius Sancho, Olaudah Equiano and Quobona Ottobah Cugoana, had been resident in Britain, often pursuing political activity as well as engaging in the cultural life of the imperial capital (Stein 2004: 4). Famously, Dadabhai Naoroji became the first Asian to be elected to the British Parliament in 1892. By the 1940s, Britain had become a key centre for non-European anglophone intellectuals from across the globe, with the Fifth Pan-African Congress being held in Manchester in 1945, which was attended by George Padmore, Kwame

Nkrumah and W.E.B. Du Bois among others, and which heralded the wave of decolonisation that would sweep the world after World War II. C.L.R James, moving between the Caribbean, the US and Britain, played a key role in articulating the relationship of socialism and anticolonialism in the postwar period, while some of the major voices writing in Britain from the 1930s through to the 1960s were from the colonies or ex-colonies – including Jean Rhys, G.V. Desani, Nirad Chaudhuri, Doris Lessing, Sam Selvon, George Lamming, Wole Soyinka and V.S. Naipaul. For those coming to Britain, arrival involved both cultural affiliation and critique, and Anand nicely captures this double attitude: 'though I might admire these English writers for their literary skills,' he reflects, 'I would fight for the freedom of my country forever' (Anand 1995: 24).

Two recent studies of British literature have placed decolonisation at the heart of understanding the legacy of modernism and subsequent postwar developments in British literature. In *A Shrinking Island: Modernism and National Culture in England*, Jed Esty relates the impending sense of imperial collapse to retrenchment within a localised English nationalism in the late work of Eliot and Virginia Woolf, a shift that anticipated the provincialism and withdrawal of much postwar British writing (Esty 2004). In *The Modernist Novel and the Decline of Empire*, John Marx argues that, on the contrary, modernism responded to the relativisation of Britishness associated with the globalising tendencies of colonialism, enabling a more flexible engagement with the emergent regime of globalisation associated with postwar US hegemony (Marx 2005). I would argue that the portrait of literary London offered by Anand demonstrates that these two tendencies are not in fact incompatible, but rather co-existed and in many ways reinforced one another.

In *A Shrinking Island*, Jed Esty sees the later work of T.S. Eliot and Virginia Woolf as marking a shift from the cosmopolitan or universal aspirations of an earlier moment of modernism to a particularised conception of national culture. Rather than seeking to encapsulate universal truths, their work looked instead to render the local character of an English culture that had been absent because – as the universal standard of colonialism's 'civilising project' – it was everywhere and nowhere, an abstract standard of civilisation, rationality and modernity without a location of its own (Esty 2004: 6). 'Eliot and his London contemporaries,' Esty writes, began 'to borrow the logic of cultural nationalism back from the colonies, adapting it for a belated brand of Anglocentric revivalism' (2004: 14). For Esty, then, decolonisation generates a compensatory retreat to an Anglocentric national culture, but crucially, its particularistic conception of Englishness is not in fact the expression of an integral and self-contained culture as it claims, but is itself derivative and dependent on the colonial history it abjures (2004: 27–8). Local comes to repudiate and exclude the global by using the very gestures and methodologies that were developed in the collapsing moment of imperial globalisation.[4]

In John Marx's *Modernist Novel*, the legacy of interwar British modernism moves in a fundamentally different direction. For Marx, while some writers did respond to the relativisation of British culture by 'seeking to preserve some sense of English authenticity', the broader historical significance of British modernism in fact lies in its capacity to 'imagin[e] the proliferation of local Englishes on a planet-wide scale' (2005: 10, 4). Modernism's pluralising of register and idiom accommodates a historical predicament in which English has become Scottished, Indianised, Africanised, creolised, Irished and Americanised, so that '"English" no longer names a series of monolithic ethno-linguistic entities, each of which reproduces the nation form of the others, but rather identifies a way to unify a number of competing English vernaculars through the logic of parallelism' (2005: 24). Thus, rather than reconstructing or repairing an 'inside' through the techniques once employed to regularise and make knowable a colonial 'outside' (as for Esty), for Marx 'modernist fiction swept aside the chiasmatic relationship between inside and out that had enabled the Victorian distinction between English and British' (Marx 2005: 16). Here, the globalisation of imperial British culture generates a localisation that does not coalesce in a single, insular Englishness, but through its relativisation 'helps us to imagine a loosely tied network of ongoing and reciprocal interaction between various English speakers' (2005: 20). While such a pluralisation of English is potentially opening and productive, the flexible logic of comparison and transferability it enables is also well suited for the co-ordination and management of localisation – which as Marx points out, was a key priority in establishing Western hegemony during the process of decolonisation (2005: 20–3). For the economist and Bloomsbury luminary J.M. Keynes, this logic anticipated a new global dispensation associated with US power, within which Britain could assume an important if subordinate role as 'Vice-Chairman, so to speak' (quoted in Marx 2005: 21). Indeed, Marx notes a wider 'tendency' at this time 'to conceive of American hegemony as a revision of British Empire' (2005: 23).

As we have seen in following Anand's memoir of interwar London, both the national retrenchment described by Esty and the transformative cosmopolitan identified by Marx are observable there. My suggestion is that taken together, these two accounts of the relativisation of an ostensibly universal imperial culture help to map the blocked and partial decolonisation of British post-imperial culture, understood as an 'incomplete . . . project' (Premnath 2000: 59). While Marx's emphasis is on the way in which localisation and relativisation spring-boarded British involvement in the new US world system, Esty's focus on nationalism indicates how that transnational involvement was articulated through a decidedly national framework, which often generated representations that occlude or deny that very transnationalism. Indeed, as Marx notes, if 'modernism laid the ground for the most utopian accounts of globalization . . . It also anticipated globalisation's neo-colonial aspects by identifying an English that was a cut above the rest' (Marx 2005: 4). This chapter attempts to trace significant tendencies in postwar culture by reading these two positions together, a project that in turn modifies and qualifies each of them.

Decolonisation and the Cold War: Auden's 'Fleet Visit'

The emergence of US global hegemony took place against the backdrop of the Cold War, the period of confrontation between the United States and the USSR that lasted from 1946 until the fall of the Soviet Union in 1991. The Cold War overdetermined the process of decolonisation and postcolonial nation-building, organising the political landscape around an all-consuming competition between ideologically defined blocs. Within this new paradigm, existing justifications of colonialism – as a 'civilising mission' or as a benign relation on the model of parent and child – collapsed in the face of the language of freedom, democracy and self-determination that became central to the rhetoric of all the Allied powers during World War II (Brennan 2006: 44, 46; Kaplan and Kelly 2004: 140). The American response to the new postwar landscape ran along a number of different tracks simultaneously. Immediately after the war, the United States oversaw the creation of an impressive framework of international legality centred on the United Nations, which not only introduced human rights norms at an individual level, but also outlawed colonial conquest at the level of interstate relations and promised all countries a formally equal status.[5] As the supreme guarantor of this new international regime (the 'leader of the Free World'), the US could present itself as the embodiment of the universal values of freedom and democracy, which meant that its geopolitical conflict with the USSR could be framed as an almost metaphysical conflict between freedom and democracy and an inexplicable and ahistorical totalitarian force bent on their total destruction (Hinds and Windt 1991: 246–51; see also Saunders 1999).

At the same time, the new framework of international law and the UN was accompanied by a redesigned international economic system – centred on the World Bank, the International Monetary Fund (IMF) and a set of trade protocols that would much later become the World Trade Organisation (WTO) – through which Western, and especially American, power was wielded over the former colonies and semi-colonies, now collectively termed 'the underdeveloped world'. In the words of Eugene Black, president of the World Bank, 'Economic aid should be the principal means by which the West maintains its political and economic dynamic in the underdeveloped world' (quoted in Prashad 2007: 9). Further, despite the formal ban on military aggression and the legal safeguards for national sovereignty, the US pursued a series of military interventions – often funding or supporting existing colonial powers, as in Indochina and Malaya – as well as coups and other covert actions, all of which were designed to destabilise popular national liberation movements and install governments aligned to its interests. However, as John Kelly and Martha Kaplan note, unlike the European empires before it, the US sought to 'develo[p] global military power' not in order 'to conquer and colonize other places but to ensure that doors stayed open and US interests were . . . respected' (Kaplan and Kelly 2004: 137). This new approach depended on the control of access to world markets, and so required a truly global military reach; but it tended not to require the occupation and formal control of foreign territories, working instead through proxy forces and the cultivation of client regimes, who were accorded economic privileges and supplied with advanced weaponry, logistical support and military know-how (Arrighi 1994: 276–81, 295–300).

The Cold War thus translated the binary global division of coloniser and colonised into a three-way split: in the terms famously coined by anticolonial journalist Albert Sauvy, into the First World of economically developed states, namely the United States, Western Europe, Japan and the former white settler colonies (Australia, Canada, New Zealand and South Africa); the Second World, of the USSR and countries aligned with it or under its dominance; and the Third World of residual colonies, newly independent states and other 'underdeveloped' states in Latin America, Africa and Asia (Prashad 2007: 6–9). As Kaplan and Kelly observe, the Cold War's tripartite global division amounted to 'a new kind of "Great Game"', in which the First and Second Worlds competed 'to win the hearts and minds of the elites of the . . . new nations', a 'rivalry [that] had devastating results in a series of decolonizing civil wars, from Korea to Malaya to Indochina to Central America and many points in Africa' (Kaplan and Kelly 2004: 140). Anticolonial struggle thus became enmeshed within the goals of the Cold War, which for the European colonial powers and their American backers meant the emergence of pro-Western and anti-communist successor states (Khalidi 2009: 159–200). But as Vijay Prashad explains, for the former colonies the predicament was seen quite differently: they sought not to further the aims of either the First or Second Worlds, but to escape the insidious logic of the Cold War itself, since alliance with either side meant the erosion of their newly won sovereignty and independence (Prashad 2007: 45–50).

In the new Cold War rhetoric of freedom and democracy the imperial conception of a 'civilising mission', with its exclusive identification of universal values with the particularity of British culture, appeared insupportably hierarchical, anti-democratic and ethnically exclusive (Mazower 2009: 195–6). And yet, it would be a mistake to see the two as entirely disconnected and unrelated (Porter 2006: 62). After all, the United States also identified itself with universal values, but the difference was that this identification no longer rested on the particularities of a distinctly national culture, character and tradition, but on the more abstract paradigms of America's constitutional arrangement, formal democratic institutions and economic modernisation, identified with the legally enshrined priority of private property. The very abstractness of these structures meant that they were potentially transferable without demanding the wholesale transformation of the cultural traditions and habits of the host society. In turn, this meant that there was no need for the kind of cultural hierarchy and subordination associated with European imperialism (McCarthy 2009: 194–203). Where British and French colonial administrators had obsessively ranked and defined the indigenous cultures over which they ruled according to their own standards of civilisation, the very abstractness of 'the American way of life' could appear – at least initially – as comparatively unobtrusive and indifferent. However, as W.H. Auden's short poem 'Fleet Visit' (1951) suggests, US global hegemony still rested on the exercise of power over the lives of millions of people, and its abstractness and indifference meant that it could act as though it were innocent of that fact.

Auden's 'Fleet Visit' imagines the mooring of a gleaming US fleet at a port in an unnamed and interchangeable Third World country, described generically simply as an 'unamerican place / Where natives pass with laws / And futures of their own' (Auden 2007: 205, lines 8–10). The poem relies on an implicit contrast between the earlier operation of British imperialism, whose passing is figured here by the pointed invocation of Rudyard Kipling's notorious phrase 'lesser breeds without the law', and the emergent world order, represented here by the American fleet visible at a distance in the harbour. While Britain sent its forces to (more or less) directly govern 'lesser breeds without the law', the American fleet exerts a nebulous, unseen and potential power through its offshore presence: 'They are not here because / But only just-in-case' (Auden 2007: 205, lines 11–12). So the sailors who spill out of the 'hollow ships' come ashore not as conquerors or civilisers, but as *tourists* – albeit the kind more interested in bars and brothels than the history and culture of this other place (line 2). Yet this comparison may be less benign than it first appears, for although tourists may not consciously intend to direct the society they visit, the fact that they remain outside the negotiation of interests within that society lends them an indifference to the local which, given the asymmetries of wealth and power, can have devastating consequences.

The poem turns on the split between *human agency* – figured primarily by the currently superfluous crew, but also in part by the 'natives' whose lives are being reorganised – and a more abstract concept of *structure* as potential power, or the coercive logics built into the disposition of resources, inherited patterns of affiliation and identity, and the processes and protocols of decision making. This concept is manifested most immediately in the naval architecture of the fleet, but also by extension in the broader international architecture of law and interstate relations established by the US at the end of World War II. The 'pure abstract design' invoked in the final stanza carries this double sense – referring both to maritime and geopolitical structure – and the poem's menace lies in the slippage between the two. Like the clean, modern lines of the warships placidly floating in the bay, the new architecture of the UN and its associated institutions describes a triumph 'of pattern and line' (Auden 2007: 205, line 28); but these 'structures [remain] humane' only so long as they have 'nothing to do', and so are 'Without a human will / To tell them whom to kill' (lines 21–4). This disconnection between human agency and structure, however, is not a fortunate conjuncture; for if the operators of lethal power are absolutely removed from the social life – or 'Social Beast' (line 16) – of this 'unamerican place', then the interests of its inhabitants, over which they ultimately adjudicate, become absolutely irrelevant and superfluous to them.

For all the differences between the European empires of the past and the emerging global dispensation, the 'superfluousness' of indigenous social and political interests identifies the new structure of global power as a development and modification of the earlier colonialism – or we might say, as a mode of its afterlife (Arendt 1973: 212).[6] This combination of continuity and change is captured nicely in Auden's poem. Kipling's language of 'lesser breeds without the law' is replaced by a vision of inhabitants 'with laws' and 'futures of their own'; but significantly they remain 'natives', an ominous lexical hangover from colonial times made all the more menacing by the division of the globe into American and 'unamerican' places. In the colonial binary where civilisation confronts savagery, freedom for the savage remains a remote goal that lies far in the future, and European tutelage is justified because it is orientated to this distant future. In the tripartite rhetorical division of the Cold War, however, all individuals are at all times *potentially* free; but the achievement of freedom can only occur once the emergent national polity (as defined by the ex-colonial power) is remade as an American, rather than an 'unamerican', place – which means open to US economic interests and committed to the absolute priority of private property (McCarthy 2009: 202–5).

As numerous historians have shown, after World War II European colonial powers quickly retooled and became adept at presenting their renewed commitment to colonialism in terms of Cold War rhetoric. As John Springhall writes, 'British politicians felt entitled to claim American support based upon the contribution to the containment of communism in Malaya, while French governments played upon the "red scare" to secure American arms and funding for the war in Indochina' (Springhall 2001: 209–10). Cain and Hopkins observe that the 'bogey of communism was invoked [even] where it was not already present, and this sufficed in the early stages of the Cold War to legitimize the use of force' (Cain and Hopkins 1993: 280). But my argument here is that the new rhetoric of the Cold War did much more than simply act as a cover for a last ditch defence of the old European empires. Rather, the challenge was to realign existing colonial structures with the new global dispensation so as to manage the process of decolonisation. Without detracting from the real achievement of national liberation movements in gaining independence – often in the face of considerable violence by the colonial state – decolonisation also needs to be understood as part of a larger reformulation of Western global hegemony. This reformulation saw a shift from the often direct control exercised by European empires to a system of formally sovereign states supervised by a series of international bodies directed by the United States (Lazarus 2004: 30–2). In this new hegemonic arrangement, power is no longer exercised through formal imperialism, but largely operates through economic channels, support for political proxies and various forms of military intervention, whether clandestine, 'anticommunist', 'humanitarian' or as part of the wars 'on drugs' and 'on terror' (see Khalidi 2009; Grandin 2007; Harvey 2007).

From British to US Hegemony: Greene's *The Quiet American*

Although it is tempting to see decolonisation as an inevitable, unidirectional and unequivocal process, in fact the period initially saw a renewed commitment to empire – often termed 'the second colonial occupation' – which involved a repositioning of imperial concern away from the newly independent territories of British India and towards the Middle East, Southeast Asia and Africa (Cain and Hopkins 1993: 279; Cain and Hopkins 2002: 627–32; Orde 1996: 164–70). 'Far from being in decline,' observe Cain and Hopkins, 'imperialism and empire were revitalized during the war and in the period of reconstruction that followed' (Cain and Hopkins 2002: 639). And as John Springhall notes, 'although the British trailed far behind the Russians and Americans in terms of military power, they still remained inhabitants of the world's third great power for fifteen years or more after 1945', retaining a 'large sphere' of influence through a continuing military presence until the 1960s, centred on the oil rich region of the Middle East (Springhall 2001: 210; Orde 1996: 164). The economic benefits of the second colonial occupation helped fund full employment and the new 'welfare state' – the network of social provision, social security and social entitlements, including the National Health Service, free education, welfare benefits, social housing and labour rights – which sustained the postwar consensus pursued by Labour and Conservative governments alike, until the advent of Thatcherism in 1979 (Kavanagh 1987: 26–62).

An expression of this new commitment to empire was the fact that while Britain left India peacefully, it fought a series of vicious colonial wars in Palestine, Kenya, Malaya, Cyprus, Egypt, Muscat and Oman, Borneo and Yemen. In concert with the white settler colonies of Canada, Australia, New Zealand and South Africa – which had achieved effective independence but remained politically linked to Britain through the loose international association of the Commonwealth – Britain's formal and informal colonial possessions continued to play an important economic role, constituting the Sterling Area, a group of economies that traded in sterling and kept sterling denominated balances in the financial centre of London (Cain and Hopkins 1993: 272–5). However, while the demands of sterling and of empire were initially aligned, so encouraging the second colonial occupation, by the late 1950s they had begun to diverge radically. As British trade and investment looked to the dynamic economies of Western Europe, Japan and the United States, Britain became increasingly integrated into 'the new set of complementarities linking the advanced, highly specialized economies of the world' (Cain and Hopkins 2002: 636). This divergence made business elites, the financial sector and British politicians increasingly amenable to the decolonisation demanded by national liberation movements across the developing world, and in 1967 the Labour government of Harold Wilson announced 'withdrawal from East of Suez', which effectively meant the abandonment of formal colonial rule in Africa and Southeast Asia and the closing of British military bases in the Arabian Gulf. However, the acceptance by the political elite of decolonisation manifested in 'the withdrawal from East of Suez' was not quite such a radical departure from the earlier policy of colonial renewal as it might at first seem, and taken together both the second colonial occupation and Britain's rapid departure from 'East of Suez' can be seen in retrospect as facilitating British integration into US global hegemony. As John Springhall puts it, in the decades following the war, 'the British Empire was internationalized then dismantled', providing an important mechanism for integrating strategically important ex-colonies into the new world system dominated by the United States (Springhall 2001: 12; see also Kaplan and Kelly 2004).

However, while this 'internationalization' of the British Empire could be rationalised at the level of geopolitics, it proved much more difficult to stomach at the level of ideology and culture. A crucial arena for this transition was the Middle East, and Britain's postwar role there indicates the difficulties it experienced in managing this process. As the United States assumed the mantle of the new global superpower after World War II, it made use of existing British political, military and economic structures in the Middle East by granting Britain 'paramountcy' in the region; indeed, into the 1950s Eisenhower 'insisted that Britain should be made to pay as much as possible for the defense of the Middle East' (Ovendale 1996: 31–2, 134). In reality, however, this 'paramountcy' was partial and strictly qualified, and the United States reserved the right to pursue its interests independently, especially in its relations with Saudi Arabia and Iran, and with regard to the partition of Palestine in 1948 and the Suez Crisis of 1956. The Suez Crisis in particular stages most dramatically the differences between the new logic of

US global hegemony and the colonial parameters within which Britain continued to operate.

The Suez Canal, originally built to connect European metropolitan centres with their colonies and potential colonies in Asia and Eastern Africa, had by the mid-twentieth century developed a new strategic significance as a shipping route for oil supplies from the Arabian Gulf to Europe (Brendon 2007: 142–3, 324–6; Khalidi 2005: 20–1). Britain therefore retained a vast military base to control the canal and the sea lanes that fed it. When Egyptian president Gamal Abdel Nasser, inspired by the ideals of Pan-Arabism and the anticolonial Bandung Conference of 1955, nationalised the Suez Canal in July 1956, Britain invaded Egypt in concert with French and Israeli forces (Prashad 2007: 51–2; Khalidi 2009: 191). However, once the US refused to support the invasion – which was a Cold War propaganda disaster, coinciding with the Soviet invasion of Hungary – Britain, France and Israel were forced to make a humiliating retreat (Brendon 2007: 488–98). Yet although 'British prestige was damaged by the Suez Crisis', as G.C. Peden observes, 'there was no precipitate retreat from the Middle East' (Peden 2007: 274). In fact, over the next few years Britain intervened militarily in Jordan, Lebanon and Kuwait, although now in close concert with the United States. Indeed, Britain kept substantial military forces in the Gulf and the Indian Ocean until the 'withdrawal from East of Suez' in 1967, and even then it retained 'greater out-of-NATO area capability' than this epithet would suggest (Peden 2007: 351). The Suez Crisis in 1956 is often taken in cultural histories to mark the end of Britain's pretensions to a global role, but in an important sense this is misleading. As Piers Brendon writes, 'contrary to myth . . . the imperial legions did not march home in 1956', but instead 'London's freedom of action was' now more completely 'circumscribed by Washington' (Brendon 2007: 499; Orde 1996: 192).

The Suez Crisis, then, not only crystallised the differences between British and American modes of exercising power, but also accelerated the integration of British military action into overall US strategic policy. Ritchie Ovendale records the growing realisation of the nature of Britain's dilemma, that either it must, in the words of one British official, transform Arab states 'into territories dominated by ourselves through armed compulsion' – an increasingly untenable proposition – or it must somehow 'come to terms with Arab nationalism' (Ovendale 1996: 193). Thus, in pushing Britain to adopt the US mode of exercising hegemony, the Suez Crisis intensified the search for a new ideological language to make British actions acceptable to publics both at home and abroad. In

fact, British politicians and civil servants had for some time been searching for a completely new vocabulary to make Britain's continuing global
role more palatable. Ironically, Anthony Eden, the Conservative prime
minister who oversaw the British humiliation over Suez, had as early
as 1953 begun to see that 'in the second half of the twentieth century
[Britain] could not hope to maintain its position in the Middle East by the
methods of the nineteenth century', and argued that 'future policy must
be designed to harness [nationalist] movements rather than to struggle
against them' (quoted in Ovendale 1996: 236). Harold Macmillan, who
succeeded Eden as prime minister, put it in a nutshell: 'We should try to
appear not as reactionary powers returning to the old days of "colonization", but as a progressive force trying to bring about a permanent and
constructive settlement' (quoted in Ovendale 1996: 159).

Ultimately, this new presentational strategy required that the very
syntax of political action be transformed. Instead of pitting an active
Britain against a homogeneous object – in this case, the Arab world en
bloc – 'there had at least to be the appearance of an Arab solution to an
Arab problem', so that Britain and the US now appeared as merely ancil-
lary agents facilitating an outcome advantageous to all (Ovendale 1996:
237). This new political syntax would in time reposition the domestic,
British audience: rather than being cast as an interested actor – which
potentially raised the question of the desirability, justice or pragmatic
value of their own involvement – the British public would increasingly
be invited to stand at one remove, adopting the role of an adjudicator
whose task it was to judge between the political and moral worth of
different foreign actors. This new language of international intervention
proved highly congenial to the conceptual vocabulary of the Cold War,
in which the coercive dimension of interstate relationships is refracted
through a 'quasi-existential' conflict between freedom and totalitarianism, with the result that former colonial powers could reinvent
themselves as colonially-innocent, democratic nation-states. As such,
international political intervention could be justified on the dual basis of
strategic defence and the commitment to an abstract and individualised
freedom.[7] And here it is possible to see a homology with the apparently
incompatible vectors we have observed in postwar British literature
and culture, namely the national retrenchment identified by Jed Esty
and the globalising tendencies identified by John Marx. For while the
new doctrine of strategic defence depends on a spatially discrete nation
as the homeland in relation to which strategic resources or territories
would be mapped, abstract freedom enjoys an unbounded and delo-
calised scope, within which each particular locus of intervention is just

another instance of an almost metaphysical conflict between freedom and totalitarianism.

The overlay of territorialising and deterritorialising logics within Cold War discourse complicates the trajectory mapped by Jed Esty in his account of postwar canonical British literature, and begins to suggest ways in which John Marx's conception of modernism's globalising of Englishness needs to be folded back into his account. For Esty, the alternatives confronting postwar British literature boiled down to a commitment to an anthropologically discrete national culture, as signalled by late English modernism and pursued by British Cultural Studies, and a pointedly literary staging of national decline and individual withdrawal, as exemplified by Orwell, Greene and Waugh, and to a lesser extent Lawrence Durrell and Anthony Burgess. The paradox for all these writers according to Esty, is that while their work was 'overtly based on the predicament of a provincial ex-empire', they collapse any insight into this predicament within 'the foreclosure of the existential novel' (Esty 2004: 8, 221). But to take the example of just one of these figures, Graham Greene's postwar output pursues a much more complicated arc than this judgement suggests once placed in the context of the contradictory territorialising and deterritorialising logics of the Cold War. Indeed, what makes Greene so interesting here is that his writing through the 1940s and 1950s does not simply pursue the parallel spirals of national decline and individualised existential crisis, but reflexively locates them within the double predicament of national retrenchment and participation in US global hegemony. This more complicated arc can be traced by comparing his 1948 novel *The Heart of the Matter* with *The Quiet American* published in 1955, just a year before the Suez Crisis.

The Heart of the Matter centres on the existential struggle of an isolated and theologically inclined Catholic Englishman, Henry Scobie, a struggle that is almost completely unrelated to the novel's West African characters or setting. Indeed, George Orwell objected that apart from minor details, 'the whole thing might as well be happening in a London suburb', observing that the 'Africans exist only as an occasionally mentioned background'. Further, Orwell complains, 'the thing that would actually be in Scobie's mind the whole time – the hostility between black and white, and the struggle against the local nationalist movement – is not mentioned at all', rendering his theological dilemmas abstract and artificial because unrelated to this experiential world (Orwell 2002: 1338–9). What appears to be a novel of decolonisation, then, is really a novel of national decline and self-involved existential crisis, in which late colonial Africa becomes a backdrop for the inner angst of the male English protagonist.

The Quiet American is set during the American-sponsored French colonial war in Indochina (Southeast Asia), and at first sight appears to be built around a similar protagonist, the narrator Thomas Fowler. This time, however, Fowler's inner life is bound more closely to the late-colonial war around him through his competition for the allegiance of his Vietnamese lover, Phuong, with an earnest American intelligence agent, Alden Pyle. This competition stages their different conceptions of the war and of the Vietnamese. Pyle is motivated by a sincere and zealous commitment to 'Democracy and the responsibilities of the West', and believes the war should become an idealistic mission in which sacrifices must be made – although it turns out that 'the sacrifices were all paid by others', principally the Vietnamese (Greene 2004: 10, 53).[8] Fowler, on the other hand, as an 'old colonial', perceives the war as being driven by the same destructive and self-serving aims that animated the earlier project of European colonialism, regardless of – and in an important sense, because of – the sincerity and self-belief of individual actors in higher callings and noble causes (2004: 151). He reminds Pyle of America's own history of colonialism, and points out that 'We've no business here. It's their country' (2004: 115, 99).

The novel thus invites a reading that locates its narrator's existential withdrawal within the particularism and exemplarity of Britain as a post-imperial 'shrunken island' – although I would argue, only to expose it and pull it apart. On this initial or literal reading, the historical priority of the island's imperial story appears to give Britishness a unique wisdom now that it is over and locked in the past, a wisdom associated with an inimitable national temper signalled by Scobie's various tics and idiosyncrasies in failing to manage his divorce. It is this acknowledged experience of colonialism that leads Fowler to reject involvement, and seek an existential attitude beyond enmeshment in worthy ends and grand plans: 'The human condition being what it was, let them fight, let them love, let them murder, I would not be involved' (2004: 20). On this view, Scobie's existential withdrawal appears to mark the passage from imperial past to down-sized, nationally-bounded present, a passage that secures a worldly wisdom through historical experience, while separating the present from that experience.

However, if the novel initially appears to remove postwar Britishness from the pitiless abstraction of Cold War politics, securing it within the insularity of existential self-reflection, in fact the novel's increasingly unreliable narration ruthlessly exposes this very gesture. For while

Pyle's zealous belief in the rightness of his conception of freedom and democracy is shown to have lethal consequences, the images that force themselves into Fowler's mind when surveying the bloody results of Pyle's intervention are of the casualties of the contemporary Malayan Emergency, in which British troops ruthlessly suppressed Chinese insurgents (2004: 80). And if Fowler claims a kind of worldly wisdom over the younger Pyle because he comes from one of 'the old colonial powers', against his own volition he comes to recognise himself more and more in the figure of another 'old colonialist', the truly 'repulsive', erotica-obsessed Frenchman who embodies the worst of late-colonial venality and predation (2004: 151). Crucially, Fowler's narration increasingly comes to acknowledge that his claim to know Phuong, and by extension Vietnam – the claim upon which his sexual and political competition with Pyle depends – is a fraud: 'even when I made my speech', Fowler has finally to concede, 'I was inventing a character just as much as Pyle was' (2004: 124). As the narrator's unreliability becomes increasingly evident, it introduces a retrospective uncertainty about his narration that is nowhere remediated: 'Was I so different from Pyle', Fowler wonders, only now coming to admit 'I've been blind to a lot of things' (2004: 177). As Fowler's epistemological claim to know Vietnam collapses, so does his vision of an existential retreat. With the screams of a Vietnamese guard ringing in his ears after an attack brought about by his presence alongside Pyle, Fowler admits: 'I had prided myself on detachment, on not belonging to this war, but those wounds had been inflicted by me as though I had used the sten [gun], as Pyle had wanted to do' (2004: 105).

While national retrenchment was certainly one key feature of postwar British culture as Esty emphasises, this retrenchment was at one and the same time part of a new mode of international involvement. Greene's novel suggests that this paradox was not unnoticed by writers at this time, and that the project of imagining withdrawal into the shrinking island was never seamless or entirely convincing. Indeed, in *The Quiet American* the gesture of withdrawal comes to be recognised as just that, a gesture, or a kind of enabling fiction of disavowal made possible by what it disavows.[9] The new Cold War dispensation of US hegemony is revealed as the condition of possibility for this very gesture, while in turn this gesture is identified as the mechanism that *enables* continuing British international involvement under the sign of post-imperial 'good conscience' – as a bounded nation-state motivated only by strategic national interest and the 'denationalised' universalism of freedom and democracy. The territorialised national retrenchment that is such a striking feature of postwar British culture needs, then, to be understood in tandem with a deterritorialised and globally extended conception of right and value, in which the very particularity and rootedness of national culture enables a field of action that is both boundless and imperially innocent. But as Greene's novel suggests, holding these contrary vectors together was a fraught and difficult operation.

From 'Civilisation' to 'Culture': Churchill and Orwell

The ideology of empire involved a stunningly audacious conceptual leap: Britain could enjoy the comforts of *particularity* – of being a distinct, unique and densely idiosyncratic culture peculiar to itself – while claiming that these very idiosyncrasies were *universal*, since the attributes of British civilisation were presented as the attributes of civilisation per se. The problem that faced postwar British intellectuals in responding to the collapse of faith in the immediate universality of British civilisation was how to accommodate the new sense of particularity – understood more consciously as Englishness – as just one distinctive temperament, tradition and outlook among a series of other equally such distinctive cultures, while at the same time continuing to hold that *this* particular temperament, tradition and outlook somehow approximated more closely to the universal than almost all others. It is possible to identify different attempts to imagine or figure this paradoxical extension-as-withdrawal, and in this section and the next we consider three: first, the pragmatic but rather haphazard account by Winston Churchill in his 'Sinews of Peace' speech delivered in 1946; second, an at times penetrating but deeply contradictory series of observations by George Orwell though the late 1930s and 1940s; and third, the much smoother, more polished and ultimately more sustainable vision developed by T.S. Eliot in 'The Unity of European Culture', first published in German in 1946. As the differences between these figures suggest, this was certainly not a unified programme, and nor were its protagonists necessarily conscious of addressing the problematic as it is described here. Nonetheless, I will argue that the composite cultural framework sketched here provides a significant backdrop for understanding changing British national identity in the postwar years and for charting reactions to postwar migration.

Winston Churchill's 'Sinews of Peace' speech, delivered at Westminster College in Fulton, Missouri in 1946, is usually read within an American context because of its popularisation of the phrase 'the iron curtain', which would become a key element in American Cold

War rhetoric (Wright 2007). However, it also needs to be understood as providing a significant marker for mapping the transformation in British self-understanding, not least because the transition is here partial and incomplete, and colonial and Cold War vocabularies exist uncomfortably side by side. What is perhaps most remarkable about the speech is its capacity to embed the ideological commitments of the colonial project within the Cold War lexicon of freedom and democracy. Indeed, it does so to such an extent that concrete questions of national self-determination and state sovereignty for emergent colonial nations simply disappear.

Churchill frames his speech by invoking what was to become the central opposition of Cold War rhetoric, that between 'the great principles of freedom and the rights of man' and the 'two gaunt marauders, war and tyranny' (Churchill 1974: 7286). Initially, the former appears to be the unbounded property of 'all the homes and families of all the men and women in all the lands', and thus to be a universal principle best embodied in the United Nations rather than any particular nation or group of nations (Churchill 1974: 7286). But it quickly transpires that the universal 'principles of freedom and the rights of man' are in fact 'the joint inheritance of the English-speaking world . . . which through Magna Carta, the Bill of Rights, the Habeas Corpus, trial by jury, and the English common law find their most famous expression in the American Declaration of Independence' (1974: 7288). As the culmination of this history, the Declaration comprises 'the title deeds of freedom', so that freedom becomes territorialised and owned as the particular property of 'the British and American peoples', yet remains potentially universal in being their 'message . . . to mankind' (1974: 7288). In practical terms, what this means is that for all Churchill's talk of empowering the United Nations, the monopoly on atomic weapons – and thus strategic dominance – must be retained by the United States, Britain and Canada (1974: 7287).

Churchill's coding of universal right as Anglo-American offers an uneasy fusion between the colonial discourse of 'civilisation' and the new Cold War discourse of freedom and democracy. While the discourse of civilisation identified right with a particular socio-historical entity – as 'British civilisation', for example – and so was only available to the colonial subject in an ever-distant evolutionary future, Cold War conceptions of 'freedom' and 'democracy' remain potentially available to all in each and every abstract now – at least in theory (see Hinds and Windt 1991: 150–3, 184–8, 227–8). In this speech, Churchill wants both to harness the power of the postwar discourse of freedom and democracy, and to channel its force within the confines of the older discourse of civilisation, albeit now centred on the United States in recognition of its status as 'the pinnacle of world power' (Churchill 1974: 7286). That is, he wants both to align his own project with the new abstract and deterritorialised language of the Cold War, while at the same time territorialising it or identifying it with his own national-political location, so maintaining the 'civilisational' discourse of superiority associated with colonialism.

To try and square this circle, Churchill relies on a decidedly fuzzy conception of 'the English-speaking peoples', a quasi-historical, quasi-ethnic and quasi-judicial complex whose utility lies in its presentation as paradoxically protean yet self-identical (Churchill 1974: 7286). Through the speech, this complex is presented as a cultural tradition that is at once diffuse yet integral, able to manifest itself in a shifting series of historically determinate political entities: Britain and the United States, understood as democratic nation-states that concretely embody the ideals of freedom and democracy; the United States and the British Empire, understood as a transnational military coalition whose pre-eminence reflects contingent facts on the ground; and the white anglophone world – comprising Britain, the United States and the 'Old Commonwealth' nations, the white settler dominions of Canada, South Africa, Australia and New Zealand – understood as a geographically dispersed ethnic and racial unity.[10]

Churchill's flexible Anglo-American formation underpins and organises his more familiar account of the Cold War and the Soviet 'iron curtain' (Churchill 1974: 7290). For if the Soviet Union is by its nature opposed to democracy and freedom as the speech argues, democracy and freedom must first be understood as the exclusive inheritance of an ethnically defined Anglo-American historico-political complex. The emerging political conflict, then, is interchangeably one between the universals of democratic freedom and totalitarianism, between two military blocs, and between an ethnically homogeneous alliance of nations and its other – where the first term of each of these oppositions is deemed to be the 'English-speaking peoples' of the Anglo-American alliance. But of course these three different conceptions of the 'Anglo-American' do not in fact coincide, especially when we consider the 'British' dimension of this complex.[11] When it comes to military force, Churchill refers to 'British Empire forces', a term that not only includes the armed forces of Britain and the Commonwealth nations, but also the military personnel and assets of the many territories in Africa, Asia, the Middle East and the Caribbean still under colonial control (Churchill 1974:

7289). Yet, when this same designation is applied to the field of political rights, it has a quite different range. Although Churchill invokes 'the liberties enjoyed by individual citizens throughout the United States and throughout the British Empire', these 'liberties' are not in fact enjoyed by all subjects of the British Empire (nor indeed by all citizens in the Southern States of the United States at this time), and the British Empire is manifestly not democratic (1974: 7288). This claim only makes sense if the 'citizens' who enjoy these 'liberties' are understood to be white.

The ethnic and racial coding that lies beneath Churchill's Anglo-American formation is made explicit in the speech's imaging a future 'common citizenship', which would apply to Britain, the US and 'the British Commonwealths', that is to the white settler states and not the non-white colonies of 'the Empire' (Churchill 1974: 7289). In a speech delivered three days later before the General Assembly of Virginia, Britain, America and the white Commonwealth are explicitly identified as constituting 'our race' (1974: 7295). It is only the 'British Commonwealth', and not 'the Empire', that like the United States and Britain is immune to the 'Communist parties or fifth columns' that pose such a threat 'to Christian civilization' (1974: 7291). And it is only 'the English-speaking Commonwealths' who share 'our traditions, and our way of life, and . . . the world causes which you and we espouse'. In its closing vision, the speech envisions a predominantly white world – the '70 or 80 millions of Britons spread about the world' along with 'the English-speaking Commonwealths' and 'the United States' – as the great bulwark and 'moral force' that can prevail in the Cold War (1974: 7293). Thus, while Britain and the white Commonwealth nations will provide the moral, cultural and ideological partners for the United States in the struggle for global democracy and freedom, the non-white populations of the Empire will supply military personnel and strategic assets.

That Churchill's 'Sinews of Peace' speech is now best remembered in the United States is perhaps not surprising, since the awkwardness of its synthesis of colonial and Cold War rhetorics was largely screened out, and 'the American public heard that part of his message that fitted its view of themselves and the world' (Hinds and Windt 1991: 121). Largely unencumbered by formal colonial possessions, the United States could imagine itself as the embodiment of abstract universalism by claiming to be a 'political' rather than a 'national' state – i.e. by claiming that citizenship was a function of adherence to democratic ideals rather than of ethnic or national belonging, so giving rise to a polity that was uniquely compatible with universal right (MacPhee and Poddar 2007: 9). But in Britain, such an attempt to clothe a renewed commitment to imperialism in the garb of democratic rights and freedoms had become increasingly implausible. Despite Churchill's attempt to screen the anti-democratic and economically exploitative nature of imperialism by conjuring an image of the Empire as a free and equitable alliance of ethnically kindred nations, the following year Britain ignominiously quit its Indian Empire, widely castigated as an undemocratic force opposed to the new principles of freedom and national self-determination. Some years earlier, George Orwell exposed the same disingenuous rhetoric when reviewing a similar scheme for a 'democratic' alliance against totalitarianism, this time including France along with Britain and the US: as Orwell observes, such schemes 'coolly lum[p] the huge British and French empires – in essence nothing but mechanisms for exploiting cheap colored labor – under the heading of democracies!' (Orwell 2002: 130). Shorn of its claims for the democratic credentials of the British Empire, Churchill's rhetorical vision is left only with a pragmatic alliance based on *realpolitik* and a putatively shared 'racial' identity to hold it together. As we shall see, the racial dimension of the speech, although less important for American Cold War discourse, would nonetheless remain a significant legacy for postwar British politics and culture.

Orwell's own articulation of this new paradoxical situation was, although in very different ways, just as fraught and contradictory as Churchill's – notwithstanding the fact that he was an avowed internationalist, while Churchill was an avowed imperialist. Orwell's socialism gave him an economic perspective that significantly qualified the self-evidence of national boundaries, the experientially-based assumption that the world somehow really *is* truncated into a series of discrete units at every level of social existence and history. For as Orwell observed, the everyday well-being of Britons in fact depended on an unseen transnational economic infrastructure, what he described as the 'stream of dividends that flows from the bodies of Indian coolies to the banking accounts of old ladies in Cheltenham' (Orwell 2002: 339). At moments, Orwell was able to translate this economic insight into political terms. In 'Not Counting Niggers', published in the month before Stalin's pact with Hitler, Orwell rejected the rebranding of empire as democracy by pointing out that such a project could only work by excluding the non-white populations of the Empire, as though the British polity could suddenly be imagined without them. In reality, he observed, 'the overwhelming bulk of the British proletariat does not live in Britain, but in Asia and Africa', a formulation that bends back the fact of economic interdependence in order to reconceptualise the nation-state's fundamental political categories beyond notions of nationhood and nationality (Orwell 2002:

130). But this vision buckled under the catastrophe of the Hitler–Stalin Pact, and Orwell increasingly subordinated his political understanding of the significance of transnational economic relationships to a crude cultural framework based on a comforting vision of Englishness. Thus, 'The Lion and the Unicorn: Socialism and the English Genius' (1941), perhaps Orwell's most famous wartime essay, trades in hackneyed invocations of a cosily ordinary and local Englishness, of 'old maids biking to Holy Communion through the mists of the autumn mornings', of 'solid breakfasts and gloomy Sundays . . . green fields and red pillar-boxes' (Orwell 2002: 292). Orwell was still able to argue for Indian independence, but the economic structure of imperialism was now conceived as an external matter that did not affect the internal structuring of the domestic polity. In effect, Orwell transforms his earlier conception of economic inequality – as a political conflict that reaches beyond the nation-state – into a cultural conflict that resides exclusively within it.[12]

Orwell's recasting of class conflict transforms it from a political to a cultural relation, a move that underpins his oscillation between an ordinary and highly localised Englishness and his continuing attempts to sustain a geopolitical vision in which the nation-state would not be the determining category. It is certainly accurate to say that Orwell invested in a sense of English cultural particularity after 1941, although it is also true that he maintained an internationalist vision which might logically have undermined such musings, but which instead was articulated through and warped by them. By 1944, for example, Orwell already understood not only that the British Empire was unsustainable, but that the vision of nation-state sovereignty for 'little nations' that emerged in the interwar period would be an unlikely prospect in the postwar world, predicting that 'the English [will] ultimately dwindle to a satellite people' (Orwell 2002: 639). And in an essay published in *Partisan Review* in 1947, 'Toward European Unity', Orwell sought to look beyond the attenuation of nation-state sovereignty to argue for a 'democratic socialism' – conceived as 'a community where people are relatively free and happy and where the main motive in life is not the pursuit of money or power' – that would of necessity reach beyond national bounds, since it could only 'be made to work in some large area' (Orwell 2002: 1242). Yet his reduction of economic inequality and exploitation to a cultural rather than a political issue meant that he restricted the possibility of such an alternative to the cultural ambit that most closely resembled his own. Thus, in the *Partisan Review* essay he claims that '[i]nto Asia even the word "socialism" has barely penetrated', and that '[i]n most of South America the position is essentially similar, [as] it is in Africa and the Middle East' (Orwell 2002: 1243; c.f. Prashad 2007: 20–1). Therefore, it is only in Western and Central European nations – conceived as integral cultural entities, that is as *nations*, rather than as dynamic, porous and plural political fields – that such a vision has any meaning. In this way, the different potentialities for social justice and political democracy emerging at this time within multiple determinate historical locations are collapsed into a kind of national cultural beauty contest, in which a suspiciously English conception of the West sets the only standard. As the Cold War loomed, this standard and the nascent social democratic model associated with it became increasingly marginal, and Orwell's pessimism mushroomed.

Orwell's starkly desperate novel *1984* needs to be understood within this more convoluted and conceptually confused context. The novel's implosion into masculine existential mourning is not simply an analogue of national decline, but is supervised and necessitated quite consciously and explicitly by an ambitious remapping of the globe that liquidates the very possibility of locality as a meaningful category. The novel's shrunken island, Airstrip One, is just one irredeemably non-specific point in a global system of interchangeable and perpetually warring power blocs within which both event and location are drained of all specificity. But it is the putative readers' revulsion at such a liquidation of particularity that performs what Walter Benjamin describes as allegorical reversal.[13] Just as the allegorical representation of the transience of earthly things is designed to instil in the baroque sinner the certainty of otherworldly salvation, so the absolute abnegation of the local per se – whether at the level of national sovereignty, the particularities of cultural tradition, or the idiosyncrasy of everyday life – provokes such a violent rejection from the reader that they will hold on all the more tightly to every familiar detail, every signifier of locality and particularity, that the novel allows them. The novel's pessimism, then, is not a result of Orwell's inability to keep faith with English culture as Esty claims, but a function of his intemperate commitment to it (c.f. Esty 2004: 220–1). Englishness is not abandoned, but celebrated for its residual failure to integrate into the smooth rhythms of mass society, whether communist or capitalist. But at a cost: resistance is thereby transformed into cultural idiosyncrasy, habits of mind, quirks of emotional tone and tics of character that stand immovably opposed to the political. Whereas a decade earlier Orwell had been able to grasp the interplay between politics and the culture of everyday life in *Homage to Catalonia*, now social differences are reduced to the purely cultural, and the political relationships that might counter Orwell's ethnocentrism melt away (see Orwell 1952: 5).

The difficulties experienced by Churchill and Orwell in satisfactorily articulating a sense of Britain as at once particular and universal sets in relief the different approach pursued by T.S. Eliot. Churchill sought simply to retrofit the imperial model, hoping to maintain the equation of particular and universal by expanding the limits of the particular – to include the 'English-speaking peoples' of the United States and the former white settler colonies – and rearticulating universality in terms of the new language of the Cold War – as freedom and democracy. Orwell's political commitments led him to begin to rethink universality itself, introducing conceptions of economic and social justice that would trouble the very delimitation of particularity, or the self-evidence of the nation state. But the collapse of his faith in political universality following the Hitler–Stalin Pact propelled him back into such a restricted and localised conception of the particular that *any* universal would now appear indifferently as totalitarian. T.S. Eliot could develop a much more stable and so sustainable model because unlike Churchill and Orwell, who were encumbered by the concerns of *realpolitik* and social justice respectively, Eliot could build it entirely on the more tractable ground of culture. And as we will see in Chapter 2, Eliot's conservative reconstruction of Englishness would be as influential for the left and for the development of British Cultural Studies as it would be for his natural constituency on the right.

Reinventing the West: T.S. Eliot

The late work of T.S. Eliot certainly exhibits a commitment to the localness and distinctiveness of English culture, yet Eliot's vision of locality explicitly and quite consciously depends on and finds its meaning through a framework that exceeds the local but which is always operative within it. As a student of the latter-day Right-Hegelian philosopher F.H. Bradley, Eliot was well aware that particularity requires the universal to be meaningful, or indeed particular; that is, he understood that a transferable or generalisable set of criteria is needed in order for us to recognise or appreciate the specific qualities of any thing.[14] This insight underpins his earlier poem *The Waste Land* (1922), for example, where the collapse of the universal narratives of Christianity, humanism and scientific progress render contemporary experience as a vista of empty and interchangeable fragments. In order to rehabilitate this shattering conception of modernity, Eliot's later work had to do more than simply insist on the organic meaningfulness of a unified and localised English culture. It also had to generate a quasi-universal cultural matrix within which to secure this conception of Englishness and make it meaningful, and to find a way of establishing a privileged connection between this particular local culture and the larger 'universal'.

Eliot sets out his solution in 'The Unity of European Culture', originally delivered as a series of radio talks broadcast in 1946 on German radio. The essay conjures a quasi-universal European cultural tradition upon which English culture is granted a privileged but not exclusive hold. In and of itself, the quasi-universal that Eliot conjures here is familiar enough: 'The Western world,' he writes, 'has its unity in this heritage, in Christianity and in the ancient civilizations of Greece, Rome, and Israel' (Eliot 1962: 123). But as a transnational field of related differences – what the essay describes as 'a tissue of influence woven to and fro' – this Western tradition provides a historically generated complex which transcends each particular culture, and so provides a quasi-universal scale against which the particularity of each cultural instantiation is discernible, and so counts as particular (Eliot 1962: 112). This framework will allow Eliot both to endorse the affective experience of the uniqueness and integrity of each particular European national culture – and by extension the United States, which is conceived as 'European' at the level of culture[15] – while at the same time establishing that particularity as the necessary expression of a cosmopolitan and transnational cultural complex. As Eliot writes, 'For the health of the culture of Europe two conditions are required: that the culture of each country should be unique, and that the different countries should recognize their relationship to each other, so that each should be susceptible of influence from the others' (Eliot 1962: 119). Arguing that the linguistic substratum of English culture, the English language, is itself unique in its status as a 'composite from so many European sources', Eliot claims that *this* particular national culture is the most exemplary instance of that larger European culture, and of the broader interplay between national self-identity and cosmopolitan openness.

On one level, it is important to observe that Eliot's account of the 'heritage' that would secure the 'unity of European culture', and more broadly, of 'the West' – effectively the cultural complex of Middle Eastern and Mediterranean antiquity – was not especially 'Western' nor 'European', but formed part of a larger linguistic and cultural arc that extended eastwards and southwards into Asia and Africa (Burkert 2004). But on another level, this is to miss the point. Approximating as it does to late-nineteenth-century self-understandings of Western civilisation – which claimed both Classical and Judeo-Christian culture as its exclusive patrimony – this conception of a broadly shared 'Western culture' allows Eliot to align English culture with a quasi-universal value, but without having to claim their absolute or necessary identity, as the older discourse of British Civilisation had. That is, the fact of Allied victory secures the validity of 'Western culture' as a historical *accident* and not as fateful *necessity*, or the apodictic manifestation of universal rationality. Thus, Britain's postwar pre-eminence in a war-torn Europe secures its place as the exemplary instance of this victorious 'Western culture' – after all, the British had won the war, while Eliot's German listeners had lost it. The power of Eliot's formulation lies, then, in its ability to extract the claim for the transcendent value of English culture from the unsustainable commitment to universality ventured by British imperial ideology. As such, the instantiation of transcendent value in Englishness becomes a happy accident whose very fortuitous-ness is proof both of the quasi-universal validity of 'Western culture' and of the serendipity of English idiosyncrasy and uniqueness.

The significance of Eliot's reformulation of imperial British civilisa-tion as English national culture can be traced within the context of the paradoxical imperatives of downsizing and extension we have explored above. Unlike Churchill's attempt simply to 'update' the imperial discourse of civilisation by blending it with the rhetoric of the Cold War, this formulation frees Eliot from having to identify transcendent value with the historico-political complex of Britain and its Empire as currently constituted. Yet at the same time it maintains that value as 'Western', and so irrefutably 'ours' and constitutive of 'us', even while inviting affiliation from a relatively elastic range of cultural locations. Crucially, Eliot's conception of culture allowed for class difference; or rather, by sublating class conflict as cultural difference, it seeks to contain class conflict within the all-encompassing national culture. 'There are of course higher and lower cultures', Eliot observes, and 'the culture of an artist or philosopher is distinct from that of a mine worker or field laborer . . . but in a healthy society these are all parts of the same culture' (Eliot 1962: 120). And because English exemplarity rests on its integral self-identity, and not its sharing of qualities exhibited in more attenuated ways by others, it remains irreducibly restricted and closed, and so untroubled by the transnational extension acknowledged inter-mittently by Orwell. Thus, while acknowledging 'some influence of [the] poetry of the East', including the translations by Ezra Pound and Arthur Waley that had been so important for his own poetic development, Eliot can claim an openness whilst firmly shutting the door:

The frontiers of culture are not, and should not, be closed. But history makes a difference. Those countries which share the most history, are the

> most important to each other, with respect to their future literature. We have our common classics, of Greece and Rome; we have a common classic even in our several translations of the Bible. (Eliot 1962: 114)

History indeed 'makes a difference', since if universality can be remodelled as cultural – that is, as contingently and historically located in the practices and beliefs of a socio-historical complex, albeit one that has been 'purified' and isolated – then it can enjoy the authority of transcendence while avoiding the troubling claims of political universality. For as we have seen in Orwell's case, the claims of political universality – now often presented as simply oppressive or totalising – had begun to unsettle the very bounds of the nation-state.

This double logic – of openness and closure, of exemplarity and self-identity – thus provides an extraordinarily flexible way of managing the imperatives of withdrawal and extension in the postwar world. Most strikingly, Eliot argues for the continuing authority of English exemplarity while at the same time excising the history of imperialism upon which it was erected: as Englishness, this exemplarity is conceived of as having *always resided* in the porosity of the English nation, whose boundedness was nonetheless ensured by its setting within an overarching European culture and not in the ebb and flow of British imperial extension. Eliot's solution, then, allowed for a renewed sense of English exemplarity and global pre-eminence, one that was no longer tied to the British Empire, and that was therefore able to articulate an international role without reference to it.

The Disappearance of Colonial Labour: Lamming, Selvon and Bennett

The renewed commitment to Empire and Commonwealth that marked the immediate postwar period also had significant consequences within the nation-state through the redefinition of citizenship and migration. In line with John Marx's conception of the cultural cosmopolitanism of modernism, with its urge to 'imagin[e] the proliferation of local Englishes on a planet-wide scale', British policy looked to maintain the political and economic cohesion of an expansive 'zone of Britishness' both through legal forms and through ties of kinship and culture (Marx 2005: 4). At the same time, the national withdrawal identified by Esty encouraged an exclusionary and highly racialised conception of national identity. This first tendency can be seen in the 1948 British Nationality Act and in the huge state-sponsored programme of emigration from

Britain to the dominions, or former white settler colonies, in the decades after the war; the latter manifested itself in the profound and extended redefinition of British citizenship initiated by the 1962 Commonwealth Immigrants Act, which ended the free migration of British subjects, and concluded in Margaret Thatcher's 1981 British Nationality Act.

The 1948 British Nationality Act sought to continue the extensive category of imperial British subject that had existed at the height of imperial rule where, in theory at least, all people under the British monarch's rule were British subjects. With the effective independence of the dominions, this imperial subject status was nonetheless retained in a new and updated form, that of United Kingdom and Colonies (UKC) citizen (Paul 1997: 9–17; see also Baucom 1999: 7–14). As Kathleen Paul remarks, while separate dominions were allowed to create their own national citizenships, through the institution of UKC citizenship London continued to give all inhabitants of the dominions, colonies and the United Kingdom 'equality of status and rights throughout the empire', and all were in theory 'equally entitled to live and work in Britain' (Paul 1997: 16). Until 1962, official British policy saw the 'preservation of the common nationality [as being] linked to the preservation of the empire/ commonwealth . . . under continued British influence' (1997: 19).

However, a parallel policy also pursued by successive Labour and Conservative governments at this time rather qualifies the apparently unbounded universalism of this gesture, namely the sustained programme for the emigration of UK residents to Southern Rhodesia, South Africa, Australia, New Zealand and Canada. According to Kathleen Paul, the '"white" dominions received over 1.5 million UK residents in the fifteen years after World War II', or an annual average of 125,000 migrants, all despite a pressing need for labour to rebuild the war-ravaged British economy (Paul 1997: 25). As Paul notes, although 'the needs of the imperial migration program conflicted with the needs of domestic economic recovery', the domestic demand for labour was overridden by what a 1954 government committee identified as a more urgent priority, the need 'to encourage [outward] migration as a means of strengthening the bonds of the various parts of the Commonwealth and Empire' (1997: 47, 41). According to this committee, 'whatever the demographic, economic, and strategic arguments may suggest, we feel that it is a continuing United Kingdom interest to ensure that the British character of the Commonwealth is preserved' (1997: 41). Underlying the imperial emigration programme, then, was an understanding of Britishness that undercuts that more expansive definition ostensibly extended through the legal form of UKC citizenship. As Paul observes, beneath the legal or state-based designations of citizenship, 'policy makers conceived of separate spheres of nationality: residents of the empire with white skin and European cultural descent were British stock; residents of the empire with skin of color and African or Asian heritage were British subjects only' (1997: 26).

This distinction between the visible legal category of citizenship, manifested in the universalism of state legislation, and more informal and often unspoken ethno-nationalist or racial designations that express themselves in cultural traits and the distinctions of everyday life, lay at the heart of the reality of postwar immigration. In order to meet the demand for labour, which was itself intensified by outward UK emigration to the Commonwealth, the Atlee and Churchill governments encouraged immigration from Europe rather than migration from the colonies, with large-scale programmes aimed at recruiting veterans of the exiled Polish army, 'displaced persons' (often Jewish and other refugees from Eastern and Central Europe) and Italian workers under the aegis of the Foreign Labour Committee, which recruited 345,000 European aliens to live and work in Britain (Paul 1997: 64–83). In addition, every year from 1946 to 1962 between 50,000 and 60,000 Irish workers entered the UK (1997: 90). While many refugees faced extraordinary hardships and had precious few alternatives, what is striking is that they qualified for immigration less on the merits of their specific condition than on what official papers describe as their perceived potential 'for ultimate absorption into the British community', a potential that was supported by government-led campaigns to encourage their acceptance by public opinion (1997: 85). In contrast, migration by UKC citizens from non-white colonies and former colonies was not encouraged by the government, which often worked to obstruct or slow the process down, before formally instituting limits to migration from the non-white Commonwealth in the 1962 Commonwealth Immigrants Act.[16] And rather than seeking to persuade public opinion of the benefits of inward colonial migration or the responsibilities Britain had to the millions of colonial soldiers and airmen who had fought in World War II, colonial migration was immediately constructed as a problem that needed to be contained and mitigated (Paul 1997: 134). Beginning with the 1962 Act, successive legislation worked to bring the legal or state-based definition of citizenship into line with the initially unspoken assumptions of ethno-national identity, culminating in the Thatcher government's 1981 British Nationality Act, which tied the definition of British citizenship all the more closely to 'the larger postwar discourse of blood, family, and kith and kin' (1997: 170, 180–1, 183; see also Baucom 1999: 22–3).

The history of postwar immigration legislation is the story of the successive subordination of legal or politically based universal categories to categories modelled on a putative conception of the nation, conceived as an ethnic and quasi-racial unity.

While it took time for the conflict between political universality and national exclusivity to manifest itself in legal categories, it was immediately apparent to many of the colonial subjects who came to Britain in the postwar period. Indeed, as Simon Gikandi argues, this disjunction – between an ostensibly universal and open British imperial identity, and an ethnically coded and culturally bounded English national identity – had always posed a treacherous dilemma for the colonial subject's identification with modernity, 'civilisation' and Britishness (Gikandi 1996: 32–7; see also MacPhee and Poddar 2007: 5–8). But arguably, the significance of this disjunction became all the more intellectually apparent and experientially palpable for migrants from British colonies and ex-colonies in the decade following the docking of the troop ship the *SS Empire Windrush* at Tilbury docks on 21 June 1948 with 492 West Indian migrants aboard. Although Britain's existing non-white population probably stood at somewhere between 10,000 and 30,000 in 1945, the arrival of the *Windrush* is now taken to symbolise the beginning of a new multi-ethnic society in Britain, which saw a steady trickle of migrants from the anglophone Caribbean and subsequently from South Asia over the next decade (Paul 1997: 113).[17] Those who migrated from the Caribbean before the 1962 Act are now referred to as the 'Windrush generation', and as Ashley Dawson notes, they saw their decision to come to Britain both in terms of 'helping to rebuild the devastated motherland' which many had served in World War II, and as coming to participate in 'the affluent and cosmopolitan life represented by the London of their dreams' (Dawson 2007: 2–3). As well as ex-servicemen, teachers, students and skilled workers of all kinds, they included in their number writers and intellectuals such as George Lamming, Sam Selvon, Edward Kamau Brathwaite, Stuart Hall, Beryl Gilroy, Andrew Salkey, James Berry, Wilson Harris and Edgar Mittelholzer, and the musicians Aldwyn 'Lord Kitchener' Roberts and Egbert 'Lord Beginner' Moore amongst many others.

Part of the retrospective significant of the *Windrush*'s arrival in June 1948 lies in its contemporaneous framing by prominent politicians and sections of the media as marking, in the words of Prime Minster Attlee, an 'incursion' into the national space (Dawson 2007: 9). In addition to official hostility, non-white migrants also met with racism and informal discrimination at the level of everyday life, especially in the areas of housing and employment. But as we have seen, these migrants entered into a social and cultural milieu that was complicated and often contradictory, and as Kathleen Paul argues, at least before the Notting Hill Riots of 1958 it is 'difficult' if not 'impossible to discern popular response to the arrival of additional colonial migrants' (Paul 1997: 139). Citing a study by Michael and Ann Dummett, Paul suggests that while there was 'a dedicated minority of 15 per cent . . . determined to arrest all inward migration of people of color', there was a similar-sized minority of perhaps 10 per cent of 'committed antiracists', while the remaining three-quarters of the population 'was "hesitant, ambiguous, and confused" in their attitudes toward the new visible minorities in their midst'. Paul's own study of correspondence within the British trade union movement appears to corroborate this broad picture: 'In general,' she writes, 'the letters portray a workforce worried by visible difference, surrounded by an imperial tradition of racial hierarchies, yet aware that discrimination and injustice were wrong.' She concludes that 'it was a workforce unsure how to receive additional labor, whether colonial or alien, but expecting guidance from national leaders', an audience that remained a 'potential base for education in tolerance . . . as late as the 1960s' (Paul 1997: 140).

The music of calypsonians like Lord Kitchener and Lord Beginner captures the complex mix of optimism and disappointment, inclusion and exclusion, experienced by the Windrush generation. Calypso, a musical form associated with the Trinidad carnival, traditionally had lyrics that addressed topical events and concerns, providing a means of popular expression and communication that circumvented the official channels of colonial culture (Stuart Hall 2002; Dawson 2007: 32). Once transplanted to Britain, calypso continued to provide sharp-eyed, witty and often poignant commentary on the daily lives of its practitioners and audiences, as well as celebrating the national and international events that most concerned them. In a song composed onboard the first *Windrush* voyage, Lord Kitchener famously sang that 'London is the place for me' and that 'English people are very much sociable', declaring that 'I am glad to know my mother country'.[18] The song expresses the expectations of colonial subjects who had been educated in British history, literature and culture, and had been encouraged to view Britain not as an alien occupier but as the 'mother country'. But after the experience of living in cramped, expensive and hard to find lodgings in Britain, Kitchener would sing 'Me landlady's too rude . . . she likes to intrude', comically articulating the common experience of coldness, exploitation and restrictive supervision and surveillance that defined a central area of conflict for migrants, housing.[19] Calypsos often reflected West Indian participation in British public life, marking Queen Elizabeth's coronation in 1953 for example,[20] but perhaps most pointedly in celebrating the historic West Indies victory over England in the Second Test at Lords in 1950. Lord Beginner's calypso 'Victory Test Match', first sung as joyous supporters marched in triumph to Piccadilly, articulated a sense of diasporic pride in the fact that the West Indies team had 'taken on the colonizers at their sacred game and mastered it sufficiently to defeat them at home in open play' (Stuart Hall 2002). This anti-imperialist and diasporic consciousness was also reflected in calypsos that celebrated the impending independence of Ghana,[21] and which lauded 'sweet Jamaica' as 'our heaven and saviour'.[22] Kitchener's song 'If You're not White then You're Black' offers a careful dissection of the complexities of racism and the internalisation of Englishness and whiteness as the normative categories of civilisation and national belonging. The singer complains that a mixed race associate – who in passing 'wouldn't say goodnight' because their skin is lighter than the singer's – would 'rather be among whites / Than stick up for [his] father's rights', and warns that in the eyes of the wider British society 'If you are not white, you considered black'.[23] Yet the daily experience of racism did not blunt Lord Beginner's optimism in 'Mix Up Matrimony', which declares that 'Mixed marriage is the passion / And the world is saying so', so that 'Colored Britons are risin' fast' and 'racial segregation I can see universally fading gradually'.[24]

However, the tensions around housing and sexual relations between black men and white women came to a head in 1958, first in Nottingham in the Midlands and then in Notting Hill, London. In Notting Hill on 23 August crowds of whites, instigated by fascist groups and armed with homemade weapons, attacked the local West Indian population, who in the absence of effective police protection organised collectively to defend themselves (McLeod 2004: 49–50; Paul 1997: 155; Winder 2004: 364–5). The incident that reportedly initiated the violence was an attack by a white crowd on Majbritt Morrison, the white bride of a Jamaican man, indicating the hold of racist conceptions of sexual 'pollution' and the desire to police white female sexuality (Travis 2002; Paul 1997: 155). Because of discrimination in housing, colonial migrants were concentrated in poor neighbourhoods like Notting Hill, and were therefore accused of 'taking over' such areas. The long-term political and media reaction to Notting Hill focused less on the premeditated violence by whites, and more on constructing the victims of that violence as a 'problem', a problem whose terms would set the symbolic and ideological parameters for the discussion of race and nation in Britain for decades to come. This construction combined two key elements: the perception that properly English 'places' – streets, neighbourhoods, towns – were being 'occupied' and 'despoiled' by an alien presence was intensified and expanded by a second topography of fear, that of the fear of sexual deviance and corruption (Baucom 1999: 22–3; Waters 1997: 229–31). While this combination of themes could operate at the level of straightforward biological racism – in terms of racial impurity and race war – as Chris Waters argues, it also informed more 'benign' forms of culturally-based othering, including the nascent discipline of 'race relations' pursued by anthropologists and sociologists in the 1950s and 1960s, which constructed a unified conception of national community in opposition to the 'dark strangers' who now appeared in its midst (Waters 1997: 236–7). Addressing himself to an indigenous British audience in his 1960 book *The Pleasures of Exile*, the novelist and poet George Lamming declared that 'after Notting Hill' it now had to be 'accept[ed] that racial antagonism in Great Britain, is . . . an atmosphere and a background against which my life and yours are being lived' (Lamming 1992: 76).

Lamming's inventive and genre-splicing work *The Pleasures of Exile* – part memoir, part cultural analysis, part intellectual history, part personal reflection – gives an important insight into the perspective of West Indian migrants who were being busily framed and constructed in public discourse. These migrants did not of course arrive in Britain as empty ciphers, waiting to be categorised, analysed, championed or condemned, but came from societies that had complex patterns of racial and class coding that emerged from a long history of European colonialism. As the cultural theorist Stuart Hall observes about his own upbringing, the Jamaica of the immediate postwar years 'had the most complicated color stratification system in the world . . . [and] anybody in my family could compute and calculate anybody's social status by grading the particular quality of their hair versus the particular quality of the family they came from and which street they lived in, including physiognomy, shading, etc.' (Stuart Hall 2000: 149). Instead of the simple white/ black polarity emerging in Britain, colonial Caribbean societies were organised around a finely graded continuum of differences emanating from the central value accorded to the European rulers; as Hall recalls in retrospect, 'I was formed, brought up, reared, taught, educated, nursed, and nurtured to be, a kind of black Englishman', although 'the word "black" had never been uttered in my household or anywhere in Jamaica in my hearing, in my entire youth and adolescence' (Stuart Hall

1995: 8). For Lamming, the decision to migrate to Britain was motivated
by the need to escape the system of value that judged all intellectual
effort and expression in terms of 'England's supremacy in taste and
judgment', a system 'which can only have meaning and weight by a cal-
culated cutting down to size of all non-England'. And 'the first to be cut
down', Lamming observes, 'is the colonial himself' (Lamming 1992: 27).
His decision to migrate was not so much an attempt to escape his native
Barbados as to escape the colonial assumptions that imperial culture
had embedded there. Like the others on board the *Windrush*, who 'were
largely men in search of work', Lamming sought 'a better break', which
for him and for his fellow passenger Sam Selvon meant the chance to
be a writer judged on his own terms rather than the colonial assumptions that dominated in the anglophone Caribbean (1992: 212). But for
Lamming, that did not mean a renunciation of Caribbean culture: 'I was
a West Indian poet, and I wasn't deserting that' (1992: 223).

The passage from colonial periphery to metropolitan centre – terms
that were themselves in the process of becoming confused – had profound and ambiguous effects on the early migrants, effects that are
explored in Lamming's writing about labour. 'For the West Indian of
all classes,' Lamming writes, 'work is the only sure rescue from the long
sleep which followed the emancipation of the slaves', and the voyage
to the 'mother land' provided new opportunities for work impossible in the colonial West Indies (Lamming 1992: 211). In the colonial
context, the type of work and its potential rewards were deeply bound
up with the system of class and colour stratification described by Hall,
so one of the most immediately visible markers of entering a new zone
of possibility was the realisation – experienced straightaway on the train
journey from the port of Southampton to London – 'that white hands did
nigger work in this country' (1992: 217). For the colonial migrant, who
'arrive[d] here as a man reprieved from the humiliation of an arrangement which he has known all his life', this perception went 'home, so
to speak, and it would stay there . . . in the soil of their thinking' (1992:
218, 217). It engendered the prospect of 'this new place as an alternative: open, free with an equal chance for any British citizen', a prospect
that for Lamming would remain a powerful motivating force even as it
is recognised as a dangerous 'illusion' (1992: 218). For the visible signs
of equality were accompanied by 'a cold stare, an enigmatic sneer, the
built-in compliment which is used to praise, and at the same time remind
them who and what they are' – that is, a 'stranger' (1992: 218, 217).
While some sought to deny this conflict of illusion and reality by practis-
ing 'doublethink', for Lamming 'the easiest way to achieve this denial

of a personal difficulty is to . . . translate *me* into *we*' (1992: 218, 213):
that is, to come to think of yourself as 'West Indian'. Lamming writes
that 'no Barbadian, no Trinidadian, no St Lucian, no islander from the
West Indies sees himself as a West Indian until he encounters another
islander in a foreign territory', and 'in this sense, most West Indians of
my generation were born in England' (1992: 214).[25] Yet for Lamming,
there is a sense in which that prospect of openness and equality, despite
its illusory nature, remained a powerful force 'in the soil of [the colonial
migrants'] thinking' (1992: 217). In his rereading of the colonial relationship between Prospero and Caliban in Shakespeare's *The Tempest*,
it enabled 'Caliban [to get] hold of Prospero's weapons and [to decide]
he would never again seek his master's permission' (1992: 63).

The complex role of labour in the cultural construction of colonial
migrants also plays a prominent role in the writing of Lamming's fellow
passenger and writer, the Trinidadian Sam Selvon. In a short story first
broadcast on the BBC's *Caribbean Voices* programme in 1955, 'Come
Back to Grenada', which was incorporated into his novel *The Lonely
Londoners*, Selvon linked the new definition of West Indians of colour
as 'black' with their categorisation as 'non-labor'. Whereas Lamming
articulated the importance of work from the perspective of the West
Indian migrants, as 'the only sure rescue from the long sleep which followed the emancipation of the slaves' (Lamming 1992: 211), Selvon's
protagonist George reflects on the quite different perception projected
onto the 'boys', as male migrants termed themselves: 'Them English
people think the boys lazy and goodfornothing and always on the dole,
but George know it only because the white people don't want to give
them work' (Selvon 1989: 172). This disparity between reality and
appearance becomes the basis for a racialised perception of the migrant
as 'non-labor', as superfluous to and parasitical upon the working
population of the nation. The work George can find is on the night
shift, so when observed during regular working hours he would likely
be perceived as not working; but periodically there are 'grim days' when
he is unemployed, and on such days his status as a visible 'stranger'
and 'non-worker' become fused as he walks streets populated by those
exempt from paid labour at this time, namely middle-class women and
young children: 'Mummy, look at that Black man!' screams 'a little
white child', so that 'poor George don't know what to do' (Selvon 1989:
173). For Selvon, the racialisation of colonial migrants – their identification as 'black' and as 'strangers' – is entwined with their location beyond
the bounds of the British working class and the new welfare state. The
welfare state formed the social compact in which national cohesion was

secured in return for the reduction of economic inequality and the exten-sion of social provision to the working class; to be outside the bounds of the working class was therefore to be excluded from political life. And to be outside the bounds of the welfare state was no longer simply to be just an unexpected 'stranger', but a drain on national resources and therefore a threat to the neediest within the social pyramid.

The power and significance of Selvon's insight becomes apparent if we recall the opacity of Britain's reliance on colonial labour. Throughout the period of colonialism, the British economy benefited from the raw materials and profits that colonial economies provided for British busi-ness. But as Frederic Jameson notes, the labour that produced these raw materials and profits was invisible within the metropolis: what British consumers saw was the alluring appearance of commodities like tea, coffee, sugar and luxury fabrics, designed to excite consumer desire through fantasy and narcissism, rather than the labour expended in producing them and the social violence required to keep that labour cheap and biddable (Jameson 1990). James Joyce's 1922 novel *Ulysses* famously remarks on this disparity in perception, when its protagonist Leopold Bloom idly day-dreams while perusing packets of tea:

> choice blend, made of the finest Ceylonese brands. The far east. Lovely spot it must be: the garden of the world, big lazy leaves to float about on, cactuses, flowery meads, snaky lianas they call them. Wonder is it like that. Those Cinghalese lobbing about in the sun in *dolce far niente*, not doing a hand's turn all day. Sleep six months out of twelve . . . Flowers of idleness. (Joyce 1986: 58)

As the commodity sells itself as an affordable luxury that transports the consumer out of the cares of metropolitan life, so it obscures the harsh realities of back-breaking toil on the tea plantations that produced it. Bloom's reverie conflates the exoticisation of the Orient in imperial ideology ('big lazy leaves to float about on') with the magical disap-pearance of labour in the commodity form ('not doing a hand's turn all day'), to create an outlandish fantasy of indolence and decadence in which colonial labour disappears ('Sleep six months out of twelve . . . Flowers of idleness'). But as his half-question suggests ('Wonder is it like that'), this 'disappearance' can be seen through by the exercise of reason, although rational thought may prefer to remain within the ease of self-affirming fantasy instead.[26] However, as we have seen in the case of George Orwell, left intellectuals had indeed begun to draw attention to the dependence of the apparently integral British polity on colonial labour. As Orwell had written, not only did a 'stream of dividends . . .

flo[w] from the bodies of Indian coolies to the banking accounts of old ladies in Cheltenham', but 'the overwhelming bulk of the British proletariat does not live in Britain, but in Asia and Africa' (Orwell 2002: 339, 130).

The paradox that Selvon captures in his short story 'Come Back to Grenada' is that the disappearance of colonial labour was *intensified* and not weakened with the arrival of colonial workers within the national space. That is, the arrival of colonial labour in Britain functioned less to encourage awareness of the broader dependence of the British polity on colonial resources, and more to engender the perception of colonial workers as superfluous labour or 'non-labor'. This paradox also underlies Louise Bennett's caustically comic poem 'Colonization in Reverse'. More than a decade after Lord Kitchener's 'London is the Place for Me', Bennett's poem famously rewrites migration to the 'motherland' as 'colonizin / Englan in reverse', a process in which colonial subjects will 'populate / De seat a de Empire' and 'settle ... de mother lan' (Procter 2000: 16). As Ashley Dawson argues, the poem's 'witheringly ironic attitude towards the imperial legacy' emerges from a keen historical consciousness that sees 'the relation between Britain and Jamaica [as] grounded in exploitative and at times violent colonial power' (Dawson 2007: 3, 4). In the poem, migration is clearly economically driven, but as Dawson notes, 'the passage to Britain was not simply another arduous trek in search of a decent wage, with all the pain of ruptured family relations and cultural alienation' that that involves: for behind the immediate disparity of economic resources is the 'tight economic logic [of] this unequal imperial dispensation', wherein 'resource extraction took place at the colonial periphery' while 'manufacturing and the accumulation of capital took place primarily in the metropolis' (2007: 4). Colonialism does not simply impose temporary exploitation, but builds into the colonial economy structural asymmetries that leave a lasting legacy of 'underdevelopment' (2007: 5).

There is plenty of irony to go around in the poem's broad humour, which as Dawson explains is based in the character of 'Miss Lou, the opinionated and cantankerous persona whom Bennett employed in many of her dramatic monologues', a character deployed to multiply opportunities for satire rather than to articulate a single, literal perspective (2007: 4). Her celebration of Jamaican migration – 'What an islan! What a people! / Man an woman, old an young / Jus pack up dem bag' – both lauds the achievement of those migrants in overcoming the hardships of relocation and laments their loss to the island (Procter 2000: 16). Equally, Miss Lou's praise for a character Jane, who prefers to 'read love-story book' and lie 'all day' on 'Aunt Fan couch' because 'dey payin she / Two pounds a week fe seek a job / dat suit her dignity', works on different levels. At one level, it takes a wicked enjoyment in this petty instance of counter-exploitation, when the exploited finally get the chance to take a little back. But at another level there is a more tragic irony here, in that Jane is following a script already written in Britain, in which 'jamaica live fe box bread / Out a English people mout''. In this larger irony, colonial labour power – which helped to sustain Britain through World War II and rebuild its wrecked economy afterwards – disappears, transformed instead into the ungrateful and belligerent guest who takes the very 'bread' from the host's mouth, so threatening the life of the nation:

> What a devilment a Englan!
> Dem face war an brave de worse,
> But me wonderin how dem gwine stan
> Colonizin in reverse. (Procter 2000: 17)

Behind the poem's exuberant cheerfulness, then, lies a bitter irony that operates through the stereotypes of colonial non-labour now emanating from Britain – of indolence, ingratitude, bad faith and the parasitical draining of national strength. The irony depends on the gap between the supposed 'horrors' of this reverse colonisation as conjured within the racist imaginary, and the realities of colonialism in the Caribbean, with its history of genocide, slavery, forced migration and indentured labour, and its legacies of poverty and underdevelopment. This irony depends, then, on a continuing awareness of that colonial history, an awareness readily available in the Caribbean. But in Britain, one of the most immediate effects of the perceptual transformation of colonial labour into non-labour is *the disappearance of colonialism itself*. For once exploitation and the legacy of underdevelopment are erased, then colonialism appears as a fortuitous confraternity of nations, as lightly shrugged off as it was once supposedly entered into.

Decolonisation in Reverse: From Larkin to Powell

The political complexities of the period – which saw the second colonial occupation, decolonisation, the Cold War and the emergence of US hegemony – are accompanied by an equally complex, unstable and often paradoxical range of cultural responses. As we have seen, for Eliot an exemplary Englishness could only be reconstructed by excluding all reference to the Empire, while at the level of popular racism the transformation of colonial labour into non-labour effected a parallel erasure of imperialism. Yet at the same time, it was much harder for many to renounce the affective appeal of empire, and extensive popular support for the Empire continued into the 1950s and 1960s (Springhall 2001: 211–12). After all, colonialism had been a major component of British national identity for over two centuries (see Colley 1992; Catherine Hall 2000; Baucom 1999). When set against his broader authorship, Philip Larkin's poem 'Homage to a Government' (1969) nicely captures the subterranean connection between the postwar retrenchment of British national identity and its continuing commitment to and dependence on the Empire.

Larkin's poetry characteristically locates pathos in the local and mundane, a prosaic world that is perennially in decline but which none-theless implies a scale of value that is all the more powerful for being imminently absent (Paulin 1997). Thus, in 'An Arundel Tomb' (1956) the voice of the poem observes the sculpted figures of a feudal lord and lady atop a fourteenth-century table tomb in Chichester Cathedral, charting the deepening failure of subsequent generations of cathedral visitors to understand the now gone social world that produced them. While sculpture freezes its subjects in time, later generations figure as the 'endless altered people' whose 'succeeding eyes' can 'look' at but 'not read' the meanings encoded in the tomb's statuary (Larkin 2003: 116). The incomprehension of this 'unarmorial age' works upon the sei-gneurial effigies like a semantic acid, '[w]ashing at their identities' and erasing the social meanings that once anchored them in the feudal world. Instead of the fixed hierarchical order of feudal England, now visitors see only their hands clasped as a sign of love, reducing the meaning of tradition from the sober message of stable hierarchy and order to the sentimental concerns of the contemporary: 'Time has transfigured them into / Untruth', the poem's persona laments, archly noting the irony that the 'stone fidelity / They hardly meant has come to be / Their final blazon', or symbolic epithet. But in fact the poem's ostensible narrative of semantic entropy is belied by the persona's sure grasp on the meaning now supposedly lost: for despite the depredations of modernity, the poet still knows how to read the tomb, understanding that its true meaning lies in 'The Latin names around the base' – that is, in the maintenance of a social hierarchy once based on patrilineal descent (2003: 117). It is to the masses that the meaning of England is opaque, just as the working-class 'crowd' in 'Going, Going' (1972) prefers an empty quan-tity over meaningful quality, demanding 'more – / More houses, more parking allowed, / More caravans, more pay' (Larkin 2003: 133). And yet although unknowing, these masses remain reverent of that tradition and obedient to its secular rituals – such as visiting historical monuments on wet Bank Holiday weekends. Ironically, then, 'An Arundel Tomb' accommodates class differences within an overarching hierarchy based not on feudal lineage but on proximity to national tradition. The newly mobile working class are blind to the meaning of English tradition but remain loyal to its empty forms, while the ironic voice of the poet sustains the meaningfulness of that tradition in the very moment of announcing its apparent loss. But in 'Homage to a Government' it becomes clear that this ability to incorporate social differences is not as integral and self-enclosed as Larkin tends to claim, but depends on an 'elsewhere' to 'underwrite' its 'existence'.[27]

By the 1960s, the second colonial occupation had served its purpose in rebuilding the shattered British wartime economy, and Britain increasingly looked to Europe, the United States, Canada, Australia and South Africa for markets and trading partners rather than to its remaining colonial possessions, a shift that dovetailed with the unraveling of the Sterling Area between 1967 and 1972 (Cain and Hopkins 2002: 634–7). At the same time, political demands for independence and the increasing burden of military and administrative costs meant that the permanent projection of British military power beyond Europe – or 'East of Suez' as it was termed – became unfeasible. British withdrawal from its colonial base at Aden on the Arabian Peninsula in 1967 in the wake of a bloody counter-insurgency war known as the Aden Emergency, quickly followed by withdrawal from its Gulf protectorates in 1971, signalled for many the effective end of the Empire.[28] In a pointedly ironic register, 'Homage to a Government' laments not just that 'Next year we are to bring the soldiers home / For lack of money', but that 'now it's been decided nobody minds' (Larkin 2003: 141). The poem's concern, then, is primarily domestic, focusing on the collapse of national will incumbent on what is presented as the listless acceptance of the vicissitudes of history:

> Next year we shall be living in a country
> That brought its soldiers home for lack of money
> The statues will be standing in the same
> Tree-muffled squares, and look nearly the same.
> Our children will not know it's a different country.
> All we can hope to leave them now is money. (Larkin 2003: 141)

The poem's blank repetition mimes the evacuation of meaning from national space, whose monuments will henceforth 'look nearly the same' but which have, like the statuary of 'An Arundel Tomb', been drained of the meaning that once animated them. What is different, however, is that the observer no longer provides the repository for that meaning, and his glassy eye, and the voice that articulates its vision, is no longer animated by Larkin's characteristically zesty sarcasm, but is as blank and enervated as the scene it surveys. It turns out that the confident grasp of national tradition that had once seemed so rooted, personal and intimate required the military infrastructure of empire to guarantee the surefootedness of its perceptions and underpin its puckish joie de vivre.

'Homage to a Government' both acknowledges and denies the dependence of nation on empire. On one level, the charge is that the 'government' that is the recipient of this ironic 'homage', the Labour administration of Harold Wilson, reflects the modern mindset which Larkin summarised in an interview as 'idleness, greed, and treason', and so is concerned only with its own well-being (Larkin 1983: 52): 'We want the money for ourselves at home, / Instead of working', recounts the voice of the poem, and since the 'places' where British troops are stationed 'are a long way off, not here', selfish concerns easily trump broader responsibilities. But these responsibilities, it turns out, are not really to these other 'places', but to 'ourselves', and here lies the root of the denial – or self-deception – at the heart of the poem (1983: 52). In a not-so-distant echo of Rudyard Kipling's poem 'The White Man's Burden' (1899), which had argued that imperialism was an arduous and costly task undertaken only out of selfless duty, decolonisation is rebranded as the resignation of that demanding 'work' and the slothful embrace of self-indulgence and greed. The little word 'work' thus carries an immense burden of meaning, for what the poem terms 'working' is in reality the economic exploitation of the colonies for the benefit of British reconstruction. In this semantic economy of 'burden' and 'responsibility', the relation of colonial labour and exploitation is reversed: colonial labourers become exploiters, while imperial exploiters become altruistic workers on behalf of others.

The poem's ostensible concern for these other 'places', then, is not a concern for them as societies with their own dynamics, conflicts and potentials, but for the British ability to impose order: they are simply so many anonymous and interchangeable 'places' that must be 'guarded, or kept orderly'. This self-centredness is masked by the poem's blank irony, which mimics the 'we' it condemns – the 'official' Britain of the self-serving political state, which has reneged on its supposed colonial commitments. Thus there is a split in that 'we' between the voice of the 'government' or state, and that of the common sense of the people, or what we might call the 'nation' properly speaking. In ironically ventriloquising what are clearly to be regarded as the establishment nostrums that justify the state but defy the common sense of the nation – that 'from what we hear / The soldiers there only made trouble happen', and that these 'places' can now 'guard themselves, and keep themselves orderly' – the poem invites us to understand the opposite: that the soldiers did not 'make trouble happen', and that these places are in reality incapable of 'guard[ing]' and 'keep[ing] themselves orderly'. There is a gap between the statist views that the poetic voice cheerlessly articulates and the implicit 'national' good sense that the poem almost invisibly invites its readers to endorse, although it is a narrow one. There is no longer room enough to accommodate the more historically rooted and socially differentiated conception of national tradition invoked in 'An Arundel Tomb'; instead, it seems only capable of encompassing *ressentiment* at the state that has so betrayed the common sense of the 'nation'.

The conflict between state and nation in Larkin's 'Homage to a Government' matches the tension identified at the heart of European imperialism by the political philosopher Hannah Arendt in *The Origins of Totalitarianism*, first published in 1951. For Arendt, imperialism conflicts with the basic character of the nation-state to the extent that the nation-state approximates to a properly political space, defined by constitutionality and negotiation between a plurality of different political actors (see MacPhee and Poddar 2007: 9–15). Imperialism reflects the 'private' needs of capital accumulation and economic expansion, while the nation-state, albeit imperfectly, involves a level of respect for enduring patterns of social differentiation and some recognition of a 'national' or public interest in contradistinction to the imperatives of the private realm. For Arendt, the decision by the British state in the second half of the nineteenth century to put its resources fully behind the economic expansion of imperialism thus marks the subordination of the state to economic imperatives, or the subordination of the political to the social.[29] Despite the fundamental incompatibility of the national-political and the economic-imperial, during the late nineteenth century different sectors of society came to identify the *private* economic imperatives of imperialism with the *public* interest of the national-political, and imperialism rapidly came to be regarded as the 'panacea' for all the ills of the nation-state (Arendt 1973: 151). 'In theory,' Arendt writes, 'there is an abyss between nationalism and imperialism'; but 'in practice', she observes, 'it can and has been bridged by tribal nationalism and outright racism' (1973: 153).

This 'confusion of imperialism and nationalism' constitutes what Arendt regarded as the dangerous and damaging 'boomerang effect of imperialism upon the homeland' (Arendt 1973: 153, 155). The misrecognition of economic expansion – which for Arendt is fundamentally private in character – as the public good, gives rise to a particularly impoverished conception of 'community' at the political level, but compensates at the experiential level through its valorisation of the mysterious, ineffable and emotional character of ethno-national identity, a mystery that finds its ultimate expression in the fantasies of 'race thinking' (1973: 158–61). Thus, although ostensibly expanding the remit of the nation, the confusion of imperialism and nationalism in fact results in the degradation of the substantive political framework of the nation-state – characterised by legality, constitutionality and publicity – the growth of quasi-private bureaucracies, the strengthening of the supranational force of the economic and the increasing role of ethno-nationalism as a basis for national belonging (1973: 153, 267). In subordinating state to society, imperialism uncouples the terms of the nation-state and subordinates 'state' to 'nation'.

In certain senses the creation of the welfare state during the second colonial occupation began to renovate the impoverished political community bequeathed by nineteenth-century imperialism. But at the same time, as the writing of George Lamming and Sam Selvon reminds us, this restructuring of community was shaped by an increasingly ethnically and racially based conception of nation, one which paradoxically tended to erase the history of imperialism that had engendered it. Larkin's 'Homage to a Government', on the other hand, identifies what it sees as the betrayal constituted by the withdrawal from empire with the rising social visibility of the working class and with state welfarism and the reduction of social inequality. Against the renovated postwar welfare state, Larkin opposes the 'nation', an ineffable field of belonging that exists primarily as a sense of continuity with a hallowed past, a set of contemporary cultural habits and predilections, and belief in an organic or 'natural' conception of social hierarchy and individual worth. These elements are cemented together by a powerful resentment against statist and bureaucratic regulation, which are seen as jeopardising them.

Arendt's conception of the reformulation of the relationship between state and nation under imperialism provides an illuminating analytical approach for understanding the power and appeal of Enoch Powell and the discourse of Powellism associated with him. Powell was a Conservative Member of Parliament and former Cabinet minister who had taught classics at Sydney University, and had for a period harboured ambitions of becoming viceroy of India (Heffer 2008). After an unsuccessful bid to become leader of the Conservative Party in 1965, Powell sought to rebuild his political fortunes through a series of high-profile speeches on immigration that harnessed popular racism to a neoliberal and anti-statist agenda. Most notorious was the speech he delivered on 20 April 1968 to Conservatives in Birmingham before invited news cameras, which subsequently became known as the 'Rivers of Blood' speech. Although Powell was initially censured by the Conservative Party leadership for the overt racism of the speech, his ideas provided the intellectual basis for Thatcherism – the new popular language of conservatism associated with Prime Minister Margaret Thatcher – many of whose tenets were in turn adopted as political 'common sense' by the 'New Labour' programme of Tony Blair and Gordon Brown (see Mercer 1991; Kavanagh 1987: 69–71; Evans 2004: 128–34; Bourne 2007; McKibbin 2006). However, the political and cultural significance of Powell lies not simply in the fact that he developed a style of culturalist racism more acceptable to mainstream British society, but that he articulated this racism as a coherent element of a much larger restructuring of national identity that responded to the new tensions and challenges we have explored above (Gikandi 1996: 70). As a sympathetic writer commented at the time, by the late 1960s Powell was charged by the Conservative leader Edward Heath with 'one of the most crucial and pressing missions – the destruction of the Imperial legend which [had been] so important a part [of] the mythology of British Toryism' (Utley 1968: 103). Where Larkin's conception of national unity required an international military infrastructure to scaffold its sense of class hierarchy, Powell would dispense with both class and empire under the all-consuming banner of ethno-nationalism.

Intellectually, Powellism works by stripping away most of the complexity of social life, so that all social and political interaction can be reduced to the interaction of a few highly predictable but absolutely inexplicable elements (Powell 1967: 20). The basic mechanical ingredients of this worldview are the multiplicity of atomised individuals on the one hand, and on the other the state. While atomised individuals relate to one another through the market, understood as the sole arena for 'the free discretion and self-determination of individuals', the state is an alien force whose fundamental predisposition is to 'loc[k] [its] citizens up in [ideological] prisons' and 'to hoodwink' them so as to control and restrict 'the natural course of human behaviour' (1967: 22, 14). Powellism was thus 'forward thinking' in anticipating the subsequent turn to 'neoliberalism' in the new global disposition, the political ideology associated with Thatcherism and Reaganism that 'proceed[s] on the assumption that the world market is the overriding force of contemporary economic development and that nation-statist policy has therefore become irrelevant' (Lazarus 2004: 25). However, it was also 'forward thinking' in recognising the need to compensate for the potentially asocial character of this drastically pared down vision of human existence, and so Powell supplements these two mechanical elements (individual versus state) with a third, magical concept – the 'nation'. As many commentators have pointed out, Powell anticipates Benedict Anderson's conception of the nation as an 'imagined community', in that for Powell the nation is based on 'collective self-consciousness' rather than being definitively tied to 'Race, language, [or] geography': a nation 'is that which thinks it is a nation' (Powell and Maude 1970: 7; c.f. Anderson 1983: 15–16). However, it needs to be remembered that Powell's concept of the nation differs from Anderson's in its absolutism and immutability. Once constituted, 'national consciousness . . . remains the same', a fixity that depends on the insistence that 'history bears a tantalizing similarity to biology' (Powell and Maude 1970: 8, 9). '[N]ational consciousness . . . remains as mysterious as that of life in the individual organism', Powell writes, a formula that secures its predictability while exempting it from analysis: 'transmitted from generation to generation by a process *analogous to inheritance*', the nation becomes the unchanging and all-determining 'body in whose bloodstream one is oneself a single corpuscle, the collective mind in whose thoughts, for an instant, one shares oneself' (1970: 9; emphasis added). An unchanging mystical unity ('the body') composed of already homogeneous units ('corpuscles') secures the reality and primacy of 'the nation' over and against the (nation)-state. Thus, while (nation-)states are basically illusory and insubstantial entities, 'nations' – properly understood as the 'mysterious' unity of already identical atoms – 'are the units of mankind as a political animal', and all else – class consciousness,[30] social justice,[31] democratic rights[32] – 'are no part of history' (Powell and Maude 1970: 7). As Kobena Mercer astutely points out, what Powell refers to in individualistic terms as the 'deep and dangerous gulf in the nation' is more accurately understood in terms of the decoupling of the elements of 'state' and 'nation' which comprise the nation-state: that is, as 'the antagonism between "the people" as the silent majority' which constitutes the 'nation' proper, 'and the "establishment" which . . . represents "the state"' (Powell 1991: 383; Mercer 1991: 435).

The primacy of the 'nation' in Powellism entails the disappearance of the ongoing significance of imperialism, both in terms of its transitional role in securing Britain's place in the new US hegemony and in terms of its continuing legacy of underdevelopment and inequality. The distance of the present from the glories of the past becomes proof both of the glory of that past and of its absolute absence in the present:

> We are told that the economic achievement of the Western countries has been at the expense of the rest of the world and has impoverished them, so that what are called the 'developed' countries owe a duty to . . . underdeveloped countries. It is nonsense – manifest, arrant nonsense, but it is nonsense with which the people of Western countries . . . have been so deluged and saturated that they feel ashamed of what the brains and energy of Western mankind have done, and sink on their knees for being civilized and ask to be insulted and humiliated. (Powell 1991: 247–8)

In its melodramatic theatricality, this passage both avows and disavows imperialism by converting it entirely into a question of the celebration or disparagement of the abstract Western individual and its supposed achievements. The Empire is remembered as the product of 'the brains and energy of Western mankind' and as the natural manifestation of 'being civilized'; but as merely the expression of such fleeting inner qualities, it cannot be conceived as having collective or structural effects or legacies. As Simon Gikandi observes, its passage into an absolutely sealed and inaccessible history – marked by the degradation of the Western individual, so brow-beaten that it now calls for its own humiliation – is secured (Gikandi 1996: 74; see also Gilroy 2005: 106–9). 'By the 1960s,' Powell writes, 'Britain was, what she had for long not been, once again an offshore island of Europe,' a judgement that completely erases the integration of British economic, foreign and military policy into the new US hegemony which Powell on other occasions denounced with such vehemence and acuity (Powell and Maude 1970: 235; c.f. Powell and Maude 1970: 237 and Powell 1991: 421–39). Britain as 'nation' becomes a lonely, pariah figure – not unlike Powell's own self-mythologising – rather than a major nuclear-armed state with a veto at the UN Security Council and preferential access to markets and investment opportunities around the world.

In fact, the Empire left a profound imprint on Powell's own political thought through its decoupling and opposition of state and nation. This impact helps to explain his contradictory vision of Britain: as at once a globally-integrated state, and an outcast and traduced nation. Initially Powell was 'an ardent imperialist', as attested by his membership of the Suez Group of Conservative MPs who opposed military withdrawal from the Empire. Over the period between the evacuation of British troops from the Suez Canal in 1954 (two years before their unsuccessful return during the Suez Crisis) and his admission to the Conservative Shadow Cabinet in 1965, Powell began to feel 'that the British Empire had dissolved and would not be reconstructed' (Schoen 1977: 4; Utley 1968: 103). Under the Empire, Powell could allow state action some legitimacy as long as it centred on military and administrative support for private economic expansion; but now that he saw the game would soon be up, he increasingly viewed the state as fundamentally antagonistic and detrimental to the nation, 'sinking national sovereignty' in all kinds of international compromises and supranational 'organizations' – whether the United Nations or the Commonwealth – and entangling itself in social provision and 'State control of every aspect of the economy' (Powell and Maude 1970: 225, 227).[33] By 1970, when he claimed that 'the writ of Britain [had] ceased to run ... outside the British Isles' and 'her influence ha[d] virtually ceased to exist', Powell would complain that the British state had ballooned, while 'Her very identity as a nation [is] called into question'. As such, it is 'the people of Britain', in contradistinction to the British state, who must 'find a new concept of themselves which would support and satisfy them' (1970: 238).

While, as Douglas Schoen observes, such anti-statism developed a powerful momentum in the United States with the McCarthyism of the early Cold War years, similar popular appeal was lacking in Britain at a time when the welfare state was associated with reducing economic inequalities and providing much-needed public services (Schoen 1977: 277–8). However, in his speeches of the late 1960s Powell discovered a popular language for articulating the conflict between state and nation – namely immigration. As Kobena Mercer argues, 'immigration provided symbolic leverage for the broader articulation of [Powell's] neoliberal anti-statism' (Mercer 1991: 435).[34] In these speeches, the legal category of United Kingdom citizenship, until 1981 still residually tied to the UKC citizenship of the 1948 Act, comes to represent in palpable terms the conflict between the more abstract entities of 'state' and 'nation'. 'The West Indian or Asian does not, by being born in England, become an Englishman,' declares Powell: 'In law he becomes a United Kingdom citizen by birth; in fact he is a West Indian or an Asian still' (1991: 393). Thus, the visible phenotypical differences between 'white' and 'non-white' are conflated with the cultural differences associated with ethnicity, and in turn this conflation is used to lever open a gap between 'law' and 'fact', or between the arbitrary, artificial and thoroughly dangerous dogma of the state and the self-evident 'commonsense' of the nation (see

Gikandi 1996: 76–7). The emerging discourse of Powellism turns on the move between these different levels. Ethnic differences are used to transcode the visible differences of phenotype referred to in everyday terms as 'race', and in doing so they become fixed as effectively unalterable divisions of culture, allegiance and belonging – that is, as markers of ethno-national identity which 'remai[n] the same' and are 'transmitted from generation to generation by a process analogous to [genetic] inheritance' (Powell and Maude 1970: 8, 9). This ethno-national identity then becomes the bulwark against the 'state', or political appeals to rights, citizenship and full social participation.

This shift from the language of biological race to an ethno-nationalism based on fixed cultural categories has been termed by Etienne Balibar 'neo-racism'. Balibar describes it as a 'racism without races' since it depends

> not [on] biological heredity but the insurmountability of cultural differences, a racism which, at first sight, does not postulate the superiority of certain groups or peoples in relation to others but 'only' the harmfulness of abolishing frontiers, the incompatability of life-styles and traditions. (Balibar 1991: 21)

Thus, while the racial ground of these ethno-national distinctions is still observable in the background – Powell refers specifically to the danger to British national identity of 'Asiatic and negro immigration', rather than European immigration, and employs the homogeneous race-based category of 'Afro-Asians' (Powell and Maude 1970: 238; Powell 1991: 386) – it is obscured, and questions of identity and belonging are increasingly articulated in the language of fixed ethno-national differences (Gikandi 1996: 76). The discourse of Powellism is therefore able to distance itself from the increasingly discredited and unsustainable biological definitions of race, depending instead on a diffuse complex of cultural discourses – gender roles and sexual norms, patterns of behaviour, religious practice and belief, language, clothing and styles of visual appearance, among others – to set the limits of community, tradition, belonging and difference (Mercer 1991: 435). Yet as Balibar observes, neo-racism can distance itself from nature only because *culture can also function like nature*; that is, because cultural differences are naturalised and rendered immutably fixed (Balibar 1991: 22). The political force of this 'racism without races' lies not only in its capacity to neutralise the existing defences of anti-racism by accepting and endorsing cultural diversity – although as a series of fixed and unbridgeable differences – but also in its ability to provide an explanation for racism which naturalises racism itself (Balibar 1991: 21–2). As Balibar explains, given these fixed cultural distinctions it appears only 'natural' from the perspective of neo-racism that there should be a '"spontaneous" tendency [for] human groups . . . to preserve their traditions, and thus their identity' – although 'in practice' it is the 'political category of the nation', whose 'anthropological significance . . . is obviously rather dubious', that is granted this inviolable status (1991: 22). Thus, 'in accordance with the postulate that individuals are the exclusive heirs and bearers of a single culture', in order 'to avoid racism . . . you have to respect the "tolerance thresholds", maintain "cultural differences" or, in other words . . . segregate communities' (1991: 22–3). The shift from immutable biological to immutable cultural differences means that neo-racism *naturalizes not racial belonging but racist conduct*' (Balibar 1991: 22; c.f. Gikandi 1996: 77). That is, what is to be defended from the viewpoint of neo-racism is not the scientific or physiological basis of particular 'races', but the felt integrity and exclusivity of the dominant 'national' grouping within the nation-state. In Britain, that dominant grouping has been defined at the associational level with 'Englishness', even when it is articulated as 'British' national identity, a confused and confusing structuring of identity that enables the presentation of an English ethno-national identity in the guise of more 'reasonable' British civic nationalism (MacPhee and Poddar 2007: 1–9; Baucom 1999: 7–29). Thus, Powell could at once denounce with incandescent outrage the situation (as he saw it) that it was now 'heresy to assert the plain fact that the English are a white nation', while at the same time claiming that 'I hold no man inferior because he is of different origin' (Powell 1991: 247, 404). Indeed, he would even claim to be innocent of the very category of 'race' (Powell 1991: 245–6).

Balibar's analysis of neo-racism establishes a relationship between decolonisation and the shift from biology to culture, and it accounts for the centrality of immigration to neo-racist discourse. As we have seen, by the late-nineteenth century imperial rule sought legitimation through its claim for the 'natural' superiority of Europeans over less 'civilised' or more 'decadent' racial groups. During the same period, immigration to Britain was predominantly white, coming largely from Ireland and Eastern Europe, and hostility to immigrants tended to take the form of cultural xenophobia, as exemplified for Balibar by anti-Semitism (Balibar 1991: 21, 23–4). Colonial and Commonwealth migration after the war took place within the complex of factors we have examined above: the eclipse of the imperialist ideology of the 'civilising mission' by the new internationalist discourse of the Cold War, with its vocabulary of democracy and freedom; a renewed focus on national culture and a localised national identity; the cultural excision of the Empire within various new transnational models; and the disappearance of colonial labour through the casting of non-white workers as 'non-labour'. In these conditions, older imperialist ideologies of race were folded into existing patterns of culturalist xenophobia with their vocabulary of 'invasion' and 'occupation', so that race and culture were conflated.[35] Ironically, what are lost here are the very cultural connections that had tied colonial subjects to the 'mother country', and which had encouraged that migration in the first place. As Paul Gilroy observes, the disappearance of Empire and of colonial labour 'feeds an additional catastrophe: the error of imagining that postcolonial people are only unwanted alien intruders without any substantive historical, political, or cultural connections to the collective life of their fellow subjects' (Gilroy 2005: 90).

This damaging conflation of culture and race is evident in Powell's notorious 'Rivers of Blood' speech, whose occasion it should be remembered was the impending passage of legislation designed to outlaw racial discrimination in housing and employment, so securing at least some limited political recognition for the rights of all those residing within the domestic polity. The speech openly invokes racist stereotypes – soon 'the black man will have the whip over the white man' we learn, while 'wide-grinning piccaninnies' are said to roam the streets (Powell 1991: 374, 378) – although they are carefully put in the mouths of others, who are nonetheless described as 'ordinary, decent, sensible people' and 'fellow Englishm[en]' (1991: 377, 374). The weight of the argument, however, rests on the 'grave but . . . avoidable evils' constituted by the immigration of 'Commonwealth citizens' – that is, by UKC citizens coming from the predominantly non-white countries of the 'New Commonwealth' (1991: 373, 375). Yet if this suggests that such 'evils' are a temporary product of acclimatisation and acculturation, or that difficulties might obtain in the case of both white and non-white Commonwealth migrants, the speech goes to great length to reject such possibilities. What 'creates the extreme urgency of action now' is not the situation of new arrivals but the impending increase of 'immigrant descendents, those born in England, who arrived here exactly by the same route as the rest of us' – that is, British people who are not 'white' (1991: 374). Here colour and culture are run together, although they are not identified absolutely: 'where there are marked physical differences, especially of colour', Powell insists, 'integration is difficult', although he concedes the possibility that 'over a period' it is 'not impossible'. But theoretical possibility does not reality make, for 'to imagine that such a thing enters the heads of the great and growing majority of immigrants and their descendants is a ludicrous misconception, and a dangerous one to boot' (1991: 378). In transfixing culture as nature, Powell determines both the relation of state to nation and the possible outcome of successful immigration as 'integration'. Progress towards a successful multi-racial society cannot be made through the securing of universal political rights that would enable the mutual recognition of different social actors and the negotiation of their political, economic and cultural differences; for, according to Powell, such an extension of political rights has *already* been accomplished, with every 'Commonwealth immigrant' already 'a full citizen' in 'a country that knows no discrimination between one citizen and another' (1991: 376). The securing of state-based rights as envisaged, albeit imperfectly, by the proposed Race Relations Bill therefore does not address the problem because the 'problem' lies not in the political realm but in the immutable alienness of these immigrants to the 'nation'. 'Whatever drawbacks attended the immigrants,' Powell claims, 'arose not from the law or from public policy or from administration but from those personal circumstances and accidents which cause, and always will cause, the fortunes and experiences of one man to be different from another's' (1991: 377). But if, as Powell argues, the achievement of social harmony cannot be realised by the recognition and negotiation of differences through the opening up of the political realm, then it can only be effected through the exclusion of such differences from it – that is, through the absolute homogeneity and self-identity of the nation.[36]

After Empire

This chapter has focused on the period up to 1971, which saw the dissolution of the Sterling Area and the withdrawal of British forces from the Arabian Gulf. It has argued that rather than seeing a uniform process of decolonisation, we have to view this period as a transitional phase that produced a much more complicated and variegated range of cultural and literary responses than is often assumed. While Indian and Pakistani independence has understandably loomed large in retrospective cultural histories of the period, an exclusive focus on these epochal instances of decolonisation nonetheless risks neglecting the importance of Britain's transition into the new global dispensation under United States hegemony. Britain was launched on this new role by the second colonial occupation, which like the spent stages of a rocket was incrementally jettisoned until its final abandonment in the early 1970s.[37]

This transition had to cope with a dizzying array of economic, social and political shifts: the loss of prestige and self-confidence associated with decolonisation in South Asia and the growth of American power across the globe; the transition from imperial conceptions of the 'civilising mission' to the Cold War discourse of 'freedom' and 'democracy'; the integration of working-class demands through the creation of the welfare state and the new social mobility and cultural visibility of the working class that went with it; the increase in transnational mobility and its extension to colonial and postcolonial subjects; the (re)integration of the British economy into a transforming global economy and the deepening penetration of American popular culture into Europe that accompanied it; and the challenge to existing patterns of social morality and gender roles that accompanied all these shifts and the political struggles which they engendered.

As we have argued in this chapter, this more complex and contradictory process generated a whole range of cultural and political responses whose dynamic vectors, as we shall explore in Chapters 2 and 3, would continue to play themselves out in the subsequent decades after 1970. While national retrenchment became a ubiquitous and secular cultural tendency as articulated by Jed Esty, it was accompanied by a transformed sense of exemplarity and global extension, as identified by John Marx. This combination would give rise to some striking and even baroque attempts to configure national and global, which indeed are often the ones we remember today. In Orwell's *1984*, for example, global and national are combined in the exemplary anonymity and subordination of 'Airstrip One', a formulation which insists that even the most residual invocation of national particularity implies insertion into the context of global power. Eliot's cultural criticism, though less dramatic in scenario and more sober in tone and style, would provide an even more audacious fiction, relocating English particularity to a plane of transnational culture in which the history of imperialism and its legacy in the new global dispensation simply did not obtain. It is not true, then, that postwar British culture can be neatly choreographed as the renunciation of the global and the consequent withdrawal into the national. What emerges even from this brief sketch is a much messier, more complicated and more contradictory picture. In Orwell and Eliot, for example, national and global are combined in different ways, but in each case what disappears is not the global per se, but imperialism as a historically specific formation whose legacies are still operative: in Eliot, the history that 'matters' is no longer the past or future history of British global power, but an imperially innocent Western culture; and in the case of Orwell's *1984*, it is 'we' (the British) who have been colonised. For writers like George Lamming, Sam Selvon and Louise Bennett, who made their way in a transatlantic world defined by the rising power of the United States and the declining power of Britain, such claims for Britain's colonisation would appear as a considerable, but perhaps not entirely unexpected, irony. In the hands of Enoch Powell, this complex of vectors would be organised in order to effect a kind of *de*colonisation in reverse, which combines an ethno-nationalist conception of Englishness with the anti-statist neoliberalism of transnational corporate capital. If we understand colonisation not simply as forcible settlement in another territory but also as the economic exploitation of that territory and its population, then Powellism demands more than an end to Commonwealth migration and the 'repatriation' of non-white British people. It also implies the disintegration of that state sovereignty which might hinder transnational capital's power and foster alternative forms of economic and political self-organisation.

Notes

1. In arguing for the strategic use of a restricted focus here, I am mindful of Edward Said's important discussion in chapter three of *Culture and Imperialism* of the dangers of excluding non-European dynamics; see Said 1993: 191–209.
2. For a discussion of the relevance of Bloch and Benjamin to postcolonial studies, see Keya Ganguly's 'Temporality and Postcolonial Critique' in Lazarus 2004: 162–79.
3. The reference is to Orwell's 1940 essay 'Inside the Whale'; see Orwell 2002: 211–48.
4. Esty's framework sees a structural division in the postwar period between 'a culturalist discourse of national transformation' and 'a broader individualist discourse of national decline' (Esty 2004: 216). This first, culturalist discourse is primarily embodied by the British – or as Esty has it, 'English' – Cultural Studies of Richard Hoggart and Raymond Williams, and by the work of a wave of writers from various colonies and former colonies who migrated to Britain in the immediate postwar years, exemplified by the writing of Sam Selvon, George Lamming, Doris Lessing and Nirad Chaudhuri (2004: 183, 208, 199). This second discourse of national decline includes most of the major, established literary figures of the day – W.H. Auden, George Orwell, Phillip Larkin, Graham Greene, Evelyn Waugh, Malcolm Lowry and to a lesser extent Ted Hughes and Geoffrey Hill – as well as the dominant academic school of literary criticism, associated with F.R. Leavis and the journal *Scrutiny* (Esty 2004: 216).
5. See Sands 2005; see also Prashad 2007: 10–11, who emphasises the role of Third World states in building the new human rights architecture; and Mazower 2009, who stresses the ambivalent aims involved in the founding of the UN. The status of all member nations was never even formally equal given the special role of the Permanent Members of the UN Security Council.
6. As Auden's friend and fellow expatriate Hannah Arendt argued that very same year, the indifference of power and its removal from the social life of the ruled

was one of the most original and dangerous features of European imperialism, and one that had now entered into the very architecture of modern politics. 'Aloofness,' Arendt writes, 'was a more dangerous form of governing than despotism and arbitrariness because it did not ... tolerate [any] link between the despot and his subjects', instituting instead 'an absolute division of interests to the point where they are not even permitted to conflict' (Arendt 1973: 212). In this reading, the point of Auden's poem is not to claim that the new order is simply the same as the old colonialism; rather it is to reveal the complex way in which the removal of colonial relations may facilitate a new structure of power asymmetry, one in which the very certainty of the powerful in their own imperial innocence creates the conditions for the repetition and intensification of colonial violence; see Kolko 1994.

7. My reading here draws on Gilroy's important account of 'postcolonial amnesia' (Gilroy 2005: 89–90), but also suggests that we need to include the Cold War as a crucial but unacknowledged locus for the construction of this amnesia; see also Said 1993: 282–303; Brennan 2006: 41–7; Khalidi 2009: 1–17.

8. Pyle's academically inspired alliance with General Thé in order to create a 'third force' to oppose the Vietnamese national movement, the Viet Minh, closely resembles the political project developed by Ngo Dinh Diem, the CIA and academics at the Michigan State University Vietnam Advisory Group: see Ernst 1998. Diem's regime was brutal, repressive, corrupt and deeply unpopular, and fell to a coup in 1963.

9. This element of self-reflexivity is not allowed for in Esty's analysis, although it is evident in the essay by Anderson that provides its intellectual inspiration; see Anderson 1992: 96.

10. The term 'Old Commonwealth' refers to the predominantly white settler colonies that were formally granted independence (as imperial 'dominions') by the Statute of Westminster in 1931; conversely, the 'New Commonwealth' refers to predominantly non-white colonies that became independent in the period between 1947 and 1970. Churchill is drawing on a history of 'Anglo-Saxon' racial ideology that goes back to the end of the eighteenth century, and which is itself a transnational and transatlantic formation; see Horsman 1981.

11. This was understood by contemporary political critics, who objected to the speech's contamination of the emerging Cold War rhetoric with the older discourse of colonialism: see Hinds and Windt 1991: 97–100.

12. As Raymond Williams observes acutely, the 'complicated processes' of British politics and society are made 'too easy, too settling, too sweet' (Williams 1971: 24). For Williams, the 'difficulty' always lay in Orwell's 'image' of the British social formation as 'a family', a formulation that both erased class conflict and sealed the nation from the world through a fantasy of genetic collectivity that resembles Churchill's (Williams 1971: 22).

13. In his *Trauerspiel* book, Benjamin describes how the absolute arbitrariness of allegorical meaning comes cumulatively to figure its opposite, the certainty and self-presence of meaning within Christian eschatology: 'For it is precisely visions of the frenzy of destruction, in which all earthly things collapse into a heap of ruins, which reveal the limit set upon allegorical contemplation ... In [allegory] transitoriness is not signified or allegorically represented, so much as, in its own significance, displayed as allegory. As the allegory of redemption. Ultimately in the death-signs of the baroque the direction of allegorical reflection is reversed; on the side of its wide arc it returns, to redeem' (Benjamin 1977: 232). My suggestion here is that Orwell's *1984* might profitably be read as a latter day *Trauerspiel*, or work of mourning.

14. See 'Sense-Certainty: Or the "This" and "Meaning"', in Hegel 1977: 58–66.

15. Despite his criticisms of Irving Babbitt, Eliot follows him in identifying the United States with the European basis of Western culture; see Eliot's essay 'The Humanism of Irving Babbitt', in Eliot 1975: 277–84.

16. Colonial recruitment was pursued by some public services and nationalised industries, including London Transport and the National Health Service; see Winder 2004: 335.

17. Paul estimates colonial migration into the UK in the decade after the *Windrush*'s first trip at around 180,000, approximately half of the figure for continental European immigration over the same period; see Paul 1997: 132. Chris Waters suggests a figure for migration that is much lower than this, although he implies that the existing black population of Britain was much higher than Paul's estimated range (Waters 1997: 209).

18. 'London is the Place for Me', Lord Kitchener with Freddy Grant's Caribbean Rhythm, Melodisc 1163, London, 1951. Available on the compilation *London is the Place for Me: Trinidadian Calypso in London 1950–1956*, Honest Jon's Records, 2002.

19. 'My Landlady', Lord Kitchener with Freddy Grant's Caribbean Rhythm, Melodisc 1208, London, 1952. Available on the compilation *London is the Place for Me: Trinidadian Calypso in London 1950–1956*, Honest Jon's Records, 2002.

20. 'I Was There (At The Coronation)', Young Tiger with Cyril Blake's Calypso Serenaders, Melodisc 1229, London, 1953. Available on the compilation *London is the Place for Me: Trinidadian Calypso in London 1950–1956*, Honest Jon's Records, 2002.

21. 'Birth of Ghana', Lord Kitchener with his Calypso All Stars, Melodisc 1390, London, 1956. Available on the compilation *London is the Place for Me: Trinidadian Calypso in London 1950–1956*, Honest Jon's Records, 2002.

22. 'Jamaica Hurricane', Lord Beginner with the Calypso Rhythm Kings, Melodisc 1183, London, 1951. Available on the compilation *London is the Place for Me: Trinidadian Calypso in London 1950–1956*, Honest Jon's Records, 2002.

23. 'If You're Not White You're Black', Lord Kitchener with Fitzroy Coleman's Trinidad Ragers, Melodisc 1260, London, 1953. Available on the compilation *London is the Place for Me: Trinidadian Calypso in London 1950–1956*, Honest Jon's Records, 2002.

24. 'Mix Up Matrimony', Lord Beginner with the Calypso Rhythm Kings, Melodisc 1229, London, 1952. Available on the compilation *London is the Place for Me: Trinidadian Calypso in London 1950–1956*, Honest Jon's Records, 2002.

25. By 1960 Lamming came to see himself as Caribbean rather than West Indian due to the 'British colonial limitation' and the desire to include French and Spanish speaking cultures: Lamming 1992: 215.

26. J.M. Bernstein describes this as 'seeing through and obeying' (Bernstein 1991: 12–13). In Joyce's text, it is the imperial consumer – figured in this instance by Bloom – and not the colonial labourer, who is the 'Lotus Eater' lost in reverie and forgetful of the realities of its own social world.

27. This claim for integrity is articulated most clearly in 'The Importance of Elsewhere', from which these terms are taken; Larkin 2003: 105. 'Homage to a Government' reveals that the self-evidence of Larkin's 'everyday' in fact requires the supplement (in the Derridean sense) of empire.

28. Britain's military involvement in Yemen included funding a secret, quasi-autonomous mercenary force, which – had it been orchestrated by anti-Western forces – would most likely now be described as a 'terrorist group' (see Jones 2004: 199–214). Significantly, a number of the troops who returned from Aden

in 1967 were redeployed to Derry in the North of Ireland following the Battle of the Bogside (Tillotson 1995: 99–101).

29. In Britain's case the situation was more complex and contradictory than Arendt suggests, as Disraeli's turn to popular imperialism coincided with, and was in some senses a response to, the Reform Act of 1867; see Metcalf 1995: 55–60.

30. See Powell and Maude 1970: 214, where class appears as a temporary and artificial phenomenon during the first decade of the twentieth century, although on the very same page Powell exhibits a clear class preference for 'the classes from which [military] officers were drawn' (1970: 214–15).

31. See Powell and Maude 1970: 238, where the creation of the welfare state and lessening economic inequality are described as 'a revision downwards' of natural dignity and worth.

32. Powell regrets the fact that as a consequence of the process of British decolonisation 'one man, one vote . . . was now *de rigueur* for Parliament', threatening as it did white rule in Rhodesia which the reader is invited to accept as part of the right order of things; Powell and Maude 1970: 234. See also my discussion of his speech 'The Enemy Within' in Chapter 3.

33. As Simon Heffer observes, although in government Powell argued 'for a programme based on liberal economics and the dismantling of the socialist state . . . he had to make compromises', and as Minister of Health he supervised a hospital building programme and oversaw recruitment of NHS personnel from the Caribbean and South Asia; Heffer 2008.

34. I do not mean here, nor do I take Mercer to mean, that the legacy of colonial racism was incidental to Powellism or that his focus on 'race' was simply a pretext for a prior neo-liberal agenda – although his attention to immigration can indeed be dated to the late 1960s. Rather, as Simon Gikandi succinctly puts it, 'Powell [was] aware, more than any other public figure in post-imperial Britain, of the ways in which blackness functions as the mediator between an English identity that is split between an imperial positivity (which thrives on nostalgia) and a post-imperial negativity projected onto immigrants' (Gikandi 1996: 70). In the postwar world, the political programme of this combination of nostalgia and *ressentiment*, in Britain and elsewhere, is neo-liberalism.

35. Indeed, this fixed concept of 'ethnic identity' can be seen as part of the 'boomerang effect' identified by Césaire and Arendt, since as Thomas Metcalf observes it had been developed initially in India with the creation of a special Muslim electorate (Metcalf 1995: 224).

36. In these terms, what Powell calls 'integration' is therefore the absolute abnegation of 'those personal circumstances and accidents which cause . . . the fortunes and experiences of one man to be different from another's' (Powell 1991: 377). Given that Powell regarded such 'integration' to be impossible, he argued for a policy of 'repatriating' non-white British citizens, although the question of where British-born citizens were to be 'repatriated' is a telling one.

37. An important qualification to this account is Britain's continued jurisdiction in the North of Ireland, a residue of its colonial occupation of Ireland.

Chapter 2

Decolonising the Discipline

The enlarged geographical and historical perspective provided by postcolonial studies changes the way we read literary texts and cultural formations, often challenging existing readings or offering alternative readings that supplement and complicate them. Therefore, to understand the significance of postcolonial studies for analysing postwar British literature and culture, it is important to reflect on some of the central ideas and paradigms of postcolonial studies. Like any other conceptual or disciplinary field, what sounds like a fixed body of accepted knowledge or theoretical practice in fact includes a range of different theoretical assumptions, frameworks and interpretations. In this chapter we will look at how decolonisation, migration and the emergence of diasporic cultures have prompted different approaches to national and racial identity, the role of culture in social and political life, and the idea of national literature. This involves considering how different theoretical paradigms have been enlisted to interpret and characterise these developments, whether drawn from cultural studies, identity politics, the analysis of social experience or postmodernism. A recurring theme through this chapter, which we focus on in the final section, is the relationship between 'national' and 'global', an issue that raises the question of whether 'British literature' remains a cogent and coherent framework for analysis at all.

However, as in the case of any other conceptual field, we also need to bear in mind that the theoretical parameters of postcolonial studies are themselves historically produced and do not simply arise in a realm abstracted from social experience. And in the case of postcolonial studies in Britain, its main theoretical parameters emerged and developed within the historical period of our study, and more specifically during the 1980s and 1990s. That is, as an intellectual field in Britain postcolonial studies arose during the period of Thatcherism and its aftermath (Mercer 1991: 424; Premnath 2000: 62–3).

Postcolonial Studies as Insurgent Field and Contested Concept

Critical analyses of the political and social impact of European colonialism existed before the current field of academic activity we now call
'postcolonial studies'. Initially such writing was produced primarily by
non-European intellectuals engaged in anticolonial liberation movements or in defining the cultural life of the new nations, such as Solomon
Plaatje, W.E.B. Dubois, C.L.R. James, Aimé Césaire, Léoplod Senghor,
Frantz Fanon, Amílcar Cabral, Walter Rodney, Kamau Brathwaite and
Chinua Achebe (Lazarus 2004: 69; Moore-Gilbert 1997: 5). Equally,
in the early part of the twentieth century Marxist theorists including
Karl Kautsky, Rudolf Hilferding, Rosa Luxemburg, Nikolai Bukharin
and V.I. Lenin developed analyses of imperialism as an international
economic system driven by the expansionist dynamic of capitalism
(Johnson and Poddar 2005: 174).[1] As Robert Young records, postcolonial studies developed from both these traditions of anticolonial
national liberation and Marxism (Young 2001: 6–10). However, it
emerged as a recognisable field within Anglo-American academia only
in the late 1970s and early 1980s, when the term became associated
specifically with the application of French poststructuralist theory to
analysis of the culture of colonialism (Moore-Gilbert 1997: 34). Where
the term 'postcolonial' had previously served as a chronological marker,
designating the period *after* colonialism, through the 1980s it came to
describe a broad theoretical disposition primarily located within the
disciplines of literary and cultural studies (Lazarus 2004: 2). While what
we now recognise as postcolonial studies covers a very wide range of
approaches and positions, according to the editors of a recent study of
the current state of the field, two broad tendencies can be identified: first,
a 'disciplinary shift' away 'from sociological and economic analysis' and
towards 'cultural and interpretative and theoretical/semiotic/discursive
analysis'; and second, the rejection of 'metanarratives', or the broad historical and philosophical structures of explanation that underpinned the
accounts of reason, freedom and progress that are associated both with
the Enlightenment and with its critics, such as Hegel and Marx (Loomba
et al. 2005: 34). However, the development of postcolonial studies is
not simply an intellectual phenomenon but also an institutional one. In
providing one locus for the institutional development of postcolonial
studies, the post-imperial British context has also shaped the intellectual
terms of this new field.

The academic discipline of English literature as it developed in Britain
in the decades following the war was largely unconcerned with the

impact of imperialism on literary and cultural representations. In contrast, intellectuals from the colonies had long connected the representations and claims to knowledge of imperial culture with the imperatives and processes of colonial rule. For example, in an essay arguing for West Indian independence written in 1933, the Trinidadian intellectual and activist C.L.R. James connects British accounts of the supposed 'savagery' and 'childishness' of 'the average Negro' to the need to justify and legitimise colonialism. Since colonial rule contradicted the conceptions of legality and democratic rights central to British self-perception and its concept of the 'civilising mission,' such representations provided a way of reconciling – albeit at the imaginary level – the contradictions between colonial ideology and the exercise of political power (James 1992: 49–53). Thus, James demonstrates that what claim to be representations of colonial subjects are in fact projections of anxieties *within* British imperial culture, and have precious little to do with those they purport to represent. However, as Bart Moore-Gilbert recounts, 'within Europe and America . . . these interconnections were almost completely ignored throughout the period from 1945 to the early 1980s' (Moore-Gilbert 1997: 22). In Britain, academic scholarship traditionally focused on what was described as 'the literature of empire', or canonical British literature set in colonial locations, while from the 1960s it also began to address what was termed 'Commonwealth literature', or literature written in English by writers from the newly independent colonies (sometimes referred to as the 'New Commonwealth') and the former British dominions (sometimes referred to as the 'Old Commonwealth'). The sobriquet 'literature of empire' effectively worked as a cataloguing descriptor, identifying empire as the location or backdrop for the literary works under consideration (like 'literature of the city'), while the histories of imperial rule and the dependence of the metropolis on the resources and economies of colonial possessions were deemed external to the author and to the work of art (Moore-Gilbert 1997: 23). 'Commonwealth literature' initially focused on writing from all of the former colonies, protectorates and dominions of the British Empire. But like the political organisation after which it was named, the arbitrary grouping it implied raised fundamental critical problems from the outset: namely on what basis such diverse societies, with such different cultural traditions, such divergent histories of settlement and imperial control, and such a variety of languages, should be grouped together; and according to what framework(s) of comparison they were to be read in conjunction (Johnson and Poddar 2005: 107).

According to Bart Moore-Gilbert, the first conference on

Commonwealth literature, held at Leeds University in 1964, established an Anglocentric framework for comparative reading, with 'British literature' constructed as 'the norm against which "local" Commonwealth literatures were to be measured', although only 'local literatures' written in English were considered (Moore-Gilbert 1997: 27). Many metropolitan critics such as Norman Jeffares and B. Argyle argued that contemporary writing should focus on 'human' issues supposedly applicable to all, rather than on 'local' concerns – a formulation which took a certain particular, class-bound and metropolitan viewpoint as natural and universal, and marginalised all other viewpoints by casting them as relevant only to a narrow set of 'local' circumstances. As Moore-Gilbert observes, this meant that 'rather than looking to define a Nigerian national literature, for example, critical emphasis was to be placed on establishing the connections between individual writers like Soyinka and Achebe and, firstly, the British tradition, secondly, other Commonwealth novelists, and only last, if at all, between such figures and other Nigerian authors' (Moore-Gilbert 1997: 27). In one sense, British literature was thus given a central, normative role, and yet in another it was excluded from the purview of Commonwealth literature altogether: as fully representative of the 'universal' and 'human', it was to correct and modulate these other 'local' literary cultures through comparison, but was exempt from any such correction or modulation itself. However, from the outset the central and normative position of British literature did not go uncontested. In his contribution to the proceedings of the 1964 conference, for example, the Nigerian novelist and critic Chinua Achebe 'rebutted many of the critical assumptions' about the disconnection 'between politics and literature evident in Jeffares's opening address', and stressed his distance and that of other African critics from 'the normative critical values operating in the metropolitan English department' (Moore-Gilbert 1997: 29). This distance crystallised on 24 October 1968 when Ngugi wa Thiong'o and two other colleagues called for the abolition of the English department at what was then University College Nairobi, arguing for its replacement by a new department of African Literature and Languages (Lazarus 2004: 85). The organisational structure of University College Nairobi, then part of the University of East Africa, was inherited directly from the University of London, which had awarded its degrees until 1964 and which maintained a consultative relationship for a period thereafter. Despite formal independence in 1963, the syllabus, the disciplinary definition of literary study and the language of its privileged objects of study remained in very direct ways shaped by colonialism. The project pursued by Ngugi, and subsequently articulated more fully in 1986 in his *Decolonizing the Mind*, was in contrast to build a distinctly African field of literary expression written in African languages that would reflect the different histories and cultures of the continent (Lazarus 2004: 86).

Over the next decade or so, a combination of shifts within Britain and beyond contributed to the emergence of postcolonial studies as a new framework for reading and teaching the cultural history and literary legacy of British colonialism, with the publication of Edward Said's *Orientalism* in 1978 often taken as a convenient starting point. Significantly, this new concern for imperialism centred on English departments, and focused on literature and culture rather than on the political and economic analysis of colonialism. In part this reflected changes in publishing, as writing from the 'new literatures' – as post-independence literature was called – became more widely available both in Britain and in Africa and the Caribbean. Heinemann launched its African Writers series in 1962 under the editorship of Chinua Achebe, which was conceived as an educational resource that would produce affordable texts for use in classrooms both in Africa and in Europe and the United States. It was followed in 1970 by their Caribbean Writers series, and later that decade by Longman's Drumbeat series. These developments by established publishers were complemented by the emergence of grassroots publishers founded by migrants to Britain: New Beacon Books, founded in 1966, was associated with the British-based Caribbean Artists Movement, while Bogle L'Ouverture, founded in 1968, published Walter Rodney's important study *How Europe Underdeveloped Africa* in 1973, and went on to publish authors such as Andrew Salkey and Linton Kwesi Johnson (Moore-Gilbert 1997: 7). Within the academy, colonial discourse analysis developed in response to the older study of the 'literature of empire', and sought to 'expos[e] the making, operation and effects of colonialist ideology', as for example in Benita Parry's *Delusions and Discoveries: Studies on India in the British Imagination 1880–1930* published in 1972 (Lazarus 2004: 68; Morre-Gilbert 1997: 25). But the institutional shift that in many ways contributed most powerfully to the development of postcolonial studies as it is recognised today was one which at the time seemed to have little immediate connection with the Empire or the former colonies, namely the 'crisis in English studies' that took place in the late 1970s and 1980s, and which saw the redefinition of the parameters of English as a discipline. A parallel but distinct reassessment of the discipline also took place in the United States, so it is important to identify the specific character of this development in Britain.

The 'crisis in English studies' emerged in the wake of the student radicalisation of the 1960s, as former student radicals joined the profession and looked to transform its fundamental intellectual underpinnings. English was especially open to this process because of its particular intellectual heritage: dominated by T.S. Eliot and by the 'Cambridge English' associated with F.R. Leavis, it stressed the moral dimension of culture, yet its disciplinary morality remained closely bound to the era of empire, whose structural assumptions about gender inequality, class hierarchy, race and social justice were presented as the universal edicts of civilisation. In the wake of the social and political shifts of the 1960s, such claims to universality became increasingly implausible for a new generation of students and junior lecturers (Eagleton 1983: 15–46). While initially this disciplinary redefinition looked to Western Marxism and feminism for its inspiration, increasingly the source that was to supply the intellectual renewal and regeneration of English studies was the post-structuralism of French thinkers like Roland Barthes, Louis Althusser, Michel Foucault, Luce Irigaray, Hélène Cixous and Jacques Derrida. Post-structuralism, and especially deconstruction, held a particular power for remaking English studies in its entirety because its authority seemed to depend not on an external political project or commitment – like socialism or feminism – but on the very properties and propensities of language itself (Lazarus 2004: 74). As such, it tended to bracket or exclude social experience, and focus instead on the capacity of the inherent undecidability of language to exceed static definitions and destabilise normative categories. As the discipline moved to embrace the insights of French post-structuralism and reinterpret them within the parameters of British and American culture respectively, the emergent field of postcolonial studies would bring this new theoretical sensibility to bear on the culture of British colonialism and on contemporary writing from the former colonies. Thus, although Said's *Orientalism* in fact explores the dynamic tensions *between* social experience and the protocols of representation and categorisation, what proved most influential was the study's deployment of Foucault to present a remarkably systematic account of the European discursive construction of 'the Orient' (Moore-Gilbert 1997: 15; Brennan 2006: 103, 138).

At first, however, the 'crisis of English studies' was not seen as being connected with the post-imperial location of contemporary Britain, but was framed almost exclusively in class and gender terms that were securely bound within the domestic space of the nation. As Bart Moore-Gilbert notes, none of the radical accounts of the discipline at the time – such as Terry Eagleton's *Literary Theory* (1983), Chris Baldick's

The Social Mission of English Criticism (1983) or Peter Widdowson's collection for Methuen's widely read New Accents series, *Re-Reading English* (1982) – 'found space to address in any detailed manner either the cluster of interests . . . identified with colonial discourse analysis or the already well developed fields of "new" or postcolonial literatures in English' (Moore-Gilbert 1997: 6). It was not until 1989 that Gauri Viswanathan's important study *Masks of Conquest: Literary Study and British Rule in India* established the centrality of empire to the construction of English as a discipline in the nineteenth century *prior* to its adoption in Britain. As Viswanathan argued there, 'we can no longer afford to regard the uses to which literary works were put in the service of British imperialism as extraneous to the ways these texts are to be read' (Viswanathan 1989: 169). The same year, Methuen's accessible New Accents series finally devoted a volume to postcolonial studies in the shape of Bill Ashcroft, Gareth Griffith and Helen Tiffin's *Colonial Discourse and Post-Colonial Theory*, signalling the migration of postcolonial studies from more specialised scholarly discussion to the undergraduate curriculum.

A sense of the range of factors that underpinned the shift from Commonwealth literature to postcolonial studies over this period can be seen in Salman Rushdie's 1983 essay '"Commonwealth Literature" Does Not Exist'. Rushdie's essay captures the belated imperial conde-scension of the literary and academic establishment with consummate comedy, and skewers the intellectual incoherence at the root of the insti-tution of Commonwealth literature, describing it as a kind of literary 'ghetto' (Rushdie 1991: 62). Rushdie argues that the disciplinary field of Commonwealth literature generates a double exclusion: first, of lit-erature from the former colonies not written in English (1991: 69); and second, of British literature itself: 'the effect of creating such a ghetto . . . is to change the meaning of the far broader term "English literature" . . . into . . . something topographical, nationalistic, possibly even racially segregationist' (1991: 63). By dividing off British writing as 'English literature' proper, the label 'permits academic institutions, publishers, critics, and even readers to dump a large section of English literature into a box and then more or less ignore it' (1991: 66).

However, if Rushdie echoes some of the earlier criticisms of Commonwealth literature articulated by figures such as Chinua Achebe and Ngugi wa Thiong'o, much of the focus of the essay moves in a dif-ferent direction. Just as important for Rushdie is scepticism about the concept of national tradition, which he now identifies with the develop-ment within Commonwealth literature of a desire to find 'Authenticity'

(1991: 67). Works 'are almost always praised for using motifs and symbols out of the author's own national tradition, or when their forms echo some traditional form, obviously pre-English', Rushdie claims, arguing that such an approach assumes 'that the writer can be seen to be wholly internal to the culture from which he "springs"' (1991: 66). In contrast, he looks to the dissemination of English around the globe – which he identifies as much as an 'effect of the primacy of the United States of America' as 'the result of the British legacy' – as the emergence of a 'world language' that makes such claims to authenticity untenable: 'those people who were once colonized by the language are remaking it, domesticating it, becoming more and more relaxed about the way they use it', Rushdie writes (Rushdie 1991: 64). Such a globalised conception of English begins to allow for traffics and interconnections that are no longer orientated towards or mediated through the centre, but which might, say, involve the influence of Indian writing in English on the Latin American novel and vice versa.

However, if Rushdie clearly moves beyond the bounds of Commonwealth literature with this conception of global English, there is a sense in which the disparagement of 'localism' – or the concern to articulate a specifically national set of traditions and memories – that existed in Commonwealth literature resurfaces in his approach. The essay aligns writing in English, and participation in the global English book market that it enables, with 'eclecticism', a principle that is staked against its binary opposite 'Authenticity'. 'Eclecticism' is defined by the essay in rhetorically attractive terms, as 'the ability to take from the world what seems fitting and to leave the rest', a formulation that offers a vision of cultural admixture that stresses the voluntary and untroubled nature of this choice. In contrast, what does not fall under the rubric of 'eclecticism' is labelled 'Authenticity', which is presented as absolutely exclusive and self-enclosed, a return to a restricted localism or national-ism that 'demands that sources, forms, style, language, and symbol all derive from a supposedly homogenous and unbroken tradition' (1991: 67). The thrust of Rushdie's argument resolves the literary and cultural options that confront writers into a stark opposition, between 'the reality of mixed tradition' and 'the fantasy of purity', a starkness whose clarity might make us suspicious (1991: 67–8).

Rushdie's essay is worth recalling because it captures something of the promise and power of the emergent field of postcolonial studies, as well as many of the emphases and assumptions that have proven to be contentious and controversial. Not only does Rushdie challenge the subordinate status of what is labelled as 'Commonwealth literature', but he also returns that challenge to question the dominant conception of English literature, its canon of writing and its cultural assumptions. The essay's broad conception of a range of global Englishes and its inclusion of the global market of literatures in translation reveals the untenability of the colonial paradigm of 'metropolis' and 'periphery' that organised Commonwealth literature, so acknowledging the richness of cultural interchange outside the ambit of what had been conceived of as the imperial 'centre'. Equally, its rejection of notions of cultural purity or authenticity articulates a powerful critique of ethno-nationalist and racist conceptions of culture and their vision of a fixed, integral and univocal historical tradition. And the essay's ability to imagine a different conception of cultural affiliation outside national boundaries or the dominating traditions of European culture and 'the West' – 'between writers from . . . poor countries [and] deprived minorities in powerful countries' – proved especially attractive to those in the West who were unconvinced by Eliotean conceptions of the unity of European culture, and who acknowledged the injustice of European colonialism and the reality of contemporary Western hegemony (1991: 69). Although not proceeding in strictly post-structuralist terms – the essay's argument ultimately rests on a claim for the knowability of the 'real' state of literature in English (1991: 70) – Rushdie's valorisation of what he terms 'eclecticism', but what would be recognised more widely today as 'hybridity', lent a real-world political dimension to post-structuralist theory, which otherwise threatened to become rather abstract and formal. As Andrew Smith observes, 'hybridity' has become a central term in postcolonial theory, and means not 'the mixing of once separate and self-contained cultural traditions', but the recognition that all cultural traditions are always already impure and the result of admixture, and therefore that any attempt to identify a 'separate and self-contained' culture is itself a coercive move (Lazarus 2004: 252).

However, in illustrating this transition from its own more limited writerly or literary scope to the larger political, historical and philosophical claims made by some strands of postcolonial theory, Rushdie's essay also points to some of the concerns subsequently voiced by critics from both within and outside postcolonial studies, as we will explore in this chapter. Both Aijaz Ahmad and Neil Lazarus, for example, have criticised the tendency in postcolonial studies to reject the project of national liberation, arguing that such a blanket rejection fails to differentiate between the different potentials of specific nationalisms: as Ahmad writes, '[f]or human collectivities in the backward zones of capital . . . all relations with imperialism pass through their own

nation-states, and there is simply no way of breaking out of that imperial dominance without ... restructuring ... one's own nation-state'
(Ahmad 1992: 11; see also Lazarus 1999: 68–143). While we will return
to this issue at the end of the chapter, it is nonetheless worth observing
that what might be valuable, productive and plausible for an aesthetic
manifesto – an a priori concept of hybridity as the schema, or organising frame, of judgement, for example – may prove to operate in quite
different terms when deployed in order to orientate political judgement
or account for the range of popular experience and aspiration.[2] The
essay's conception of judgement – 'the ability to take from the world
what seems fitting and to leave the rest' – is *aesthetic* in the strict sense,
since it assumes that the site of judgement is free and undetermined, that
the criteria for discrimination are spontaneous and singular, and that the
consequences of decision do not risk the future capacity for exercising
judgement (Rushdie 1991: 67). But if, as in some versions of postcolonial studies, a conception of hybridity developed in the cultural realm
comes to supply the model of judgement *for all others*, then we need
to consider more carefully the applicability of aesthetic judgement to
political and social action. To take a recent case almost at random, the
decision to privatise water and other resources in Bolivia in 1999 suggests the problems involved in this approach: privatisation was imposed
by the IMF and the World Bank as a condition for much-needed loans;
negotiations between local municipalities and transnational corporations were not conducted between equal parties; the opportunity for
popular involvement in the decision-making process was not transpar-
ent or equally open to all; and allowed to stand, the decision promised
further to weaken popular decision-making over resources for decades
(see Assies 2003; Kohl 2002).

We must bear in mind, then, the differences between the conditions
of aesthetic and political judgement. While globalisation and the overcoming of boundaries may appear in some versions of postcolonial
theory as the unqualified source of plurality, and the limits of the nation
and of tradition may seem eminently dispensable, critical voices within
postcolonial studies have pointed to the dangers of ignoring the agency
of popular sovereignty within the postcolonial nation in the context of
transnational corporations backed by US power. According to Benita
Parry, the 'location' of postcolonial studies 'within English and Cultural
Studies' departments dominated by 'the linguistic turn' of the 1980s
'license[d] the privileging of "discourse" as the model of social practice,
and consequently ... promote[d] an incuriosity about enabling socio-
economic and political institutions' (Lazarus 2004: 74, 69). Arif Dirlik,

a consistent critic of postcolonial studies as a field, goes further to reject the term 'postcolonial' itself, arguing that it 'mystifies both politically and methodologically a situation that represents not the abolition but the reconfiguration of earlier forms of domination'. As such, he charges that postcolonial studies diverts 'attention from contemporary problems of social, political, and cultural domination', and from 'a global capitalism that, however fragmented in appearance, serves nevertheless as the structuring principle of global relations' (Dirlik 1997: 503).

What's Wrong with 'National Culture'? Williams and British Cultural Studies

While in retrospect the 'crisis of English studies' in Britain in the late 1970s and 1980s was an important factor in the development of postcolonial studies as we recognise it today, it is worth returning to Bart Moore-Gilbert's observation that the key critical histories of the discipline of English generated by that moment failed to recognise the constitutive role of empire in the formation of English studies. In turn, this means that they remained blind to the role of decolonisation in prompting that crisis. Instead, as Gauri Viswanathan notes, these revisionist histories explained 'the growth of English studies as a product of middle-class ascendancy' and the consequent need for the 'containment of lower-class aspirations', and thus as a purely domestic affair, a matter internal to what was simply assumed to be 'a fully formed national culture shaped by internal social developments' alone. But in 'fail[ing] to take into account the use of the colonies as a test site for secular experiments in education', Viswanathan observes, such an approach could only ever be 'a partial one' (Viswanathan 1991: 48–9). This elision of the role of empire in the development of the discipline of English literature evident in the revisionist histories of the early 1980s has been identified by Viswanathan and others as marking a much more fundamental theoretical limitation that tracks back to the emergence of British Cultural Studies in the 1950s, and specifically the work of Raymond Williams. As Viswanathan argues, 'we ... have to go back to Raymond Williams to trace the genealogy of a critical approach that consistently and exclusively studies the formation of metropolitan culture from within its own boundaries' (1991: 49). And the stakes here are indeed significant: as Viswanathan demonstrates, not only is such an approach 'incapable of accounting for imperialism as a function of metropolitan culture', but it also works 'to render colonial territories without material presence or substance' by failing 'to extend [Williams' own] notion of contestation to transcultural or cross-referential situations' (1991: 57, 51).

Yet while this is true of Williams' influential work of the 1950s and 1960s, his position shifted in parallel with developments in the New Left, the political movement that emerged outside of the traditional Labour and Trade Union movement in the 1960s, and which increasingly sought to come to terms with the role of imperialism in constructing Britain's distinctive social and political trajectory. Thus, Perry Anderson's important essay of 1964, 'Origins of the Present Crisis', argued that by the end of the nineteenth century the 'reflux of imperialism' had 'saturated . . . British society' and was to '"set" [it] in a mould it has retained to this day' (Anderson 1992: 23–4). This paradigm shift is reflected in Williams' 1973 study *The Country and the City*, which offers an extraordinary reversal of his own earlier orientation:

> In an intricate process of economic interactions [starting in the eighteenth century], supported by wars between the trading nations for control of the areas of supply, an organized colonial system and the development of an industrial economy changed the nature of British society . . . The effects of this development on the English imagination have gone deeper than can easily be traced . . . But from at least the mid-nineteenth century, and with important instances earlier, there was this larger context within which *every idea and every image was consciously and unconsciously affected.* (Williams 1973: 280–1; emphasis added)

And, in light of charges that much of contemporary Anglo-American postcolonial studies ignores 'the structure of the new global capitalism' and so 'avoids confrontation with the present', it is significant that Williams follows Anderson in insisting on the continuing history of global inequality and exploitation, and on Britain's continuing participation in it (Dirlik 1997: 517, 513). 'It is now widely believed in Britain that this system has ended', Williams notes, only to argue to the contrary that formal 'political imperialism was only ever a stage', one that 'has been effectively succeeded by economic, monetary, and commercial controls which again, at every point that resistance mounts, are at once supported by political, cultural, and military intervention' (Williams 1973: 283). If, as Paul Gilroy argues, the version of cultural studies that emerged by the early 1990s had not pursued the implications of Williams' later insight, remaining instead within the 'ethnocentrism and nationalism' that informed Williams' original formulation of culture 'as a whole way of life' in the 1950s, it is worth returning to Williams' initial programme for cultural studies as presented in his widely invoked but not often closely examined essay of 1958, 'Culture is Ordinary' (Gilroy 1993: 5).

Williams' 'Culture is Ordinary' proposes a conception of culture as 'a whole way of life', a conception encapsulated in the formulation repeated throughout the essay that 'culture is ordinary' (Williams 1989: 4). As a number of observers have noted, Williams' approach drew on the expansive 'sense of culture' proposed by Eliot in *Notes Towards the Definition of Culture*, first published in 1948. But it tends to be forgotten that for Eliot this was an explicitly theological notion: 'there is an aspect we can see in religion as *the whole way of life of a people*, from birth to grave, from morning to night and even in sleep, and that way of life is also its culture' (Eliot 1962: 31; see for example Dworkin 1997: 82, 107). Williams' conception of culture was an attempt to secularise this idea. 'Every human society has its own shape, its own purposes, its own meanings', Williams writes, which it 'expresses . . . in institutions, and in arts and learning'; therefore, 'the making of a society is the finding of common meanings and directions, and its growth is an active debate and amendment under the pressures of experience, contact, and discovery' within which the resultant common meanings and directions 'are written into the land' (Williams 1989: 4). As the expression of 'a whole way of life', culture is not fixed, and yet because this 'whole way of life' is conceived as being 'written in the landscape', it has a kind of glacial solidity and cohesion which integrates 'new observations and meanings' within a slow and steady process of 'test[ing]', 'amendment' and self-adjustment. This solidity and cohesion gives Williams' conception of culture the ballast required for it to assume a much wider political role. It underpins the sense of collectivity and solidarity which he sees in the 'ordinary' culture of British working-class life, and which underpins his rejection of vanguardism (Williams 1989: 8–9; see also Williams 1957: 32). And it provides the basis for the democratising politics of welfare socialism proposed by the essay – its conception that 'the ordinary people should govern' – a project that aims to wrest education, the arts, cultural heritage and cultural production from the control of elites and private capital (1986: 8, 14–18). But it is also this solidity and cohesion which, as Jed Esty argues, 'relied' on 'a latently organic notion of Englishness' that itself needs to be recognised 'as a post-imperial effect' and as part of the 'late modernist domestication of [imperial] anthropology' (Esty 2004: 20).

In fact, Williams' account of culture in 'Culture is Ordinary' is much less unified than the essay suggests. Despite his claim that 'a culture is' the unity of 'common meanings, the product of a whole people, and

offered individual meanings, the product of a man's whole committed personal and social life', the essay multiplies cultural oppositions
and fractures: between working-class and bourgeois culture (Williams
1989: 7); between both of these and a 'common English inheritance'
that is distinct from them (1989: 8); between the present exclusivity of
contemporary high culture and the possible future 'common culture'
(1989:10); and implicitly, between the 'English' culture mentioned here
and the other national cultures (including Welsh) that go unmentioned.
But the central fracture in the essay is marked by what Williams terms
'commercial culture' – film, advertising, pop music – which is included
only to be excluded: 'for years I had violent headaches whenever I
passed through London and saw Underground [subway] advertisements
and evening papers', Williams confides (1989: 9). Williams' rejection
of 'commercial culture' is telling not because it convicts him of sharing
the snobbery of 'high' culture – indeed, he was a key figure in gaining
academic respect for the study of non-elite cultural forms – but because
it reveals something much more fundamental about his conception of
the 'cultural' itself.[3]

Williams' refusal of 'commercial culture' springs not from an aesthetic judgement but from its association with social disintegration,
the collapse of the intricate yet collectively powerful web of memories,
habits of expression and behaviour, shared hardships, acts of solidarity, and moments of communal and individual triumph or loss through
which working-class communities had experienced the arbitrariness
of forces beyond their control and field of vision, and which Williams
invokes at some length in narrating a bus journey through the Black
Mountains of Wales at the opening of his essay. It is this social texture
– which *need not necessarily* be constructed in romantic terms – that
is written in the landscape (MacPhee 2011a). But as he later acknowledges, 'farther along the bus journey, the old social organization in
which these things had their place has been broken' and '[p]eople have
been driven and concentrated into new kinds of work, new kinds of
relationship' (1989: 6). Indeed, the historical centrality of this extraordinarily powerful social disintegration pervades the essay in ways that
make it difficult to understand how it can maintain its affirmation
of the unity, cohesiveness and endurance of 'ordinary' culture. As
Williams recounts:

With the coming of industrialism, much of the old social organization
broke down and it became a matter of difficult personal experience that we
were constantly seeing people we did not know . . . [P]eople were physically

massed, in the industrial towns . . . [and the] improvement in communica-
tions, in particular the development of new forms of multiple transmis-
sion of news and entertainment, created *unbridgeable divisions* between
transmitter and audience. (Williams 1989: 11; emphasis added)

But we might reasonably ask how we are to square such 'unbridgeable
divisions' with the unified vision offered by what, by the fourth page of
the essay, has become not an epistemological claim to truth but an aspiration or article of faith: 'Culture is ordinary: through every change let
us hold fast to that' (1989: 6).

This acute sense of the 'social chaos' wrought by modernity is everywhere just below the surface in 'Culture is Ordinary', to the extent we
might say that its exclusion from the essay's conception of culture is its
unacknowledged structuring principle. As Williams notes, 'commercial
culture came out of the social chaos of industrialism', which is why he
spends so much energy in excluding it from the realm of culture, and why
he rejects the cultural forms of middle-brow elitism and media punditry:
'But of course it is not culture' he says of each of these (1989: 12, 5–6).
But if the claim upon which Williams' whole conception of 'culture and
society' is built – its capacity to provide a holistic account of culture, of
culture as 'a whole way of life' – depends on culture's location in and
reciprocal constitution by the panoply of social processes, it becomes
evident that the essay's conception of culture can only function by with-
drawing from the socially disintegrative aspects of modernity; that is, by
excluding or taming the social. In a remarkably telling articulation of the
relationship between culture and society, Williams writes that a common
culture 'will give our society its cohesion, and prevent it [from] disinte-
grating', a formulation that places 'culture' outside of 'society' and conceives their connection as external and occasional. In this view, 'culture'
is not itself *already* social since it can somehow stand outside of the disintegrative tendencies of the social – which is why it can provide a remedy
for social atomisation, a remedy that comes, as it were, from elsewhere.
Williams wants to develop a conception of culture that would emerge
from the social, as 'a whole way of life'; but without fully acknowledging
it, he must first remake the social in the image of the culture he wants to
find there. Or to put it another way, Williams claims that his 'culture' is
social, but in fact it exists already as a model *outside* of the 'society' it is
to mend and make whole.

There is then a double exclusion in 'Culture is Ordinary': first, the
exclusion of empire, as identified by Viswanathan, Gilroy, Esty and
others; and second, the exclusion of a conception of social experience

that includes its disintegrative dimension, as variously articulated within a broad continental European tradition of modern social thought that runs from Hegel and Marx through, among others, Nietzsche, Weber, Durkheim, Simmel, Benjamin, Arendt, and Adorno and the Frankfurt School.[5] As Perry Anderson argued in his 1968 essay 'Components of the National Culture', armed with an 'unshakeable' sense of its own stability due to its vast empire, the British bourgeoisie 'was naturally and resolutely hostile to any form of thought that might put the social system . . . in question' and gladly 'forwent any large questioning of society as a whole' (Anderson 1992: 60, 57–8). Unlike its continental European counterparts, the British intellectual tradition that Williams inherited 'never produced a classical sociology', and so did not grasp the *social* character of experience. Instead, experience was relegated to an inner world whose dimensions were simply given, and which provided the ground for an individualised conception of art and culture that lay somehow outside of the social (Anderson 1992: 56–7). As Anderson observes, nineteenth-century Britain generated 'a literary tradition' that could denounce the stultifying and inhuman effects of capitalism at the level of culture, but could 'never generat[e] a cumulative conceptual system' to address social experience in a broader sense (Anderson 1992: 58).[6] This was the 'culture and society' tradition that culminated in the twentieth century in T.S. Eliot, a tradition not only studied by Williams but one that influenced him profoundly (Dworkin 1997: 80). Williams' conception of culture as 'ordinary' was of course designed to escape from this tradition by placing 'culture' back within social life. But this was a move that had already been made by Eliot, who could happily concede that culture 'includes all the characteristic activities and interests of a people: Derby Day, Henley Regatta . . . a cup final, the dog races, the pin table, the dart board, Wensleydale cheese, boiled cabbage' (Eliot 1962: 31). In excluding the disintegrative dimension of the social, Williams inadvertently retained a residual conception of culture as closed, relatively stable and unified, although now these elements were projected back onto social life. And it is perhaps not entirely surprising that such an integral conception of the social would envision itself in national terms that excluded the imperial transactions and interactions that extended beyond it.

The problem with the position that Williams developed in the late 1950s was not simply that it conceived of culture as *wholly national*, but also that it conceived of the nation as *wholly cultural*.[7] While the exclusion of empire has been widely identified and understood by contemporary cultural studies, I would argue that this second exclusion has not. And notwithstanding all their differences, at least in this respect

Williams' abstracted culturalism finds a fortuitous fit with the 'linguistic turn' of English studies and with the textually configured postmodern theory of the 1980s and 1990s. As we shall see below, this tendency to collapse social experience into textuality has left cultural studies disastrously ill-equipped to respond to the tendencies towards 'fundamentalism' in the West and elsewhere which emerged in the wake of the neoliberal offensive of the 1980s.

However, it is possible to gain a different perspective on the thinking of the 'New Left' and on what might inadvertently be excluded in Williams' account of culture from a short report which appeared in the Autumn 1958 issue of *Universities and Left Review*, the same year as Williams' 'Culture is Ordinary' appeared. The *Universities and Left Review* emerged in response to two violent confrontations that took place in 1956: the ill-judged colonial adventure of the Suez Crisis, and the crushing of the popular anti-Stalinist socialist government of Hungary by Soviet forces (Dworkin 1997: 54–5). For the emerging British New Left, the simultaneous recourse to militarism by both 'the West' and 'the East' undermined the polarised rhetoric of the Cold War, pointing instead to the need for an alternative vision of social justice and human freedom. The Autumn issue of 1958 was the first to appear after the outbreak of racist violence in Notting Hill in the late summer of that year, and what is striking about many contributions to the issue, and especially the short report on social attitudes in Notting Hill entitled 'The Habit of Violence' that opened it, is that the event seemed to bring together the issues of racism, social disintegration and empire with an immediacy and urgency that belies subsequent accounts of the universal insularity of the New Left or of British Cultural Studies.

'The Habit of Violence' consists of five introductory paragraphs and a number of 'Notting Hill documents', namely four excerpts from 'essays written by fifteen-year-old [white] girls at a Secondary School' in the Notting Hill area of West London, 'who were asked . . . to write frankly their opinions about the recent violence' ([Anon.] *Universities and Left Review* 1958: 4).[8] In large part the 'documents' articulate an aggressive and dehumanising racism that was not usually acknowledged in print at this time, a taboo that *Universities and Left Review* is clearly seeking to break: 'I think the coloured people are a load of savages', writes one girl, continuing that 'They are uncivilized, they have no manners and no sense of hygiene' (*Universities and Left Review* 1958: 4). Another affirms that 'I hate them and I would spit on every one if I had the chance', adding that 'Most of them smell like dog's muck and eat like dogs too' (*Universities and Left Review* 1958: 5). A repeated theme, which was expressed regularly in the media at this time, was that black men were involved in the prostitution of white women; another opinion that echoes wider public discourse is the perception of migrants as primarily 'non-labour': 'My mother and father work for their livings. They [black British people] don't' (*Universities and Left Review* 1958: 4). Yet one response of the four raises the responsibility of host communities for social tensions. Referring to what she calls 'the better class of coloured people', this writer reflects:

> They come to England with good intentions, not wanting to harm or trouble anyone, but to earn a good living. But what do they come to? A country where they are looked down upon like animals in most cases, people who don't want to live near them, who shun them when they have done no harm at all. It is hard for them to find anywhere to live because the English people do not want them. (*Universities and Left Review* 1958: 5)

And even in the case of those she perceives as 'the lazy ones who never do a good days work', there is a recognition of the role of white racism: 'We only have ourselves to blame for the unruly way in which some of them live . . . I am sure if we treat them in the right way a human being should be treated, they will do us justice' (*Universities and Left Review* 1958: 5).

In their introduction, the anonymous editor(s) of these documents interpret them as pointing to the impact of a number of deep-seated social tendencies that have been ignored in the political and media response to the riots. The first is social atomisation engendered by poverty: 'there is a growing and urgent problem of unemployment and concealed poverty' which has left the area without 'even the skeleton of community life'; the result 'is a failure of values . . . or the failure to project values into our relationships with other people' (*Universities and Left Review* 1958: 4). In addition there is the lasting legacy of imperial ideology and racism:

> between the lines of these essays, we can see the unmistakable profile of Britain's colonial policy over the last century. These children are relaying second-hand the catchwords of colonial policy. Behind each irrational phrase stands an impressive list of names – Kenya, Cyprus, Malaya, British Guiana, Southern Rhodesia . . . Here is the primitive barbarian, the 'black man', abused in a score of governor's houses, beaten in a hundred district officer's huts, but who has lived on to haunt the nightmare world of a fifteen-year-old girl. The terrible tragedy of colonialism – not the past only, but the present as well – has at last come 'home'. (*Universities and Left Review* 1958: 4)

Economic neglect, social atomisation and the 'boomerang effect' of colonial racism together provide the deep context for an emergent youth culture 'which has more to spend but nothing to spend it on and nowhere to go'. The introduction argues that this combination of social disintegration, cultural conformity and the pathological othering of non-whites encourages fantasies of aggression and mastery: '[w]ithin the conformist class culture that has grown up around them, they have no ways of expressing themselves: and they have taken a plunge back into the night-life of experience to find some kind of meaning for their lives' (*Universities and Left Review* 1958: 4). While postmodern theory, as we will see, casts fragmentation as uniformly liberatory, a different perspective emerges if fragmentation is located within historically specific and shifting patterns of social experience. In certain conditions fragmentation may indeed challenge existing social meanings and generate opportunities for change; but equally, in other contexts it may also engender a search for meaning that finds refuge in fantasies of racial belonging – of being submerged, in Enoch Powell's words, in a 'body in whose bloodstream one is oneself a single corpuscle' (Powell and Maude 1970: 9).

Dislocating Identity: Fanon and Hall

Remarking on the 'boomerang effect' of colonialism, the anticolonial intellectual Aimé Césaire articulated the need for understanding the constitutive role of colonialism in the development of European culture and politics (Césaire 2000: 41). One of the central theoretical texts that has been used to think about this relationship is *Black Skin, White Masks*, written in 1952 by Césaire's fellow Martinican and former student, the psychoanalyst and revolutionary Frantz Fanon. Although the book deals with the confusion of identity experienced under colonialism by the inhabitants of the Antilles islands of the Caribbean ruled by France, it has been read within postcolonial theory as offering important insights into the nature of identity more broadly, and especially in relation to the phenomenon of diaspora, or the dispersal of populations promoted by both colonisation and decolonisation. In the British context, *Black Skin, White Masks* has been applied to the construction of national and racial identity in the wake of colonial and postcolonial migration, and as such it has played a wider role in debates about culture and politics in Britain in light of the decline of the working class as a central political identity. However, the uses to which Fanon's ideas have been put have proven controversial, and a number of debates have emerged around the

conception of fragmented identity that has been developed in his name
(see Premnath 2000).

One of the central concerns of *Black Skin, White Masks* is how
colonialism encouraged non-white, colonial subjects to identify with
the metropolitan identity not simply as another particular identity, but
as universally human. Drawing on his own upbringing under French
colonial rule, Fanon recounts:

> In the Antilles, the black schoolboy who is constantly asked to recite 'our
> ancestors the Gauls' identifies himself with the explorer, the civilizing colo-
> nizer, the white man who brings truth to the savage, a lily-white truth. The
> identification process means that the black child subjectively adopts a white
> man's attitude . . . Gradually, an attitude, a way of thinking and seeing that
> is basically white, forms and crystallizes in the young Antillean. Whenever
> he reads stories of savages in his white schoolbook he always thinks of the
> Senegalese [people of West Africa]. As a schoolboy I spent hours discuss-
> ing the supposed customs of the Senegalese savages . . . The fact is that the
> Antillean does not see himself as a Negro; he sees himself as an Antillean.
> (Fanon 2008: 126)

'As long as the black child remains on his home ground,' Fanon continues, 'his life follows more or less the same course as that of the white
child,' since that social world they inhabit confirms their sense of self-
identity. But this sense of identity is shattered once the child leaves that
social world to enter the metropolitan centre, which is at once the source
of that identity, yet functions as a different regime of meaning: 'But if he
goes to Europe he will have to rethink his life, for in France, his country,
he will feel different from the rest', and will come to learn that 'in fact he
is a black man' (2008: 127, 126). Just as in Selvon's short story 'Come
Back to Grenada', Fanon sites this process of reidentification in a prosaic
and everyday occurrence, the shocked appellation by a child in the street
through which the colonial subject is marked as 'alien' and as 'black':
'Look a Negro! *Maman*, a Negro!' (Fanon 2008: 93).

Fanon's consideration of the experience of moving from colonial
periphery to imperial centre offers some important insights. Our sense
of self-identity, which we take to be an expression of ourselves – as intimate and personal, as sharing the same continuity and stability we might
ascribe to our own sense of our 'selfhood' – is shown in fact to depend
on its location within historically and geographically specific configurations of social experience. If the Antillean schoolboy was shaped or
determined in his earlier identification with the ancestral Frenchman
('the Gaul'), he is now determined by the negative identity or exclusion

projected upon him (as 'Negro'). Entry into this new regime of experience in turn buckles or warps what had taken itself to be the sure and centred ground of experience, what took itself to be anterior to experience. Fanon reports '[m]y body was returned to me spread-eagled, disjointed, redone, draped in mourning on this white winter's day' (2008: 93). Therefore, rather than thinking in terms of the paradigm of 'selfhood', which implies an integral and enclosed inner nature, we need to think in terms of 'subjectivity', a paradigm that allows for the interaction and interpenetration of social and inner experience, and which requires that we understand identity as a social and historical phenomenon. As I will argue below, Fanon conceived of subjective agency as plural, cumulative and excessive, and therefore he was able to recognise not only its determination by history and culture, but also its capacity to exceed that determination. However, the most influential readings of Fanon in the British context have stressed the semiotic dimension of this transition, and consequently they organise their conception of subjectivity around the thematics of disjunction, indeterminacy and dispersal, rather than in terms of the variable historical potentiality of social experience.

One of the most influential semiotic readings of Fanon was developed by Stuart Hall in the late 1980s and 1990s in his account of 'new ethnicities', although significantly Hall places his semiotic reading within changing historical patterns of identification and affiliation in Britain and the Caribbean. A member of the Windrush generation, Hall was a key figure in the development of both the New Left and British Cultural Studies, serving as an editor of *Universities and Left Review* and its successor *New Left Review*, and then as the director of the influential Birmingham Centre for Contemporary Cultural Studies from 1968 until 1979. More recently he played a key role in the articulation of the 'New Times' programme associated with the magazine *Marxism Today*, which argued that socialist demands for economic democracy and social justice had become redundant in the face of the splintering of working-class identity into multiple identities or 'new social movements' – black, feminist, queer, environmentalist. In his account of the emergence of what he termed 'new ethnicities', Hall connected this splintering of identity to the working through of postcolonial migration, citing Fanon's *Black Skin, White Masks* as a key theoretical precursor for his conception of a 'new cultural politics' of identity (Chen and Morley 1996: 445).

In 'Old and New Identities, Old and New Ethnicities', Hall argues that contemporary 'black' identity is not an essential quality of those to whom it is applied, nor was it carried with Caribbean migrants to Britain. Rather, it is to be understood as a semiotic construction that emerged in the process of migration to Britain, as 'one of the main reactions against the politics of racism'. 'It had to do with the constitution of some defensive collective identity against the practices of racist society,' Hall explains, and 'with the fact that people were being blocked out of and refused an identity and identification within the majority nation'. Denied 'access to an English or British identity', non-white migrants had 'to find some other roots on which to stand' (Stuart Hall 2000: 148). According to Hall, this identity must be recognised as an extremely valuable act of 're-territorialization and re-identification, without which a counter-politics could not have been constructed'; but at the same time it must also be recognised as semiotic effect rather than an expression of innate identity (2000: 149):

> Black is not a question of pigmentation. The Black I am talking about is a historical category, a political category, a cultural category. In our language, at certain historical moments, we have to use the signifier. We have to create an equivalence between how people look and what their histories are. Their histories are past, inscribed in their skins. But it is not because of their skins that they are Black in their heads. (Stuart Hall 2000: 149)

Understood as a strategic identity, 'black' becomes no longer desirable at the moment that it threatens to become 'an essentialism', or a fixed signified that circumscribes a range of divergent signifiers.

Hall's argument emerges out of a semiotic reading of Fanon's *Black Skin, White Masks* and its account of the colonial subject's fraught reidentification by the white child. If physical characteristics (or phenotype) can be understood as a 'signifier' or 'script' that is readable in terms of a particular social meaning – its 'signified' – then the reidentification of the colonial subject on reaching Paris reveals the lack of a fixed relationship between signifier and signified. For while the signifier remains constant, its signified changes from one moment to another: one moment the visual and auditory appearance of the colonial subject (the signifier) can signify civilisation as opposed to savagery through its educated French and metropolitan styling; but in the next moment, the same signifier now signifies savagery in opposition to civilisation (as 'black') through his/her skin pigmentation and non-European physical features.[9] The fact that the same signifier can signify *both* civilisation and savagery demonstrates that the value of a sign (signifier and signified together) is 'conventional', or functions in terms of tacit social agreement or usage. The lack of a fixed or innate relation between signifier and signified, a relation described instead as being 'contingent', locates the value of a sign within a conventional system of differences rather than being the expression of a fixed meaning. For Hall, the conventional character of the relation between signifier and signified demonstrates that rather than being a 'true self', 'Blackness' must be understood as historically constituted and 'learnt', as a strategic act of signification that is contingent and historically shaped: 'We said, "You have spent five, six, seven hundred years elaborating the symbolism through which Black is a negative factor. Now . . . I want to pluck [the term] out of its [conventional] articulation and rearticulate it in a new way"' (Stuart Hall 2000: 149). But if this 'black' identity is recognised as a contingent act of signification, it becomes disabling, confining and potentially damaging at the moment when it is mistaken as the permanent expression of a fixed and essential inner self (2000: 151–2). For Hall that moment has come, since its earlier strategic utility has now ossified, and it has come instead to 'provide a kind of silencing' in relation to other identities (2000: 151).

However, the very recognition of the semiotic contingency of 'blackness' – its recollection as a strategic *position* and not a fixed signified innately tied to the signifier of skin pigment – provides the conceptual *detournement* or reversal that underlies the political force of the 'new ethnicities' of Hall's title. To use the terms of Fanon's text, if 'Frenchness' or 'whiteness' or 'blackness' are not fixed meanings but temporary snapshots of the differential play of conventional meanings, then in Hall's reading they are always open to change and renegotiation. Read in these terms, Fanon's account of the relocation of the colonial migrant becomes a way of dislocating the imperialist ideology of the civilising mission: the very appearance of the migrant in the imperial metropolis – as educated and 'well' dressed, but at the same time black and not white – combines or conflates signifieds ('civilised' and 'savage') that are understood within this conventional system to be absolute and exclusive opposites. In provoking the conflation of what are claimed to be absolutely opposed signifieds, the appearance of the migrant threatens to reveal the conventionality of these apparently self-evident meanings, and therefore their dependence on a particular, contingent history. Thus, Hall argues that understood semiotically, 'black' destabilises or disconcerts 'the logic of identity' per se: 'Third generation young Black men and women know they came from the Caribbean, know they are Black, know they are British', and '[t]hey want to speak from all three identities' (2000: 152). The very fact of this hybrid or plural position is seen to carry a political charge in itself, for by inhabiting this multiple identity this new generation 'will contest the Thatcherite notion of Englishness, because they say Englishness is Black', and they 'will contest the notion of Blackness [by] mak[ing] a differentiation between people who are Black from one kind of a society and people who are Black from another' (2000: 152). What the essay means by 'new ethnicities' is not so much a new set of identities to come after and replace 'black', but an end to what Hall calls 'the logic of identity' itself (2000: 145).

What the semiotic reading of migrancy ultimately allows is the generalisation of particular historical experiences through the disruption of a supposedly all-embracing 'logic of identity'. Where political orientation has usually been conceived in terms of conceptions of justice or freedom associated with broader historical or political frameworks, Hall identifies the ceaseless play of cultural identities as a political value in itself, and therefore as a means of political orientation (Stuart Hall 2000: 145). Since the cultural 'logic of identity' is conceived *as* the operation of power, then Hall construes the *local* articulation of an alternative mode of identification as political 'resistance', and therefore as providing a criterion for political decision without the need to develop such broader, historically synthesising frameworks. 'What we lack is an overall map of how these power relations connect and of their resistances', Hall freely admits, although the lack of such a 'map' is not seen as a deficit to be made good since 'politics [has become] positional' (Chen and Morley 1996: 234). Thus for Hall, the semiotic disruption of 'new ethnicities' assumes a paradigmatic role for British politics as a whole through *Marxism Today*'s New Times project. The programme of New Times saw political demands for economic democracy and social justice as being associated with 'outdated' social subjectivities, and looked instead to the very fragmented nature of cultural consumption as the source of political agency and orientation.[10]

Yet given the importance of position and manoeuvre in Hall's account, we might reasonably ask whether the lack of such a conceptual map for orientating political judgement is quite so incidental, and indeed whether it is only a 'map' that is lacking here. Without criteria for judgement, a range of questions is left begging: as to how we are to distinguish between 'points' that 'resist' or that 'affirm' power; as to what constitutes 'affirmation' or 'resistance', or indeed what constitutes a 'position' or 'power'; and as to the basis on which we might judge each articulation of 'power' to be worth resisting or affirming. And without such a 'map', we cannot orientate any 'position' within a larger context, or know how any point of power/resistance might issue in reformulating social space; nor can we discern to what larger outcomes any act of affirmation or resistance might tend. In translating political experience into an abstract semiotics, this approach reduces all situations to the same binary opposition (coherence/incoherence, power/resistance) and erases the historically generated frameworks of social value and political justice bequeathed by earlier struggles. As Arun Kundnani objects, the 'black political identity that had been forged in the 1960s was based on a shared political stance' rather than 'primarily [being] about cultural symbols shared by a single ethnic group'. Therefore, once 'black experience, however multifaceted' is 'bracket[ed]', then a 'whole host of concepts – struggle, solidarity, social structure – that had previously been thought essential to political liberation [are] now seen as a hindrance' (Kundnani 2007: 50–1).

Significantly, Fanon's own account of the dislocation of identity does not dissipate subjectivity in the endless play of semiosis, but identifies the experience of wounding and loss as the condition for the traumatic reconfiguration of socially determined horizons of understanding. The child's exclamation ('Look, a Negro! *Maman*, a Negro!') forces the colonial subject to recognise its own location across different (although not unrelated) configurations of experience, and thus its involvement in and determination by them. As such, it combines the memory of its earlier sense of itself as the bearer of universal values (Liberty, Equality, Fraternity) with its projection as non-universal or particular (as 'black' and not 'white'), and so inhabits both European universalism and its denial in the imaginary history of European racist mythology (Fanon 2008: 92). Yet although this experience is painful and wounding, it is in a sense also expansive: Fanon retains a sense of himself as *both* bearer of universal values *and* as non-universal or 'black', a new composite identity that is in part thrust upon him but which is also shaped by his own capacity for decision. 'There were some who would equate me with my ancestors, enslaved and lynched', he recounts, and responds by 'decid[ing] I would accept this' (2008: 92). In making this decision, Fanon recasts the self that has been shaped, projected and determined to generate an identification that goes beyond the terms of its determination: 'I considered this internal kinship from the universal level of the intellect – I was the grandson of slaves the same way [the] President [of France] was the grandson of peasants who had been exploited and worked to the bone' (2008: 92–3). For Fanon, then, what the colonial subject comes to recognise through the experience of dislocation is that although it is shaped or determined by conditions that exceed it, subjectivity is not identical with that structuring of social experience. Though not fixed or unitary as it had once assumed, subjectivity nonetheless accumulates its particular negotiations with each new social transaction, collecting and collating its disparate experiences and so maintaining a kind of differential continuity. Equally, in recording his capacity for decision in response to this dislocating experience, Fanon demonstrates that subjectivity retains an agency capable of initiating or beginning action *that exceeds its determination*. For Fanon, then, dislocation is not exclusively semiotic, but also experiential. Therefore, rather than simply erasing earlier configurations of meaning and value, the accumulation of disjunctive experience provides the context for a reformulation of subjective agency.

Hall's analysis of the development of black identity has been highly influential, and is important in tracing changing articulations of ethnic and racial identity (both 'black' and 'white') in postwar Britain. However, his attempt to read off a new cultural politics from this semiotic reading is much more problematic, as the questions we have raised above suggest. Notably Ambalavaner Sivanandan's essay 'The Hokum of New Times' offers a forthright critique of Hall's interpretation of the politics of identity, which not only offers an alternative interpretation of the political shifts associated with Britain's post-imperial status, but also raises some important questions about how we move from questions of cultural identity to social experience and politics. Conversely, Hall's position has also been intensified or radicalised in the hands of Homi Bhabha, whose work has had an extraordinarily powerful impact on postcolonial studies in Britain, and indeed the United States. The next two sections will therefore address the difficulties involved in the transition from culture to politics, first by looking at Sivanandan's critique of Hall, and then at Homi Bhabha's account of the subversive potential of the migrant within the post-imperial nation.

The New Circuits of Imperialism: Sivanandan

Ambalavaner Sivanandan's work is not usually included in accounts of the development of postcolonial cultural studies in Britain, although he has played an important role institutionally and intellectually in challenging the imperial legacy within British society, and is himself a novelist and the editor of the influential journal *Race and Class*. Sivanandan's 1990 essay 'The Hokum of New Times' offers a clear critique of the political programme implied by *Marxism Today*'s New Times thesis, and especially its rejection of economic democracy and social justice as political projects able to draw together a diverse and inclusive political subjectivity. In doing so, it offers a different conception of Britain's postcolonial legacy, one that sees Britain as part of a 'new colonialism . . . with its centre of gravity in the United States of America' (Sivanandan 2008: 179). For Sivanandan, neocolonialism operates not through the formal structures of empire but through the 'new circuits of imperialism' enabled by the intensification of capitalist globalisation (Sivanandan 2008: 179, 193). At a more philosophical level, the essay criticises the semiotic basis of Hall's model of fragmentation, and articulates instead a conception of social experience within which fragmentation must be understood in plural terms. It therefore stresses the differences and difficulties involved in moving from the cultural to the political by insisting on social experience as the uneven and inauthentic medium through which such passage must occur. This concern for social experience also underpins a further philosophical departure from contemporary theoretical approaches in arguing for a 'stronger' concept of subjectivity than is possible within the anti-humanism of post-structuralism. Combined with a fuller account of the social terrain, which includes both state and civil society and the national and the transnational, this stronger concept of subjectivity is conceived as offering a means of political orientation, which remains a problem for Hall's articulation of New Times.

Like Hall, Sivanandan views current changes in economic organisation and the disintegration of 'the working class ... as we knew it' as engendering a profound shift in the nature of politics (Sivanandan 2008: 34). But where Hall tends to present this new situation (which he terms 'post-Fordism') as a development internal to the production process, Sivanandan locates it within a larger conception of the relationship between capital and labour understood in a global framework (Chen and Morley 1996: 224–5). Where national labour movements in their 'pristine form, shape, size, homogeneity of experience, [and] unity of will' had been able to win concessions from capital (labour rights, minimum standards of living, welfare provision and democratic rights), capital now responds by 'do[ing] away with mass production lines and the mass employment of workers on the same factory floor', 'move[ing] the workplace around, from one cheap labor pool to another', and from one continent to another (Sivanandan 2008: 27, 25). The essay therefore charges Hall with operating within a restricted perspective that 'leaves out of his reckoning the massed up workers of the Third World, on whose greater immiseration and exploitation the brave new western world of post-Fordism is being erected' (2008: 25–6). For Sivanandan, the profound changes that Hall had seen neutrally as 'New Times' are to be understood as constituting the 'new circuits of imperialism' that emerge in the wake of decolonisation (Sivanandan 2008: 193).

According to Sivanandan, these new circuits of imperialism do not evidence the de-linkage of the cultural from the economic, but constitute instead 'the emancipation of Capital from Labour' on a global scale

(Sivanandan 2008: 47). As he observes, 'Capital no longer needs living labour . . . in the same numbers, in the same place, at the same time', an asymmetry which allows it to 'hold Labour captive' (Sivanandan 2008: 27). Within this perspective, economic flexibility and fragmentation are not simply neutral phenomena, but are conceived in terms of the reformulation of social experience as social disintegration (Sivanandan 2008: 24). As 'all the bits and pieces' of relatively stable communities are 'dispersed and dissipated', the 'emancipation of Capital from Labour has left a moral vacuum at the heart of post-industrial society, which is itself material', and consequently increasing numbers of people feel a desperate need for 'direction, guidance, [and] ballast', and look for 'certain certainties' (Sivanandan 2008: 28, 47, 20). The social is thus conceived as the medium through which economic transformations are articulated, repatterning and reconstituting the texture, arrangement and composition of social subjectivity. Yet at the same time, the social is the medium through which this articulation is experienced and responded to in a myriad of ways that emerge out of accumulated collective experience and the various actions initiated through political decision. Or to put it another way, economic fragmentation cannot be automatically read off as giving rise to the deconstruction of a fixed 'logic of identity', or to insight into the contingency of meaning or social institutions. Instead, it may give rise to a range of responses, which might include the desire for exclusive identities that reduce the complexity of social experience to rigid and intolerant certainties.

According to Sivanandan's essay, then, economic flexibility, outsourcing and social fragmentation do not necessarily lead to the empowered freeplay of subjective identities envisaged by Hall. Indeed, given the emancipation of capital from labour, the collapse of existing forms of community and the weakening of legal rights and state institutions designed to shield people from economic exploitation and the vagaries of social life, Sivanandan argues that the option most strongly encouraged by circumstances is the development of an atomised and armoured individualism. The erosion of larger strategic identities (whether 'black', or 'working-class', or 'Third World', or in terms of gender and sexuality) therefore results not so much in the destabilisation of an overarching 'logic of identity', as in the development of 'a small, selfish, inward-looking self that finds pride in life-style, exuberance in consumption, and commitment in pleasure' – what the essay terms 'a politics of identity instead of a politics of identification' (Sivanandan 2008: 46, 36).

If, that is, such a course is an option: for individualism is not experienced in the same way across the social landscape, and as the essay observes, 'civil society [is] not an even terrain of consent, [but] drops sharply for the poor, the black, the unemployed' (2008: 40). Hall's call to shift the focus of politics to the arena of consumption and the play of signification in civil society is seen by Sivanandan as blind both to the inequalities of civil society and to the role of the state, whose 'power does not need to be used at every turn' but whose unacknowledged presence functions 'to change the politics of the new social forces [and] personal politics [into] a politics of accommodation' (2008: 39). The absolute separation of state and civil society, Sivanandan argues, is only possible for those whose economic position frees them from their interface, while for those who rely on state provision and protection, these realms form 'a continuum' (2008: 53). And at the point where atomisation and social disintegration become *unlivable*, culture can come to play a deadly role, offering fantasies of power and aggression and wholeness and purity – what in Western political science have in the recent past been associated with the imaginary of racism and fascism. As Sivanandan writes elsewhere, 'where the poorest sections of our communities, white and black, scrabble for the leftovers of work, the rubble of slum housing and the dwindling share of welfare, racism is at its most virulent, its most murderous'. It is here, among those 'asset-stripped of the social and economic infrastructure that gave [them] some sense of worth and some hope of mobility, that ... the breeding ground for fascism' emerges (Sivanandan 2008: 58). We might add by way of qualification that the social, moral and existential 'vacuum' of atomised individualism may just as strongly draw those with wealth and education to the search for 'certain certainties' offered by fascism and fundamentalisms of all kinds (Sivanandan 2008: 47, 20).

Sivanandan's critique of Hall, then, is not simply a restatement of the familiar paradigm of economic determinism. Its account of the actualisation of economic change through the medium of social experience offers a way of reflecting on the new parameters of subjectivity from a perspective that attempts to correlate these parameters with domestic and global patterns of social disintegration, inequality and injustice. This perspective generates some surprising observations, perhaps most of all the paradox that the moment which Hall sees as deconstructing the 'logic of identity', and so moving beyond the modern subject, in fact remains caught within a narrow and inward-looking individualism, so consumed with signifying its multiple identities within the realm of consumption that it cannot see the operation of the state or the movement of capital beyond its borders. However, Sivanandan's own position does not rely on a notion of an integral and fixed subject, nor seek its return.

'Of course the self is fragmenting', the essay acknowledges, observing that what held it together – 'the homogenizing influence of class' – 'was a flattening process, a reductive process, mechanical, and as destructive of the creative self as Capital' (2008: 47). Instead, Sivanandan argues in terms that echo Fanon, who conceives subjectivity beyond the terms of absolute fragmentation and absolute unity: as providing a kind of continuity through the accumulation of differential experiences, which combine the memory of universality with the experience of exclusion and oppression. Rather than simply seeing the historical redundancy of the working-class movement, Sivanandan therefore understands it as bequeathing criteria for political judgement: 'there are still the values and traditions that have come down to us from the working-class movement', he writes 'loyalty, comradeship, generosity, a sense of community and a feel for internationalism, an understanding that unity has to be forged and re-forged again and again and, above all, a capacity for making other people's fights one's own' (2008: 48). The 'capacity for making other people's fights one's own' implies a continual process of reciprocity where the particular (the specific demands or needs of certain groups or individuals) renews and reformulates the universal (generalisable rights and protections available to all). Thus, Sivanandan argues that when 'opened out to and informed by other oppressions', the 'specific, particularistic oppressions of women qua women, blacks qua blacks and so on' are able to make 'a claim to universality', but one that emerges and is applicable only in the particular historical moment of their conjunction or comparison. Rather than dispensing with the socialism of the working-class movement, Sivanandan argues that the new social movements have the potential to reinvent socialism by transforming its claim to an ossified universality into a plurality of historically determinate *moments* of universality: 'What is so profoundly socialist about these new social forces is that they raise issues about the quality of life (human worth, dignity, genuine equality, the enlargement of the self) by virtue of their experience as women, blacks, gays, etc., which the working-class movement has not just lost sight of, but turned its face against' (2008: 30).

Having said this, Sivanandan's essay tends to restrict the potential of culture to the absorption of subjectivity in consumption, or to the imaginary inflation of the subject in the fantasies of racism, fascism and fundamentalism (2008: 44). But given the need identified by the essay to maintain traditions of collective memory and develop 'communities of resistance' in the face of the disintegrative effect of social fragmentation, this dismissal appears to foreclose an area of analysis that should logically have a place in Sivanandan's approach (2008: 48, 35). Despite this limitation in Sivanandan's account of culture, his critique of Hall raises a number of questions for attempts to translate cultural analysis into politics. Although Hall locates his initial semiotic analysis in tension with social life, in attempting to read off a politics from it through the framework of New Times, he flattens out the multi-dimensional character of the social, reducing it to the formal contingency and dislocation of the semiotic. Contingency is thus regarded as itself *inherently* radical or politically progressive. Sivanandan's critique warns that without a 'map' of the variegated and shifting ground of state and civil society and of the national and transnational, or the capacity to generate criteria for judgement, subjectivity remains caught within a fragmenting social space which it cannot survey and whose different possible outcomes it cannot discern or evaluate. Although Sivanandan's own position, especially in its most polemical moments, tends to restrict the social role of culture, his approach might be interpreted differently.[11] While his conception of social experience cautions against the urge to reduce the social to the cultural, its emphasis on social disintegration also identifies a social role for cultural practice.

The Politics of Migrancy: Bhabha

While Hall's attempt to extrapolate a new cultural politics from the deconstruction of an all-consuming logic of identity has been criticised from the political left, it has also been taken up and radicalised within the broader paradigm of postmodernism that became dominant in the Western academy in the late 1980s and 1990s. This latter approach is most closely associated with the figure of Homi Bhabha, who is often cited along with Edward Said and Gayatri Spivak as one of the three central theorists of postcolonial studies (Moore-Gilbert 1997: 3). Although this enthusiasm for postmodernism has now ebbed, Bhabha's contribution to postcolonial studies remains operative in the incorporation of many of postmodernism's theoretical assumptions and predispositions into postcolonial studies. As he puts it in one essay, 'I have tried . . . to rename the postmodern from the position of the postcolonial' (2004: 252). Bhabha's work on contemporary culture valorises the hybridity of migrancy and diasporic culture within what is conceived as the homogeneous space and time of the nation.[12] Bhabha's approach explicitly builds on Hall's semiotic reading of diasporic culture, but seeks to 'radicalise' it by bracketing historically changing economic or social configurations (such as 'post-Fordism' or the history of black identity in Britain) in order to generalise migrancy as the fundamental condition of signification and representation (2004: 253). Our discussion here will focus on the implications of this approach for thinking migrancy, diaspora and the nation.

Bhabha understands the predicament of the new multi-ethnic and multi-cultural society of postwar Britain within the framework of 'the nation as narration' developed in 'DissemiNation: Time, Narrative, and the Margins of the Modern Nation' (Bhabha 2004: 204). Here, the modern nation-state is interpreted as 'a narrative strategy' that claims to construct a stable subject position (the narrator/people) through the narration of known events (the history of the people) (Bhabha 1994: 204). In exhibiting a 'centered causal logic' and a 'homogeneous, visual time', the grand narrative of the nation is understood as suppressing the 'hybrid articulation of cultural differences and identifications' introduced through migration (1994: 200–2). However, Bhabha argues that the very homogenising act of narration introduces an element of provisionality within the narrative of the nation, which 'makes untenable any supremacist, or nationalist claims to cultural mastery' (1994: 215). In narrating its history, the narrator (the people/nation) is said to manifest its own unity and self-identity, the 'originary' national identity that grounds its authority; yet the act of narration, of telling the national story, is at the same time supposed to unify the people and generate a stable, exclusive and finalised national identity – that is, to produce the very unity, fixity and self-identity that is its own 'cause' or ground. The coherent and cohering position of the narrator ('the position of narrative control') is therefore undermined by the 'time-lag' inherent in narration – the gap between the identity that is said to emerge through the process of narration, and the claim that this identity is already grounded in the pre-existing fixity and stability of the narrator, the people/nation (1994: 263, 213–15). That is, although the nation claims mastery because its definition is supposed to be integral and self-sufficient, an expression of its own meanings, origin and destiny, in fact this unity and mastery is impossible.

According to Bhabha, the impossibility of such a unity and wholeness necessarily drives the narration of the nation towards racial discrimination and the stereotyping of the visibly ('racially') different Other in order to shore up the illusion of its wholeness – or at least to provide a fantasy of wholeness through the psychic discharge of aggression. Here Bhabha looks to the episode from Fanon's *Black Skin, White Masks* that proved so central to Hall, although in Bhabha's reading the focus shifts from the experience of the colonial subject to the role its appearance plays in the narration of the imperial nation. The colonial subject's appearance within the metropolis unleashes a stream of racist imagery that 'confirms' the identity of the metropolitan subject (as French, as 'white') through the most extreme othering of the colonial subject, an othering that demands the multiplication of racist stereotypes: 'The Negro is an animal, the Negro is bad, the Negro is mean, the Negro is ugly; look, a nigger, it's cold, the nigger is shivering, the nigger is shivering because he is cold, the little boy is trembling because he is afraid of the nigger' (quoted in Bhabha 2004: 117; see Fanon 2008: 93). The aggressive othering performed by the discourse of the stereotype thus involves the de-linkage and re-linkage of elements within the signifying chain: where in the Antilles the colonial subject's crisply pronounced French and smart dress had signified Frenchness and belonging to the nation, now in the metropolis its appearance signifies a savagery that defines the boundary of the nation. Yet this strategy is for Bhabha fatally flawed, and proves to be its own undoing. The very act of re-signification involved in constructing the 'stereotyped Other' reveals that the homogeneity and mastery of the nation is a function of the contingency of signification, and that the nation is only 'narration': 'By acceding to the wildest fantasies . . . of the colonizer, the stereotyped Other reveals something of the "fantasy" (as desire, defense) of that position of mastery' (Bhabha 2004: 117). The nation's desire for unity and wholeness, then, is a construction that requires – and so is in a sense *dependent on* – the fantasy of 'the stereotyped Other', a revelation which for Bhabha has a profound political force. 'The unreliability of signs introduces a perplexity into the social text', he argues, a 'perplexity' that orientates political judgement and even supplies political 'agency' within a postmodern framework that rejects all forms of coherent subjectivity or subjective agency (1994: 271, 274). 'My contention', Bhabha writes, is that by 'eluding resemblance', or identity with the narrative of 'nationness', the figure of the migrant 'produces a subversive strategy of subaltern agency', that functions as 'a pulsional incident' or 'a split-second' moment of disruption *within* the master narrative of the nation (2004: 265).

Bhabha's approach has been instrumental in focusing literary and cultural interest on diasporic culture and the figure of the migrant writer. Yet little attention has been paid to addressing the adequacy or implications of its construction of diaspora and migrancy. When placed within the history of postwar British culture, what is most striking about Bhabha's conception of diasporic culture is that, for all its language of temporality, it is profoundly static. The political force of migrancy and the diasporic relies on its claim that the revelation of the 'constructedness' of nation, race and civility is in itself a substantive political act; as Iain Chambers puts it, 'the idea that knowledge is constructed, produced through the activity of language . . . subverts all appeals to the idea of a "natural" truth and its obvious factuality' (Chambers 1994: 33). But as Kobena Mercer points out, contemporary articulations of British nation and race 'are not based on genetic or essentialist notions of racial difference, but on the cultural construction of little England as a domain of ethnic homogeneity, a unified and monocultural "imagined community"' (Mercer 1991: 438). While it is true that nineteenth-century and early twentieth-century imperial ideology claimed a basis for its conceptions of race in a 'science' of biological differences, and liberal imperialism claimed an intrinsic validity for European culture, during the period of decolonisation these strategies have become marginal. As we have seen in Chapter 1, in its most flexible formulation at the hands of Enoch Powell, the British nation is avowedly, explicitly and we might say triumphantly, trumpeted as 'constructed': a nation, Powell writes, 'is that which thinks it is a nation' and only that (Powell and Maude 1970: 7). In this light, Bhabha's account of the allegedly revelatory power of the 'disjunctive' or 'incommensurable' within the discourse of the nation is tied to a historical moment in the articulation of race and nation that has passed. Its conception of 'subversion' assumes a stable and never changing 'master narrative' of the nation and civilisation, within which 'disruption' is perennially conceived as 'a pulsional incident' or 'a split-second' moment within the 'synchronic' or fixed plane of signification (Bhabha 2004: 265; MacPhee 2011b). As Gautam Premnath argues, Bhabha's theoretical paradigm remains frozen in 'a parasitical relationship to the very antagonism it stages', between 'the (First World) metropolis' and the perennial interruption of 'the figure of the (Third World) migrant'. As a result, it 'cannot address' the emergence of 'a new global logic' that functions in quite different terms from the older model of British imperialism (Premnath 2000: 63).[13]

More troublingly, Bhabha's position exhibits a restrictive conception of the migrant that results in a curiously nation-bound conception of 'diasporic culture', as becomes evident if we return to his reading of Fanon. For Fanon, while coloniser and colonised share the colonial discourse of race and nation, this discourse is articulated within two different (although related) regimes of social experience – that of the colonial subject from the Antilles and that of the imperial metropolis. Consequently, Fanon's text emphasises the experience of shock in the discordant meeting of two incompatible regimes of meaning. The exclamation of the child ('Look, a Negro! *Maman*, a Negro!') marks a complex and cumulative experience of remembrance, wounding and decision, through which the colonial subject remembers itself as a bearer of universal values at the very point where it is excluded as non-universal ('Negro'), and yet decides simultaneously to accept and reject this (re)designation. For Bhabha, in contrast, the migrant's othering is not conceived as the conflict between two regimes of experience; it is simply the functioning of the same plane of signification that positions or 'constructs' both colonial migrant and metropolitan child through the same discourse of the stereotype ('Mama, the nigger's going to eat me up'), one as the civilised and imperilled subject of the nation, the other as the savage and the cannibal. Since the heterogeneity and multiplicity of historical experience are excluded by the terms of this analysis, the migrant has meaning only as the 'Other' of the master narrative of the nation, as 'a pulsional incident' or 'a split-second' moment of disruption, and therefore has no identity, no memory, no desire (Bhabha 2004: 117). But such a rendering marks an extraordinary reduction: in the terms of the British philosopher Gillian Rose, 'the other' is thus 'denie[d] identity' and so is cast as 'passive beyond passivity, more radically passive, that is, than any simple failure to act' (Rose 1996: 37). With no memory, no accumulation of experience (even as wounding or loss) and no desire, it has no capacity for political judgement, no ability to decide or to act outside the discrete moment of the punctual now, and no capacity to reinvent itself or the conditions within which it finds itself.

This reduction of the figure of the migrant in Bhabha's reading of Fanon becomes especially troubling when understood within the historical location of diasporic communities in contemporary Britain – that is, within 'the perspective of . . . marginalized, racially discriminated against members of the post-Thatcherite underclass' invoked in 'The Postcolonial and the Postmodern' (Bhabha 2004: 253). In rendering 'postwar diaspora, refugees, the international division of labor' as being wholly 'constructed' by 'signs', these terms are entirely restricted to the synchronic (or temporally static) field of signification defined by the 'nation as narration'. This move reduces the historically variegated and geographically expansive social experience of diverse communities within contemporary Britain to a perennially monochromatic interruption or disjunction within the master narrative of the nation. But as Gillian Rose warns, 'the other too is distraught and searching for political community – the other is also bounded and vulnerable, enraged and invested, isolated and interrelated' (Rose 1996: 37). That is, what appears from the perspective of the homogeneous master narrative of the nation to be 'the arbitrariness of the sign, the indeterminacy of writing, the splitting of the subject of enunciation', may appear within its own terms quite differently: as the desire for recognition, justice and rights, or as the claim to community that both reconfigures the politics of the nation-state and draws on affiliations that reach far beyond it (Bhabha 2004: 252).

Bhabha's position not only suffers from the problems of political orientation we have seen in discussing Hall, but compounds them by erasing the heterogeneity of social experience within which different possible futures might be imagined and negotiated (see MacPhee 2011b). Indeed, despite their differences, both Hall and Sivanandan recognise that the experience of non-white migrants and their descendants in Britain cannot simply be rendered as 'a pulsional' or 'split-second' moment of disruption, but has involved cumulative histories of political struggle that have reconfigured the space of the nation (Bhabha 2004: 265). Migrants and minority communities have demanded citizenship rights and equality of opportunity within the terms of the modern discourse of civil and human rights, and have developed modes of affiliation and identity that connect with, for example, African American struggles, the development of black identities in the Caribbean and a range of anti-colonial nationalisms. In Bhabha's reduction of 'the space of the political' to 'the realm of representation and the process of signification', these histories, and the different possible futures that they envisage, are erased (Bhabha 1994: 273).

The stakes involved here are perhaps illustrated most dramatically in the position of South Asian Muslims in Britain since the 'Rushdie affair', which has seen the emergence of a specifically 'Muslim' identity as a political marker for a diverse range of communities. As Parveen Akhtar argues, this Muslim political identity has emerged in response to economic deprivation, symbolic marginalisation, and an increasingly vociferous Islamophobia, or anti-Muslim racism. Economically, it offers 'a collective identity that enables [communities] to negotiate and improve their position', while providing 'active resistance to symbolic exclusion' at the level of social representation (Abbas 2005: 167–8). This identity has generated complex interconnections and affiliations that operate simultaneously both *within* and *beyond* the nation; as Ron Geaves notes, 'one important aspect of the Salman Rushdie affair was to transform the politics of identity from' a 'local ethnic micro-politics' to 'an overt Muslim religious identity that allowed a bridge between local micro-politics and global Islamicization' (Abbas 2005: 70). Yet while this transnational affiliation has worked in some cases to engender 'an oppositional path to British society' that 'reject[s] its values and promot[es] the cause of an Islamic nation or *khalifat*', according to Geaves it has also 'opened up the possibility of active participation in British society in an anti-racist, equal rights discourse', a process deepened through Muslim involvement in the Stop the War Coalition, which campaigned against the US/British invasion of Iraq. Here, alignment with a transnational identity paradoxically 'herald[ed] a new stage in Muslim participation in citizenship' in Britain, as subsequently reflected in the emergence of the Respect Party, a left-wing political party founded by socialists and members of the Muslim Association of Britain and other groups (Abbas 2005: 70, 72).

The emergence of such a complex British Muslim political identity suggests that diasporic cultures are not static, undifferentiated or univocal, and do not function simply as a perennial moment of 'interruption' or 'disjunction' that sits passively isolated from the political dynamics of the nation or the wider world beyond it. In this light, Bhabha's postmodern rendering of diasporic culture fails to recognise how the traumatic experience of social marginalisation for Muslim communities has propelled engagement in the civic politics of the nation; and nor does it register the involvement of transnational affiliations and international political events in this process. It therefore proves ill-equipped to address the potential for the reconfiguration of the social and political space of the nation in relation to contexts that lie far beyond it. Such a failure becomes especially problematic given the widespread tendency in media and political discourse to pathologise British Muslim communities as isolated and culturally alien in the wake of 9/11 and the 7/7 bombings in London, and the subsequent emergence of a state programme of surveillance that 'conceive[s] of Muslims as living in a moral universe that is separate from the rest of the population' (Kundnani 2007: 51, 123–40; Kundnani 2009: 40).

Frameworks: National, Transnational, Global

A repeated theme of this chapter is the interrelationship between national and transnational, between the culture, politics, social institutions and economy of the domestic realm and those of 'other' places that at first sight appear simply to be elsewhere. While the early work of Raymond Williams had sought to define a properly *national* culture, this urge was itself a response to decolonisation and the relative marginalisation of British power within US hegemony – that is, it depended on the very 'elsewhere' in which it participated, yet from which it sought at another level to separate itself. Although functioning in different ways, the work of Hall, Sivanandan and Bhabha all employ a *transnational* framework, an approach that identifies the dependence of the national or domestic on contexts and dynamics that exceed it. Therefore, rather than seeing the national as a discrete and integral unit, such an approach sees all national entities as interconnected and porous. From its inception, postcolonial studies has articulated a transnational perspective, since its fundamental insight revolves around the continuing significance of European colonisation for both formerly colonised nations and former imperial powers. Thus, cultural justifications of colonial authority or the development of diasporic cultures are conceived not simply as additional topics to consider within the existing disciplinary frameworks of 'English Literature' or 'British Studies', but require that these frameworks be rethought and reformulated.

However, if the involvement of the national and the transnational makes a case for the coherence and relevance of the present volume, it might in at least two other senses also throw that rationale into question. At one level, the very interpenetration of national and transnational may raise the question of the meaningfulness of national frameworks per se. Given the mobility of writers and the geographical dispersion of reading publics, the global reach of the contemporary publishing industry and of cultural texts, artifacts, trends and attitudes, and the emergence of diasporic cultural communities that reach across national boundaries, we might reasonably ask whether a properly transnational approach would not do away with a nationally-bound 'British literature', so rendering the first part of this book's title redundant. At another level, recent economic shifts in the global economy, which presage a recalibration of the balance of economic power away from what is called variously the 'West' or the 'global North' (the United States, Western Europe, Japan, Australia and New Zealand) and towards key players in the 'global South' (especially China, India and Brazil), might lead us to question the applicability of the second part of our title, namely postcolonial studies itself. Although postcolonial studies has argued against the imperial paradigm of 'centre' and 'periphery', seeing it as erasing the agency of postcolonial populations and reifying cultural differences and identities around a Eurocentric framework, it also argues to varying degrees that this paradigm has a belated effect or afterlife in the postwar international dispensation associated with US power, which continues to marginalise and disempower the societies of the global South. As Ali Behdad writes, '[t]he colonial model of centre and periphery . . . may not be at work today, but the geographical division of developed and underdeveloped worlds continues to persist' (Loomba et al. 2005: 69). But if formerly colonised countries (in the case of India and Brazil) or quasi-colonised countries (in the case of China) begin to outpace the economies of the global North and take over their role in extracting raw materials from and dominating markets in the 'underdeveloped' world, it becomes reasonable to ask whether this belated effect of European colonialism remains relevant. If in the first case we need to question the applicability of 'postwar British literature' in our title, in the second we need to consider the applicability of 'postcolonial studies' itself (Loomba et al. 2005: 62). In both cases we need to introduce a third term into our discussion of the 'national' and the 'transnational,' namely 'globalisation'. In recent years, 'globalisation' has been used to describe a new epoch of modernity that is understood as making redundant both the paradigm of postcolonialism and that of the nation-state.

Globalisation is a contested term that does not have a single accepted meaning, but for a working definition we might start with that given by Arjun Appadurai, a scholar closely associated with contemporary globalisation theory. For Appadurai, globalisation designates 'a world fundamentally characterized by objects in motion', or even more pithily 'a world of flows'. Such 'objects' are said to 'include ideas and ideologies, people and goods, images and messages, technologies and techniques' (Appadurai 2005: 5). Appadurai sees meanings and practices emerging at the level of the locality, the 'neighborhoods' or local 'life-worlds' that are 'constituted by relatively stable [patterns of] associatio[n] . . . shared histories, and . . . collectively traversed and legible spaces' (Appadurai 1996: 191). These meanings and practices are then dispersed through the migration of people – whether for economic benefit or as refugees – and the reach of mass and new media (1996: 188–99). Thus, while 'more educated and elite members of diasporic communities' participate in 'electronic and virtual communities' via the internet, '[l]ess enfranchised migrants' might use more traditional media (newspapers, radio, audiocassettes, DVDs) to remain connected to larger, translocal and transnational communities: 'A Sikh cab-driver in Chicago,' to follow his example, 'might listen to cassettes of fiery devotional songs and sermons delivered at the Golden Temple in the Punjab' even if they lack literacy skills or access to the internet (1996: 197). For Appadurai, such informal transnational networks contrast with the operation of the nation-state, which seeks to police and homogenise these 'neighborhoods'. Yet this aim is inevitably frustrated by the increasing mobility of people and media, which generate 'translocal solidarities, cross-border mobilizations, and postnational identities' that fatally undermine and supersede the 'imaginary of the nation-state' (1996: 192, 198, 166).

According to Appadurai, globalisation 'extends the earlier logics of empire, trade, and political dominion' associated with European colonialism, but it is nonetheless to be differentiated from this earlier epoch of modernity and marks 'a general break' in existing patterns of historical development (Appadurai 1996: 4, 3). In 'globalisation', mobility assumes an absolute character, so eclipsing the element of stability identified by Appadurai with the nation-state (Appadurai 2005: 5). Thus, given that 'individual attachments, interests, and aspirations increasingly crosscut those of the nation-state', Appadurai argues that 'the very epoch of the nation-state is near its end' (Appadurai 1996: 10, 19). Yet not all nation-states are as equally redundant as all others, and the United States emerges as 'eminently suited to be a kind of cultural laboratory and a free-trade zone for the generation, circulation, importation, and testing of materials for a world organized around diasporic diversity' (1996: 174).

The sensitivity of globalisation theory to transnational cultural connections, movements and trends, and to migration and the crucial role played by diasporic communities is clearly indispensable for contemporary literary and cultural studies. However, some of the broader claims that current theories of globalisation make in extrapolating from these concerns have been contested, especially the apparent celebration of the tendencies they portray. The writer and activist Arundhati Roy, for example, makes an important distinction between 'corporate globalisation' and popular forms of transnational solidarity and empowerment, such as the World Social Forum or the mobilisations around the globe against the invasion of Iraq, which she terms the 'globalisation of dissent'. For Roy, the singular form of the term 'globalisation' implies a blanket association with hybridity, plurality and mobility, and so obscures the standardisation inherent in corporate globalisation and its tendency to disempower locality through the manipulation of the asymmetries of power and reach. Where Appadurai tends to celebrate the conquering of distance implicit in mobility, Roy observes that 'corporate globalization has increased the distance between those who make decisions and those who have to suffer the effects of those decisions', leaving the latter without access to the centres of decision making. Indeed, Roy argues, the increasing use of spectacular violence or 'terrorism' by non-state actors is itself a function of the widening asymmetries of power and of the distance between constituencies that are involved in decision-making and those who are excluded. 'For those of us who are on the wrong side of Empire,' she writes, 'the humiliation is becoming unbearable' (Roy 2004).

Equally, Fredric Jameson has pointed to the need to think together the differential openness of globalisation as a 'communicational concept' alongside its coercive role in 'the forced integration of countries all over the globe . . . into [a] new division of labor' when considered as an 'economic' concept (Jameson 1998: 55–7). Jameson observes that the mobility of objects, ideas and texts is not equal nor necessarily without deleterious effects on localities, as witnessed by the 'prestige' enjoyed by 'American mass culture, associated as it is with money and commodities', which may in turn be 'perilous for most forms of domestic cultural production' (1998: 59). In contrast to Appadurai's privileging of the United States as a model for global culture, Jameson observes that 'there is a kind of blindness at the center' that arises from the 'fundamental dissymmetry in the relationship between the United States and every other country in the world'. This 'American blindness . . . tend[s] to confuse the universal and the cultural', and 'to assume that in any given geopolitical conflict all elements and values are somehow equal and equivalent', or that 'in other words, [they] are not affected by the disproportions of power' (1998: 59; see Westad 2007: 154–5).

In 'On Globalization, Again!' Ali Behdad identifies two further problems with celebratory theorisations of contemporary globalisation that speak both to the continuing role of postcolonial studies as a framework for cultural and political analysis, and to the continuing relevance of the concept of the nation. He begins by qualifying the status of globalisation as 'an utterly novel phenomenon', so challenging the absolute character of the break perceived by Appadurai (Loomba et al. 2005: 66). As Behdad points out, following among others Janet Abu-Lughod, globalisation is not a specifically contemporary phenomenon, nor even one that dates from the European world system associated with modern capitalism. As Abu-Lughod writes, 'the first nascent world-system had come into existence' by the second century CE, and stretched from the Mediterranean eastwards and southwards to include North Africa, West Asia and 'overland and by sea . . . as far away as India and China' (Abu-Lughod 1989: 43). European imperialism, then, was just one moment of globalisation, or one particular world-system. It grew out of and exploited preceding patterns of global interaction and power, and has itself given rise to a new world system, the globalisation we witness today and which provides the exclusive object of recent globalisation theory (Arrighi 1994; Arrighi 2007; Cain and Hopkins 2002: 662). For Behdad, the point is not to equalise the various historical world systems nor to ignore the significance of far-reaching historical changes, but rather to challenge the absolute character of the break envisaged by Appadurai in his claim for the uniqueness of contemporary globalisation, which implies the redundancy of the postcolonial paradigm. Instead, Behdad recommends a 'genealogical' approach for 'mapping ... the important connections that exist between our contemporary global flow and its colonial counterpart in the nineteenth century' (Loomba et al., 2005: 70). 'The quick academic shift from postcolonialism to globalization', he argues, risks 'short-circuit[ing] the possibility of understanding the ways in which the geographical and cultural displacements of people and things by European colonialism informed the ... cartography of globalization today' (Loomba et al. 2005: 70–1).

Just as he questions the absolute character of the break between contemporary globalisation and earlier world systems, so Behdad questions the way in which Appadurai opposes globalisation and the nation-state. 'Neither the internationalization of politics nor the globalization of capital implies the disappearance of the national form or of state government', Behdad argues, noting that 'globalization has actually reinforced their role as arbitrators in international processes', whether in becoming 'local agents of corporate interests' as in some instances, or where they are 'answerable to their citizens', in providing 'local shields against global capitalism' (Loomba et al. 2005: 74, 73). Behdad is here drawing on the work of Saskia Sassen, who argues against the prevalent trend of construing 'the national and the nonnational [as] mutually exclusive conditions' (Sassen 2000: 229–30). Sassen argues instead for a 'conception of the dynamics of interaction and overlap that operate both within the global and the national and between them', wherein '[e]ach sphere, global and national, describes a spatiotemporal order with considerable internal differentiation and growing mutual imbrication with the other'. As such, '[t]heir internal differences interpenetrate in ways that are variously conflictive, disjunctive, and neutralizing' (Sassen 2000: 216). While this interaction certainly involves 'an incipient and partial denationalization of [the] national', nonetheless 'the global economy . . . roots itself into national territories and institutions' even as it 'transcend[s] the authority of the national state' (Sassen 2000: 216, 230).

Sassen's conception of the relationship between global and national is, as we might expect, extremely complex, but we can nonetheless draw out some insights that are relevant to our discussion here. It is important first of all to understand that the form of the nation-state was from the outset a function of the interaction between transnational relationships and local dynamics, rather than being the purely internal expression of a discrete and self-conscious people or nation. Nation-states only exist as part of an interstate system, and not as isolated entities on their own: this is true if we are concerned with the formation of European nation-states like Britain in the eighteenth and nineteenth centuries as Linda Colley records, or with the postcolonial states that emerged as the 'globalized outcome of the rise of US power after World War II' (Colley 1992; Kaplan and Kelly 2004: 131). Under the conditions of the Cold War, decolonisation meant both liberation from imperial domination, and integration into the US world system (Arrighi 2007: 152–3). 'The nation-state was . . . made obligatory', Kelly and Kaplan argue, as 'a tool not only for the expression of national will but as a means to radically limit national aspirations' (Kaplan and Kelly 2004: 134). In this double understanding, the nation-state form is *both* what ties populations into the world system and subordinates them to its principles, *and* what provides a measure of sovereignty or self-determination for them – although the potential and consequences of this double condition are of course very different for more and less powerful states or populations. Within this predicament, the nation-state is therefore capable of functioning in very different ways according to its relative power and the political will of its population. It can work to shield its population from the deleterious impacts of the world market, as it did in Britain in the period up to 1979, or more recently in the cases of Bolivia and Venezuela; or it can act to intensify global economic forces by enforcing acceptance of their impacts and 'liquidating' existing protections, as in the case of Britain in the 1980s, or more recently, India (Arrighi 2007: 147; Roy 2004). Thus, we should neither dispense with the concept of the nation, nor try and ignore the transnational connections that criss-cross it. Rather, as Partha Chatterji argues, 'the journey that might take us beyond the nation must first pass through the currently disturbed zones within the nation' (Chatterji 1998: 57).

However, these relationships are not themselves static and do not exist in isolation. Since the 1980s the United States, with the support of other Western states and notably Britain, has used the post-Bretton Woods economic framework, and especially the World Trade Organisation, further to liberalise trade and strip away the capacity of national governments for action, significantly reformulating the pre-existing balance between global and national (Arrighi 2007: 117). One consequence of the relative weakening of state sovereignty has been the discrediting of existing nation-state identities and the resurgence and/or invention of alternative identities, a tendency inextricably bound up with the specific roles of the nation-state in each case. In the British context, where the enforcement of global dynamics under Thatcherism in the 1980s and 1990s was associated with a strident English national identity, this has given rise to significant devolutionary, if not separatist national identities, in Scotland and Wales. Yet in assessing these developments we need to be careful not simply to 'nationalise' them, but to maintain a perspective that can correlate dynamics within the nation-state and those beyond it. Thus in the case of Scotland, Ray Ryan argues that the 'cultural effort to assert a national distinctiveness' needs to be understood in relationship both to Thatcherism and to 'the leveling impact of globalization', and takes place in light of transnational comparisons – with Ireland and with colonial contexts much further afield – as much as in terms of national memory (Ryan 2002: 67, 132–3).

Ryan's analysis of devolutionary cultural nationalism in Scotland helps to bring this discussion of the national and the global back to the literary and cultural concerns that are the focus of this study, and in doing so reminds us not to forget the involvement of state and nation. While Benedict Anderson, among others, famously tied the shared (middle-class) reading public of newspaper and novel to the emergence of European nations, the development of diasporic cultures and transnational media and publishing makes this national public – to the extent that it ever existed – much more differentiated and attenuated, experiencing the present in plural ways and connected to other times and places, other traditions and other contemporary concerns (Anderson 1983: 47–9). As Jahan Ramazani argues, quoting James Clifford, we need to grasp the interaction and interpenetration of global and national in contemporary British literature, and view it 'as *rooted* and *routed* in particular landscapes, regional and interregional networks' (Ramazani 2009: 163; emphasis added). That is, we must address how cultural developments are both located ('rooted') within a specifically national or regional context, while at the same time drawing in (or 'routing') contexts of meaning and reference that extend far beyond a single locality or community. Susheila Nasta captures this double concept of being 'rooted' and 'routed' in stressing how the work of contemporary British Asian writers needs to be understood as staging 'a series of cross-cultural literary interventions which both exist within and outside the borders of a colonial and postcolonial genealogy, forming alliances and interconnections which complicate and reconfigure [existing] critical geographies' (Nasta 2002: 5). Paul Gilroy describes one historical framework for such an approach by placing British culture within the transnational cartography of the 'Black Atlantic': 'The most heroic, subaltern English nationalisms and countercultural patriotisms are . . . better understood,' he argues, 'as being generated in a complex pattern of antagonistic relationships with the supra-national and imperial world for which the ideas of "race", nationality, and national culture provide the primary (although not the only) indices' (Gilroy 1993: 11).

Within this kind of approach, at least as I understand it, the transnational dimension does not erase or make redundant the imbrication of literary texts within a 'national literature'. But nor does it deny the plurality of frameworks of reading and production (we may therefore need to place a literary text within various 'national' literatures simultaneously) or circumscribe the circulation of texts across such putative national boundaries. What it does do is demonstrate that any such 'national literature' (understood as the product of both the descendants of former colonial subjects and those who benefited from colonialism) cannot be regarded as purely 'national', but must also be understood as taking place at the same time in other contexts beyond the nation. Ray Ryan's discussion of the relationship of plurality and the state is helpful in identifying the stakes at play here. As Ryan argues, we should not oppose pluralism to the singular nature of the nation-state, for within such a construction 'pluralism . . . allows no substantive judgments on issues that might query the underlying assumptions of the role of the state', and in particular the nation-state's 'potential for defining a justice that is not inalienably separated from the communal history of the nation' (Ryan 2002: 293). A history that, we might add, is national only because it is global. The next chapter will look at a selection of literary works from across the postwar period that explore the implications of this approach.

Notes

1. Economic studies critical of British imperialism were also produced by British intellectuals in the first decades of the twentieth century, notably by J.A. Hobson and Leonard Woolf; see Johnson and Poddar 2005: 173–4.
2. John McLeod offers a reading of Rushdie's *The Satanic Verses* focused on the problems involved in the novel's configuring of hybridity and judgement; see McLeod 2004: 147–57.
3. Williams does not share the elitism of bourgeois snobbery, and indeed the essay challenges such elitism by reflecting on his own family and friends: 'a commercial traveler, a lorry driver, a bricklayer, a shopgirl, a fitter, a signalman, a nylon operative, a domestic help . . . Talking to my family, talking to my friends, talking, as we were, about our own lives, about people, about feelings . . . I found as much natural fineness of feeling, as much quick discrimination, as much clear grasp of ideas within the range of experience as I have found anywhere' (Williams 1989: 12).
4. For a fuller discussion of this conception of 'social texture' see MacPhee 2011a.
5. For an account of social experience in these terms, see Caygill 1998. My reading of this tradition in terms of the disintegrative dimension of the social draws on

Gillian Rose's identification of a strand in modern European thought concerned with investigating 'the unintended psychological and political consequences of Protestant *Innerlichkeit* (inwardness)'; see Rose 1998: 87. It needs to be remembered that this tradition, with some exceptions, largely failed to connect its concern for social atomisation with imperialism.

6. Where I would differ from Anderson is in my understanding of what was excluded from this culturalist project: the absence that limited British Cultural Studies was not so much a concept of totality, as Anderson argues, for this it could recover through Eliot's theological conception of the 'whole way of life'. Rather, what was absent was an awareness of the disintegrative dimension of the social itself, so that disintegration was conceived exclusively in terms of 'culture'. Consequently, it could only appear as a lack of wholeness; see Anderson 1992: 57–8.

7. See Paul Gilroy's critique of Williams' later failure to address the political dimensions of racism in citizenship and civil rights: Gilroy 1991: 49–50.

8. These excerpts are of course framed and organised in ways that their writers presumably did not control, and it is not entirely clear how representative they are or whether the girls gave their consent to having their essays presented in this way. Therefore they must be seen as to some extent constructed, and not simply the unmediated expression of these girls, or of the local white community as a whole.

9. As this example shows, in fact phenomenological appearance is not absolutely reducible to 'the signifier', but can be read in terms of signification only analogically as a 'multidimensional' or 'excessive' signifier; see MacPhee 2002: 83.

10. New Times was associated with the 'Euro-communist' magazine *Marxism Today*, and arguably paved the way for the 'New Labour' of Tony Blair. For an overview of Hall's vision of New Times, see his essay 'The Meaning of New Times' (Chen and Morley 1996: 223–37).

11. Paul Gilroy's approach suggests ways in which culture might be rearticulated within Sivanandan's framework, since it both acknowledges the socially disintegrative character of modernity and imperialism and maps out a role for cultural practice; see Gilroy 1993: 72–110).

12. Bhabha's concepts of 'mimicry' and 'sly civility' gained a wide currency in the study of nineteenth-century colonialism because they locate an 'ambivalence' – and therefore the possibility of subversion – within colonial discourse (Bhabha 2004: 121–31, 132–44). For criticisms of the historical and political aspects of this work, see Parry 1987; Moore-Gilbert 1997: 132–5.

13. As I indicate in my discussion of Jed Esty and John Marx in Chapter 1, I do not share Premnath's assessment that 'Little Englandism' is incompatible with this new global logic.

Chapter 3

Rewriting the Nation

This chapter looks at a range of texts that explore in different ways the historical shifts, arguments and ideas considered in chapters one and two. Their selection therefore reflects the broader concerns of the study, and is neither meant to be representative of the literary output of the period (if such a thing were possible), nor to propose a new evaluative canon. The selection has, however, tried to include both texts that have been widely discussed within academic criticism, and texts that have not enjoyed the same level of critical attention. This chapter treats poetry and drama as well as novels, and draws on writers from a range of backgrounds and cultural traditions. Chronologically it tries to capture significant historical moments and to draw out the implications of the book's arguments concerning periodisation and retrospection. An important new element here, however, emerges in the discussions of Leila Aboulela's *Minaret* and Ian McEwan's *Saturday*, both published in 2005. Just as Chapter 1 responds to the risks of focusing on the period after 1979, thereby erasing connections to the late resurgence of empire, so this discussion responds to the recent enthusiasm for constructing 9/11 as a break between the contemporary moment and the earlier period (see for example Tew 2007: xvii–xviii). Against this trend, Aboulela's novel, for example, is related both to her earlier work and to other fictional reactions to the Gulf War of 1991–2 and the Rushdie Affair, as well as to a tradition of postcolonial writing that stretches back to the newly independent Sudan of the 1960s. In resisting the paradigm of post-9/11 exceptionalism, this study argues for the need to think beyond the paradigm of 'the clash of civilisations' articulated by Samuel Huntingdon (Huntingdon 1993; see Said 2001 and Fisk 2010).

In order to place these literary works in context, we need first to extend the historical trajectory examined in Chapter 1. Crucial here is the political moment of Thatcherism, whose legacy remains central to contemporary British politics. Thatcherism is a term associated with the administration of Margaret Thatcher, who served as British prime minister from 1979 until 1990. It describes not only the political programme she pursued, but also the broader ideology associated with it. As a practical political philosophy, Thatcherism combines an array of potentially contradictory elements: economic neoliberalism and the extension of corporate power; an even closer integration of the UK into US foreign policy; the centralisation of political power in the state; and a populist cultural imaginary which built a resurgent British nationalism on an idealised conception of Englishness and something akin to the nineteenth-century 'self-help' doctrine of Samuel Smiles (Evans 2004: 137–47; Kavanagh 1987: 9–14; Wright 2009: 169–73). However, the impact of Thatcherism is not limited to Margaret Thatcher's period of political office; by successfully displacing the existing postwar consensus, it has come to provide the dominant framework for a broad range of social attitudes and thinking on economics, politics and international relations in contemporary Britain. The 'New Labour' project of Tony Blair and Gordon Brown was decisively shaped by Thatcherism, albeit with some modifications and exceptions, while the present Conservative–Liberal Democratic government has laid out what amounts in many respects to a classically Thatcherite economic and political agenda, notwithstanding the rhetoric of the 'big society' and some genuine civil liberties provisions (Evans 2004: 128–34).

In effect, Thatcherism is the practical application of Powellism, minus Powell's more clinical assessment of Britain's 'special relationship' with the US and the anti-Americanism that flowed from it (Evans 2004: 42, Kavanagh 1987: 69–71). Its neoliberal economic programme meant that '[b]y design, Britain became a more unequal society under Thatcher', since 'those at the bottom of society . . . failed to benefit' from the economic rewards she delivered to the wealthy (Evans 2004: 139). As Alan Budd, one of Thatcher's advisors, subsequently admitted, 'What was engineered in Marxist terms was a crisis of capitalism which re-created a reserve army of labour, and has allowed the capitalists to make high profits ever since' (quoted in Arrighi 2007: 148). But this abandonment of the twin elements that had previously brokered national cohesion – the welfare state and the aspiration to full employment – meant that Thatcherism would need to deploy a range of alternative resources to sustain its project, which primarily involved the cultural lexicon of an English ethno-nationalism in combination with the considerable coercive powers of the state (juridical, police and military).

The social and political dynamics that found their expression in

Thatcherism provide a crucial background to many of the literary texts we consider in this chapter, and not just those written during the period of Margaret Thatcher's administration. Although the New Labour government sought to draw back from the rhetoric of conflict when it assumed power in 1997, and to deploy instead the language of multiculturalism and social inclusion, this impulse was speedily ditched after the attack on the World Trade Center on 9/11, and even more drastically after the 7/7 bombings in London in 2005. A consequential moment from the Thatcher period was the response of some British Muslims to the publication of Salman Rushdie's novel *The Satanic Verses* in 1988. Demonstrations called for the withdrawal of the book on the grounds that it constituted blasphemy, while outside Bradford Town Hall a small group of Muslims publicly burned a copy of the novel two weeks before the Ayatollah Khomeini issued a fatwa or religious ruling 'to the effect that Rushdie's blasphemy warranted the death penalty' (Vallely 1999; see Childs 1999: 397–438). Within dominant political and media discourse, Islam and all Muslims became identified as an alien presence intolerant of secular liberal freedoms and British 'fair play'. In the wake of 9/11, this perception would be remobilised in order to provide a liberal justification for Britain's staunch support for President Bush's disastrous 'war on terror'.

Late Colonial Parallax: Samuel Selvon's *The Lonely Londoners*

Samuel (or Sam) Selvon was born of mixed race Indian and Scottish ancestry in Trinidad, but unlike many West Indians of South Asian descent who maintained a cultural identification with South Asia, Selvon did not identify as 'East Indian': 'I was never Indianized', he recounts, and '[a]s a child I grew up completely Creolized, which is a term we use in Trinidad, meaning that you live among the people, whatever races they are' (Nasta 1988: 83). After serving as a wireless operator in the Royal Navy reserve in World War II, Selvon came to live in Britain in 1950, sharing the sea voyage with George Lamming among others (Nasta 1988: 65). With a United Kingdom and Colonies passport, and within the terms of imperial ideology which saw Britain as the 'mother country' for its colonial 'children', Selvon and his comrades were not 'immigrants' but migrants coming 'home', coming to find opportunity and take part in the larger, cosmopolitan or globalised culture of an expanded imperial Britishness. Except, of course, that legal definitions and imperial ideology aside, many West Indians tended to have a more sober and perceptive understanding of the stakes involved in migration to the 'mother land' in the 1940s and 1950s. Coming from colonies that were themselves multi-ethnic and deeply imbued with colonial hierarchies of colour, class and gender, they were as, Edward Kamau Brathwaite wrote in 1957, aware both of the powerful resources of a hard fought 'folk' culture, and of 'the material poverty' and 'the cultural poverty' of territories that had now become marginal to the shifting focus of the British Empire and the indifference of the new global hegemon, the United States (Nasta 1988: 20). As we saw in Chapter 1, Lamming articulates the need felt by many to escape the colonial confines of the British West Indies, an escape that ironically led to Britain. London became an important node in a 'West Indian literary renaissance' that stretched across the Atlantic to the anglophone Caribbean via the BBC West Indian Service and literary journals such as *Bim*.

Selvon's third novel *The Lonely Londoners* was published in 1956, and deals with the experience of Commonwealth migrants in London, a predicament also addressed at this time by George Lamming's *The Emigrants* (1954) and Andrew Salkey's *Escape to an Autumn Pavement* (1960), and a little later by V.S. Naipaul's *The Mimic Men* (1967) and Buchi Emecheta's *In the Ditch* (1972). Selvon's novel is distinct, however, in its use of calypso as a structural framework, and its employment of West Indian dialect or Creole for the narration as well as the dialogue. Thus, the novel deploys the formal complexity of modernism to decentre the privileged Eurocentric viewpoint so often associated with modernism. As we saw in Chapter 1, as a musical narrative form calypso is episodic, with each song focusing on a particular scene or event drawn from contemporary life. *The Lonely Londoners* lacks a conventional plot, but is instead composed of a series of surrealistic and poetic vignettes or 'ballads' from the lives of a group of black migrants – mostly West Indian men – who have come to live in London. Much of the interest of the novel comes from understanding the different characters we meet and the ways in which they respond to this new social context in all its many dimensions, from the legal and political to the economic, geographical, environmental, interpersonal, psychological, philosophical and sexual. As Selvon explains, the 'episodic quality of my novel' came from 'the quality of West Indian life in London', and was designed to communicate the disconnection and oscillation of mood central to that experience (Nasta 1988: 66). However, the novel does have a narrative trajectory, which is established through the interplay of the two main characters, Moses Aloetta – a ten-year veteran of London life who appears in two later novels by Selvon, *Moses Ascending* (1975) and *Moses Migrating* (1983) – and the newcomer Henry Oliver, who is almost immediately renamed 'Sir Galahad' in mocking tribute to his lust for life and apparently unshakeable insouciance. The pairing of Moses and Galahad allows for a complex structure of retrospection and reflection, as Moses reviews his own experience of coming to London through his now more experienced and melancholic eyes. Galahad's arrival opens the narrative, and his introduction to British life and the difficulties of surviving in London provide its initial narrative arc. The book moves from winter through to summer, and ends with Moses in reflective mood, assessing his own life decisions and location in London in light of meeting this new version of his younger self. The use of calypso as a formal unit allows a paratactic openness, but does not mean the novel lacks structure: as Kenneth Ramchand observes, a 'close analysis' reveals 'a tightness of structure . . . a subtlety in the development of theme, [and] linguistic cunning' (Nasta 1988: 227).

The novel's use of a modified form of Caribbean English is perhaps its most radical innovation. While there is a long tradition of using dialect or non-Southern British English in the novel, this usage had traditionally been confined to dialogue, lending weight to the experiential verisimilitude of the realist novel, but clearly distinguished (we might say quarantined) from the standard Southern British English of the narrative voice. The narrative voice is therefore tacitly presented as a 'universal' frame of interpretation and linguistic rectitude. Such a convention, as we notice in Rudyard Kipling's *Kim* for example, sets up a hierarchy of discourses in which 'non-standard' speech and its interpretation of the world is subordinated to an interpretation that although ostensibly universal, in fact encodes a very particular, and in this case imperialist, vision. Thus, Kim's companion Hurree Babu's self-description ('Onlee – onlee – you see, Mister O'Hara, I am unfortunately Asiatic, which is a serious detriment in some respects. And *all*-so I am Bengali – a fearful man') is reinterpreted authoritatively by the standard Southern British English of the narrative voice, which unlike the enemy Russian and French agents, sees Hurree Babu as a noble 'Asiatic' and not a victim of British oppression: 'he did not look like a "fearful man" . . . The Hurree Babu of [Kim's] knowledge – oily, effusive, and nervous – was gone . . . There remained – polished, polite, attentive – a sober, learned son of experience' (Kipling 1987: 274–5).

In contrast, in *The Lonely Londoners* both the indirect discourse of the narrative voice and the direct discourse of dialogue is rendered in what Ramchand identifies as 'a modified dialect' drawn from 'the whole linguistic spectrum available to the West Indian writer' ranging from standard British English and standard West Indian English 'to deepest dialect', which aimed in a diffuse way to 'contai[n] and expres[s] the sensibility of a whole society' (Nasta 1988: 229):

> a feeling of loneliness and fright come on [Galahad] all of a sudden. He forget all the brave words he was talking to Moses, and he realize that here he is, in London, and he ain't have money or work or place to sleep or any friend or anything, and he standing up here by the tube station watching people, and everybody look so busy he frighten to ask questions from any of them. You think any of them bothering with what going on in his mind? Or in anybody else mind but their own? He see a test come and take a newspaper and put down the money on a box – nobody there to watch the fellar and yet he put the money down. What sort of thing is that? Galahad wonder, they not afraid somebody thief the money? (Selvon 1985: 41–2)

To employ standard British English for the narrative voice would be to set up a hierarchy of experience between the language of the characters and that of the narrative voice, which would decentre and devalue the experience of the West Indian migrants, while at the same time casting it as knowable and ultimately reducible to the co-ordinates of what is already experienced by metropolitan readers. Instead, Selvon explains that he wanted to invite such readers to experience their familiar world *differently* by entering a whole new linguistic world which would be central and valuable in its own terms: 'the lilt and the music of this language form as it's spoken in Trinidad,' he says in an interview, 'is what I've been trying to capture and make understandable to English readers' (Nasta 1988: 79). This narrative mode sets up a kind of parallax in which, as Susheila Nasta observes, the 'psychologically disorientating effects of the alien surroundings on the newcomer are created implicitly in the way that language is used'. This enables the text to register the non-identity between the regime of experience from which the West Indian migrants have come and that existing in London, or 'the collision of two worlds' as Nasta puts it (Nasta 2002: 77). Thus, Galahad defamiliarises the buying of a newspaper from an unattended stack, which to a Londoner is so mundane and everyday as to be unnoticeable. This defamiliarisation reveals the inculcation of respect for property and the elision of human interaction that is naturalised in the compressed space-time of the metropolis.

The linguistic rendering of different regimes of experience is developed through the use of both the narrative voice and the more acclimatised Moses to reflect on the unequal nature of this difference, exposing how the non-identity of the migrants with the experiential realm of London allows them to be framed and rendered as an image or stereotype of the alien. The opening scene of the novel, the arrival in Waterloo Station of new migrants on the boat-train from Southampton, is presented by the narrator in terms of the contemporary construction of Caribbean migration in political and media discourse, or 'the boys' as the overwhelmingly male migrant population is called:

> [B]ig discussion going on in Parliament about the situation, though the old Brit'n too diplomatic to clamp down on the boys or to do anything too drastic like stop them coming to the Mother Country. But big headlines in the papers everyday, and whatever the newspaper and the radio say in this country, this is the people Bible . . . Newspaper and radio rule this country. (Selvon 1985: 24)

The 'boys', say the papers, 'think the streets of London are paved with gold', a formula that mixes naïveté and cultural distance with an avaricious guile, casting them as free-loaders who drain the nation to which they are culturally alien. As a reporter scouts the new arrivals for targets, the narrator's scepticism, which reflects the mistrust of official media in the colonial Caribbean, is sharpened by Moses' own bitter experience: the press had reported a strike threat by the white workforce when he had previously been employed in a railway yard, after which Moses was sacked (Selvon 1985: 29). Unaware of any hidden agenda, Tanty, a Jamaican women coming with a family group to join her nephew Tolroy, poses for the camera and gives unguarded answers to the reporter's questions. Rebuffing Tolroy's warning to keep up her guard, she asks her nephew ironically, 'Why you so prejudice? . . . We have to show we have good manners, you know' (Selvon 1985: 31). Putting on her best, wide-brimmed straw hat, she collects the family together to pose for the photograph, which appears in the next day's paper with the headline 'Now, Jamaican Families Come to Britain' (1985: 32). The unfamiliar appearance of the family is thus made to image a threat to the insular nation, apparently confirming the 'alienness' of these newcomers through an 'innocent' eye, while suggesting the spectre of reproduction and generation that was to form a key topic for anti-immigration discourse.

Through a series of such vignettes the novel traces how the construction of Commonwealth migrants as 'immigrants' (rather than as British citizens) and as 'coloured' plays an important role in the reciprocal construction of Britain as a *nation* rather than an *empire*, and thus in the process of post-imperial amnesia identified by Paul Gilroy (Gilroy 2005: 89–90). Britishness moves from being a question of 'civilisation', which is said to be available to any member of the British Empire, to membership of a racially defined national community. As we have seen, this process is shown to operate through the media and political discourse, but it also works through the patterning of perception engendered by employment practices and the welfare system. At the Employment Exchange, (or 'labour office'), where Galahad goes to find a job, Moses explains that each person's record is marked according to race and place of birth in order to enforce an informal 'colour bar' – the exclusion of non-whites from skilled, clerical, or other well-paid employment, forcing them into manual work, often temporary or on the night shift (Selvon 1985: 46). The alternative is unemployment benefit, shown to have a corrosive effect on its recipients through the 'atmosphere' of the welfare office, which 'hit Galahad hard so that he had to stand up against a wall for a minute': 'Is a kind of place where hate and disgust and avarice and malice and sympathy and sorrow all mix up . . . a place where everyone is your enemy and your friend' (Selvon 1985: 45). Cast as administrative units to be processed, organised, regulated and directed, the unemployed 'stand around in little groups . . . all of them looking destitute' (1985: 46). Although non-white migrants are becoming identified in the larger culture as work-shy and parasitic, the picture the novel paints is instead of a painful and unending struggle to work, for as the narrator muses, 'when a man out of work he like a fish out of water' (1985: 45). Poverty and work – the lack of it, its temporary nature and the hardships endured to maintain it – remain constant themes through the novel, with Galahad reduced to capturing a city pigeon to eat, although 'the feeling that he do a bad thing wouldn't leave him' (1985: 125). And yet many men manage to save money from slim wage packets to send as remittances to families back home desperate for economic support.

If the novel shows how public institutions and discourses construct a new 'immigrant' subjectivity, it also shows how the migrants remake London and its public and social spaces, a dynamic also registered in the narrator's use of Caribbean English (Nasta 2002: 77). Galahad escapes the grimy world of work through his sharp fashion sense, transforming his appearance from labourer to dandy and stepping out to see and be seen in the city streets. As the narrator reflects, 'This is London, this is life oh Lord, to walk like a king with money in your pocket, not a worry in the world' (Selvon 1985: 87). Critics have seen this reappropriation of public space as an important early moment in the hybridisation of postwar Britain, or 'Brit'n' as it is renamed in the novel: 'Galahad's ability to walk, and the confidence he exudes in circulating in the city,' writes John McLeod, 'represents a modest victory for himself . . . over

London's power of arrest' (Mcleod 2004: 36). McLeod sees the 'fete' or dance party organised by Harris, which features a steel band playing calypsos, as a key utopian moment in the novel, 'a way of envisaging just for a moment a new kind of socially inclusive space which emerges from the creolizing promise of the dance-floor: tolerant, racially inclusive, pleasurable, mobile, negotiating between ... past and present, inside and outside, the Caribbean and London' (2004: 39). Indeed, the novel is filled with such moments, as the narrator redescribes familiar sites or neighbourhoods within its own Caribbean cadence, and as the various characters criss-cross London reinventing its everyday sounds and appearance. Tanty, who 'even the English people she call Tanty', conjures a little bubble of Caribbean social relations in the backstreets of London when she 'cause the shopkeeper to give people credit' by invoking the need for 'trust' and the reality that '[w]e is poor people and we don't always have money to buy' (Selvon 1985: 79). But this bubble has very definite limits, and when she tries to spread the policy of trust to the high street shops, her strength of character and moral force no longer count against the relentless protocols of the capitalist market. And as Moses observes, although the 'boys' can cruise the parks, pubs and public spaces, 'you can't go in their house and eat or sit down and talk' (1985: 130).

In fact, in *The Lonely Londoners* every expression of self-possession, reappropriation and hybridity is hemmed in by a surrounding sense of limitation. At the very moment that Galahad enjoys the weightlessness of cruising through London in his finery, a little white child exclaims, 'Mummy, look at that Black man!' in a close echo of Fanon's *Black Skin, White Masks* and of Selvon's own earlier short story 'Come Back to Grenada' (Selvon 1985: 87). And just as we saw in reading Fanon in Chapter 2, this everyday moment of othering, repeated again and again, coalesces into a reified entity that assumes a distinct existence, but which nonetheless frames these characters and shapes their interaction with others. In a striking episode Galahad begins 'talking to the color Black, as if it is a person, telling it that is not *he* who causing botheration in the place, but Black, who is a worthless thing': 'Colour, is you that causing all this you know,' declares Galahad, asking '[w]hy the hell you can't be blue, or red or green, if you can't be white?' (Selvon 1985: 88). But as the migrants' frantic sexual exploits indicate, these reified stereotypes of colour cannot be wholly externalised, but come to govern their intimate transactions and desires. The 'boys' are valued by white women in terms of an imaginary sexual 'savagery: 'you can't put on any English accent for them or play ladeda ... or try to be polite and civilise', the narrator observes, 'they want you to live up to the films and stories they hear about black people living primitive in the jungles' (1985: 108). In turn, many of the 'boys' pursue white women, who are termed 'pretty pieces of skin' or 'things' (1985: 102). Noting that the novel has been criticised for its portrayal of a chauvinistic male perspective, Susheila Nasta argues that 'their view of women . . . reflects ultimately upon the boys' own uncertainty and insecure sense of self' (Nasta 2002: 80). Certainly the novel chronicles a stream of unfulfilling and often casually cruel relationships, and Moses for one judges that within this social world all sexual relationships are caught up in the objectification of race and the discrimination that underpins it. '[A]fter a while you want to get in company, you want to go to somebody house and eat a meal,' he muses, reflecting that '[i]t ain't have no sort of family life for us here'. 'This is a lonely miserable city,' he concludes (1985: 130).

The more optimistic reading of critics like John McLeod, while rightly emphasising an important dimension of the novel, thus needs to be qualified, and the pervasive nexus of isolation, objectification and racism that pervades the novel also needs to be emphasised. Indeed, the complexity of this highly self-reflexive modernist novel lies in tracing how these dimensions are intricately interrelated. In Moses' final reflective moment, which offers itself as a frame for reading the text, the patterns of migrant sociality are correlated with the atomisation that structures everyday experience: 'Under the kiff-kiff laughter, behind the ballad and the episode, the what-happening, the summer-is-hearts, he could see a great aimlessness, a great restless, swaying movement that leaving you standing in the same spot' (Selvon 1985: 141). Implicit in this vision is a much more penetrating account of British society than is usually ascribed to the novel, one which expands its concern for migrant experience to provide a perspective on a broader social moment.

This expansive scope is established in an important but surprisingly unexplored passage that comes about midway through the novel. Here the narrator considers the white working-class areas of London where colonial migrants – who are referred to as 'spades', now considered an offensive term – are concentrated: 'It have a kind of communal feeling with the Working Class and the spades, because when you poor things does level out, it don't have much up and down' (Selvon 1985: 75). But this is not a romantic portrait of 'organic' community: whatever elements of solidarity or 'communal feeling' emerge here have to be forged and actively produced in the teeth of social conditions that function powerfully against them. These conditions become starkly apparent within the defamiliarising gaze of the narrator:

It have people living in London who don't know what happening in the room next to them, far more the street, or how other people living. London is a place like that. It divide up in little worlds, and you stay in the world you belong to and you don't know anything what happening in the other ones except what you read in the papers ... Them people who have car, who going to theatre and ballet in the West End ... they don't know nothing about hustling two pounds of brussel sprout and half-pound potato, or queuing up for fish and chips in the smog. People don't talk about things like that again, they come to kind of accept that is so the world is, that it bound to have rich and poor, it bound to have some who live by the Grace and others who have plenty. (Selvon 1985: 74)

In an unsentimental yet humane vision of social disintegration, the narrator surveys the legacy of the war years, which have left a dazed army of war widows, 'who does be pottering around the Harrow Road like if they lost, a look in their eye as if the war happen unexpected and they still can't understand what happen to old Brit'n' (1985: 75).

In a striking image that recalls the sensibility of Samuel Beckett's prewar novel *Murphy* (1938), the narrator imagines this broader nexus of social disconnection as a kind of hard-wired infrastructure that maintains the separation of worlds and the inwardness of social atomisation. An old man 'sing in a high falsetto, looking up at the high windows, where the high and mighty living', his eyes waiting for a coin to be tossed from the window, his voice producing '[n]o song or rhythm, just a sort of musical noise so nobody could say he be begging' (Selvon 1985: 75). But the coin thrown down by a woman does not attest to an unalloyed moment of solidarity or connection, but rather works to reconfirm the isolation of these small worlds:

Could be she had a nice night and she in a good mood, or could be, after the night's sleep, she thinking about life and the sound of that voice quavering in the cold outside touch the old heart. But if she have a thought at all, it never go further than to cause the window to open and the tanner [coin] to fall down. In fact when the woman throw the tanner from the window she don't even look down; if a man was a mile away and he controlling a loudspeaker ... the tanner would have come the same way. (1985: 75–6)

The dislocated perspective of Selvon's narrator sees the disintegrative fabric of social experience in a way that escapes the empiricist gaze of an established Londoner. Though physically just a few feet away, the structuring of social experience extends the separation between listener and singer like electrical wires, which carry the voice but disallow any further engagement between their worlds. It is this disintegrative nexus of social experience that subtends the emergence of an insular concept of the nation and the remaking of British colonial subjects as 'black' and as 'immigrants'.

This expanded context enlarges the purchase of the closing vision of the novel, in which Moses sees 'black faces bobbing up and down in the millions of white, strained faces, everybody hustling along the Strand, the spades jostling in the crowd, bewildered and hopeless' (Selvon 1985: 141–2). As many critics have interpreted this passage, it clearly attests to the relentlessly destructive impact of racism,'[a]s if a forlorn shadow of doom fall on all the spades in the country' (1985: 141). While this is certainly true, it does not, on my reading, 'confir[m] by implication the peculiarity and cohesion of postwar Englishness', but instead offers a perspective comparable to Walter Benjamin's image of modern politics in 'Experience and Poverty' (Esty 2004: 203; Benjamin 1999).[1] For if on one view this vision serves to highlight the disconnection and isolation of the black faces amidst the sea of white faces, if we switch our focus, the black faces also serve to highlight the disconnection and atomisation of 'the millions of white, strained faces' who surround them, another facet of the same coin. In this reading, the incipient synthesis of racism and nationalism that emerged in the postwar years was not the expression of a homogeneous community responding to outsiders for the first time. Rather, it was a function of the disintegrative structuring of social experience that held out the promise of 'community' built on the aggressive exclusion of a visibly conspicuous 'enemy within'. But as the image 'of everybody hustling along the Strand' implies, the promise of such a 'community' cannot repair social disintegration, and indeed will serve only to worsen it. Although the novel may be judged not to 'offer any real solutions to the increasingly urgent problems of justice in a multi-ethnic nation-state' – arguably a tall order for any fictional work – *The Lonely Londoners* does at the very least adumbrate the social nexus which was to find its political manifestation in the racist violence in Nottingham and Notting Hill just two years later (Esty 2004: 211).

Bringing the War Back Home? John Arden's *Serjeant Musgrave's Dance*

If Selvon could describe the construction of an insular nation from the viewpoint of those excluded from it, such a perspective was much harder to generate from within. And yet, there were significant challenges to the second colonial occupation and the Cold War rhetoric upon which it increasingly sought to draw. While not focusing on colonial conflict, the Campaign for Nuclear Disarmament (CND), a non-party mass popular movement, rejected the automatic assumption that Britain should continue as a global power, arguing instead that it should withdraw from the Cold War alliance with the United States and pursue a non-aligned foreign policy (Hewison 1981: 165). Culturally, John Osborne's successful play *The Entertainer*, whose first performance at the Royal Court Theatre in London in 1957 starred the celebrated British actor Laurence Olivier, twinned the Suez debacle of the previous year with the declining tradition of music hall (or vaudeville) as a double metaphor for the ossified nature of postwar Britain. Britain is figured as a society that has failed to embrace generational change and is unable to depart from rigid habits of deference, social convention and propriety. *The Entertainer* centres on the dysfunctional family of a British soldier killed in the Suez invasion, and parallels the perceived inertia of contemporary popular audiences with public indifference to the casualties of the rapidly multiplying late colonial wars. The dead soldier's sister Jean, fresh from a CND march, asks 'Why do people like us just sit here, and just lap it up, why do boys die?' – only to answer by pointing to the unthinking deference symbolised by the 'gloved hand' of the Queen 'waving . . . from a gold coach' at yet another imperial pageant (Osborne 1958: 78).

Yet although posing the question, Osborne's play is also symptomatic of the limited vision it seeks to denounce. *The Entertainer* ruthlessly lampoons the tired rhetoric of imperial jingoism, now transparently empty after decades of repetition – 'Those bits of red still on the map / We won't give up without a scrap.' But in the figure of Billy Rice, the retired vaudevillian, it also demonstrates a marked nostalgia for a moment when imperial belief, and the self-respect it engendered, were still possible (Osborne 1958: 33). The problem for Osborne's play is not really empire, but the failure of its magic to continue to enthral domestic audiences, just as the music hall had lost its ability to cast its spell with the rise of cinema and rock and roll. In the moral economy of the play, the real problem is the absence of a manly individualism in contemporary society, which has been emasculated by what is conceived as a feminising welfare state and the selfishness produced by relative prosperity. The last vaudevillian Archie Rice complains that 'We're all out for good old Number One', and so we no longer 'let [our] feelings roam' but live existentially timid lives, preferring the security of routine and the familiar to a world of risk and authenticity (Osborne 1958: 86). The play is, then, primarily inward looking, concerned with an existential failure of nerve in a 'Good old England' which, apart from the fuzzy memory of wartime Canada, provides the limits of the play's world. Thus, although the body of Mick, Archie's son, is returned from

Suez for burial, the violence of the second colonial occupation does not come home in the sense that the play fails to imagine how conflict and dissatisfaction within the nation might connect in any substantive way with the late colonial project still being pursued beyond its borders.

John Arden's play *Serjeant Musgrave's Dance*, first performed at the Royal Court two years later in 1959, takes this connection more seriously. In effect, it explores Jean's question as to why 'people like us just sit here', while the state that represents them inflicts massive violence overseas in pursuit of geopolitical power. The play was prompted by reports of British atrocities in Cyprus, a colonial outpost in the Mediterranean embroiled in spiralling violence: British suppression of the anticolonial movement led to the emergence of a violent guerrilla campaign in 1955, which was in turn met with torture, internment camps, house demolitions and extrajudicial killings by British forces, including the bayoneting of villagers (Arden 1994: xviii; Brendon 2007: 614–24). Violence reached its height in 'Black October' in 1958, which 'brought Cyprus to the top of the political agenda in Britain'; yet British war crimes abroad – in Cyprus or in the concurrent Mau Mau Uprising in Kenya – remained a foreign news story rather than a central political motivator at home, and foreign atrocities failed to affect the basic parameters of domestic political thinking (Brendon 2007: 624; Anderson 2005; Elkins 2005). *Serjeant Musgrave's Dance* sought to explore this disconnect, although not unsurprisingly it was at first greeted with incomprehension by most mainstream critics. New Left writers like Stuart Hall, on the other hand, saw the vital connection it made within the contemporary context between 'the terrors and brutalities of a colonial war' and the overarching zero-sum logic of the Cold War, in which overwhelming violence was seen as the only possible response to the anticipated violence of the 'other side' (Hall 1960: 50). This connection was to become increasingly palpable through the 1960s during the Vietnam War, in which colonial and Cold wars were visibly merged, and Arden's play became a key text for the anti-war movements in both Britain and the United States.

However, the initial incomprehension that greeted the play also reflects Arden's dramatic style, which drew on the theatre of Bertolt Brecht, whose work, alongside other avant-garde European dramatists such as Eugene Ionesco and Samuel Beckett, had been able to make inroads in the relatively open world of postwar London theatre (Hewison 1981: 144–5). Where naturalistic drama sought to create a socially plausible representation of everyday life by integrating music, setting and acting within a recognisable narrative scenario and range of characterisation, Brecht's 'epic theatre' sought to dissociate the basic elements of dramatic form and set them in conflict with one another. For Brecht, the integrated, familiar and conventionally plausible quality of naturalistic drama simply confirmed the dominant 'common sense' view of the world, a perspective that he saw as implicitly supporting the existing social order. In providing a clear 'message' or 'moral', however apparently dissident, drama functioned to dull the critical perception of its audiences and promote a kind of world-weary acceptance of the order of things. In contrast, Brecht argued for a non-naturalistic, anti-illusionist theatre:

> Once the content [of the play] becomes . . . an independent component, to which text, music, and setting 'adopt attitudes'; once illusion is sacrificed to free discussion, and once the spectator, instead of being enabled to have an experience, is forced as it were to cast his vote; then a change has been launched which goes far beyond formal matters and begins for the first time to affect the theatre's social function. (Brecht 1964: 39)

Arden, who had seen the Berliner Ensemble perform in London in 1956, found in Brecht a theatrical style for which he was already searching, one that avoided the straightforward moral or message of naturalist drama (Arden and Gaston 1991: 151). '"Telling" people in the audience what the play is about is something I've always tried to avoid,' Arden has said, since it amounts to 'the author explaining what the audience is *supposed* to think about the play' (Arden and Gaston 1991: 153; emphasis added). *Serjeant Musgrave's Dance* is challenging because it does not clearly endorse a particular character's viewpoint or line of action, but presents a project that falls apart as the characters pursue different arguments and ideas.

The play revolves around a small group of deserting soldiers led by the puritanical but driven Serjeant Musgrave. They return from a distant colonial war to a coal-mining town in late Victorian England with the body of their fallen comrade, a former miner and resident of the town. The town itself is locked in conflict, as the mine-owners lay off their workforce in the face of slack demand for coal, and without work the miners now face starvation. Sickened not only by the death of their friend, but also by the resulting reprisals – in which their unit has killed five local people (including a young girl) and injured thirty-four more – the deserting soldiers have come back to stage an inverted recruiting drive. Instead of reinforcing the glamorous appearance of military service, they plan to stage a spectacle that will puncture this perception and communicate the realities of imperial violence. The long first scene of Act III operates as what the Situationists would call the *détournement* – or subversive restaging – of a recruiting meeting, which in Brechtian fashion speaks directly to the theatre audience, placing them (at least discursively) in the position of destitute workers and potential recruits for colonial service. In the *détournement* the pomp and ceremony of military spectacle and the prurient display of lethal technology are 'refunctioned' to reveal the violence of colonialism, culminating in the dramatic unfurling of a 'recruiting banner' that is in fact the uniformed skeleton of their dead comrade. '[W]e belong to a regiment is a few thousand miles away from here,' explains Sergeant Musgrave, 'in a little country without much importance except from the point of view there's a Union Jack that flies over it and the people of that country can write British subject after their names'; another soldier adds, '[w]e live in battered tents in the rain, we eat rotten food, there's knives in the dark streets and blood on the floors of hospitals, but we stand tall and proud: because of why we are there' (Arden 1994: 305). Moving from visual and spoken propaganda to the propaganda of the deed, Musgrave turns his maxim gun on the assembled mine-owners and dignitaries, arguing that the only way to bring home the reality of colonial violence is to inflict its brutal logic of escalating reprisals upon those at home who are responsible.

To Musgrave's incomprehension, however, the revelation of colonial violence in its most palpable form creates confusion rather than clarity or unity of purpose. As the deserters reveal the (initially anonymous) skeleton and tell the story of their comrade's murder and the subsequent bloody reprisals, they are met with indifference: 'we're not bloody interested,' exclaims Walsh, the most articulate of the colliers, enjoining the deserters to '[m]end your own heartache and leave us to sort with ours – we've enough and to spare!' (Arden 1994: 311). And when the skeleton is finally identified as one of their own, although the townspeople feel shock and sadness, they are repelled by the deserters' gruesome tactics. When it is revealed that they have hushed up the accidental killing of one of their own party the night before, the crowd turns against them. Losing moral authority, Musgrave is captured by the dragoons who have come to suppress the miners' protest, and Walsh, the articulate miner, accepts bitterly that 'We're back where we were' (Arden 1994: 321).

The play's refusal either to straightforwardly endorse Musgrave's project by depicting its successful transformation of the townspeople's consciousness, or to condemn it by providing an alternative solution that answers its protests in other terms, has frustrated critics, and has been interpreted either as a dramatic flaw or the expression of a nihilistic viewpoint (Arden 1994: 229; Malick 1995: 17–21). However, this lack of easy resolution might instead be interpreted as demonstrating the play's concern with describing the problem in terms that exceed existing common sense or received opinion. Throughout the play the struggle of the miners for economic justice and political participation is repeatedly paralleled with that of the colonial subjects who attempt to establish their own autonomy: 'We've earned our living by beating and killing folk like yourselves in the streets of their own city,' explains one of the soldiers (Arden 1994: 316). Yet if disempowerment and exploitation are the common condition of the British working class and the colonial populations they are sent to garrison, the very experience of disempowerment militates against fellow feeling for those in the same condition: as the miner Walsh insists fiercely, '[m]end your own heartache and leave us to sort with ours – we've enough and to spare!' (Arden 1994: 311).

Thus, disempowerment focuses the disempowered community's concern on its own particular experience as a practical necessity, inadvertently separating it from the experience of others. Musgrave's inability to understand this is articulated by Mrs Hitchcock, the pub landlady who along with the play's other female character, Annie, figures the 'life and love' that in Musgrave's eyes is inimical to the discipline and logic of masculine, military thinking. Musgrave's strategy is to use this logic – expressed in the tactical 'plan' – to expose the interests that drive the imperial project. To his mind, the closely focused interpersonal experience he calls 'life and love' threaten this strategy by 'scribbl[ing] all over that plan . . . mak[ing] it crooked, dirty, idle, untidy, *bad*', and dissolving it into 'anarchy' (1994: 273; emphasis in original). He believes that the iron 'Logic' of colonial militarism – of ever greater reprisals, ever greater shows of force – can only be overcome by returning that 'Logic' to the imperial homeland:

> Twenty-five to die and the Logic is worked out . . . I brought it back to England but I've brought the cure too – to turn it on them that sent it out of this country – way-out-ay they sent it, where they hoped that only soldiers could catch it and rave! Well here's three redcoat ravers on their own kitchen hearthstone! (Arden 1994: 314)

But as Mrs Hitchcock explains to the imprisoned Musgrave at the end of the play, he has failed to understand that his own project has in just these terms failed to respect or recognise the parameters of experience and meaning of the struggling mining community:

> Then *use* your Logic – if you can. Look at it this road: here we are, and we've got life and love. Then you came in and did your scribbling where

nobody asked you. Aye, it's arsey-versey to what you said, but it's still anarchy, isn't it? And it's all your work. (Arden 1994: 324; emphasis in original)

The world of colonial oppression and violence, however logically connected to the exploitation and disempowerment of working-class communities in Britain, can only seem alien and abstract – or worse, absolutely nihilistic or absolutely evil – if it lacks any experiential connection to metropolitan audiences. In the wake of 9/11 and the London bombings of 7/7 the play's argument clearly remains relevant.

On this reading, the play neither disavows the logical connection between colonial violence and domestic disempowerment, nor the pressing problem of finding modes of connecting them experientially. While one of the soldiers objects to Musgrave's 'Logic' by arguing that 'You can't cure the pox by further whoring', Arden responds in an interview some thirty years later: 'but the pox *has* to be cured' (Arden and Gaston 1991: 169; emphasis in original). Surveying British killings in Ireland and US military intervention in Panama and Nicaragua, he remarks that '[y]et again . . . this type of military repression . . . is backed up by the media of the country that sponsors it and is then accepted by what appears to be the majority of the population of that country' (Arden and Gaston 1991: 169).

The Fire Next Time: Linton Kwesi Johnson's *Dread Beat and Blood*

Linton Kwesi Johnson's second volume of poems *Dread Beat and Blood* (1975) provides a powerful insight into the profound changes in the social and political consciousness of black British communities that occurred in the 1970s and 1980s. Johnson built on an existing tradition of formal innovation initiated by writers like Aimé Césaire, Samuel Selvon, Louise Bennett and Kamau Brathwaite, but developed it in a markedly new direction in order to speak to 'a black British generation born in England . . . but without a place of their own in their immediate homeland' (Nasta 1988: 223). Born in Jamaica but moving to Britain when he was eleven, Johnson's poetry moves between and combines different linguistic zones: as he explains, his poetry inhabits 'the tension between Jamaican Creole and Jamaican English and between those and English English' (Johnson 1975: 8). His poetry is often identified as 'dub poetry', a term also associated with such poets as Oku Onuora and Michael Smith in Jamaica, Jean 'Binta' Breeze and Benjamin Zephaniah in Britain, and Lillian Allen and Afua Cooper in Canada. Dub poetry is a poetic form closely aligned with the rhythms and oral style of reggae, and is designed both to be read and to be performed and heard, whether with musical backing or simply as spoken word. Johnson's poetry works simultaneously as performance and as written poetry: when confronted on the page its cadences set up strong rhythms, while the text often exhibits what Mervyn Morris has called an 'eye Creole', the use of unfamiliar spellings designed to communicate the distinct pronunciation of otherwise familiar words – 'fia' for 'fire', or 'Inglan' for 'England', for example (Morris 1983: 151).[2] The declaratory and performative nature of *Dread Beat and Blood* marks a striking innovation in postwar British writing because it repositions the social location of literature, shifting the centre of address and interpretation from the literary establishment to communities who, in Andrew Salkey's words, 'share and understand a common experience of oppression and the matching language of pain' (Johnson 1975: 8). Yet Salkey also argues that the poetry's close connection with the experiences of particular communities need not be exclusive, for 'in talking to his own, so rootedly, so sincerely, [Johnson] manages also to talk to all of us; that is, to those of us who will listen and connect' (Johnson 1975: 9).

Dread Beat and Blood appeared at a moment when the expectations for equality and social recognition of a new generation of British-born black citizens were met with a political and institutional assault by the police, media and politicians. As Stuart Hall and his colleagues charted in *Policing the Crisis* (Hall et al. 1978), a moral panic over mugging came to define black youths as inherently violent and criminal. Police harassment of young black people was authorised by the 'suss' laws, Victorian-era legislation that allowed police officers to stop and search anyone on the most vaguely defined 'suspicion'. Police harassment came to be symbolised by the Metropolitan Police's campaign in 1976 and 1977 to suppress the Notting Hill Carnival, widely seen as the central pan-Caribbean cultural event in Britain (Dawson 2007: 83). At the same time, the neofascist National Font (NF), an openly violent and racist party, gained a measure of electoral support, and there was an associated rise in racist attacks over the decade. But it was Thatcherism that was to be most successful in politically harnessing white racism. In an interview on Granada TV in 1978 Margaret Thatcher signalled her identification with Britain's imperial past and her sympathy with anti-black and anti-immigrant racism, using the code word 'swamping' to present non-whites as a threat:

I think people are really rather afraid that this country might be rather swamped by people with a different culture and, you know, the British character has done so much for democracy and law, and has done so much throughout the world, that if there is any fear that it might be swamped, people are going to be really rather hostile to those coming in. (Thatcher 1978)

Deploying the culturalism of Powell's neoracism, Thatcher's statement constructs the 'British character' as a fixed entity against which 'people with a different culture' are both irretrievably alien, generation after generation, and inherently menacing, thus justifying and naturalising racism against them. At the same time, the Empire is both celebrated and disavowed: what the 'British character' has 'done throughout the world' must include colonialism and imperialism, which are manifestly anti-democratic and extra-legal; but rendered through the lens of culturalism, it is the 'British character' not the British state that is invoked, and this international role can be imagined in deeds of pluck and resolution removed from the social and the political. Intensified police harassment and skyrocketing unemployment following Margaret Thatcher's election in 1979 led socially marginalised communities to respond, and 'riots' or 'uprisings' broke out in Brixton, Toxteth and other inner city locations in 1981 and 1985.

Many of the poems in *Dread Beat and Blood*, such as 'Five Nights of Bleeding', are primarily concerned with the violence experienced by black communities at this time. Johnson looked to understand the role of violence in relation to migration and decolonisation through Frantz Fanon's later book, *The Wretched of the Earth*:

I was trying to relate the Fanonist ideas about violence in the process of decolonization to my particular situation here, seeing the internecine warfare going on between youths of my generation . . . And . . . at the same time we were being brutalized by the police and framed and criminalized. So ['Five Nights of Bleeding'] was trying to talk about that ambivalent relationship with violence. (Johnson and Caesar 1996: 67)

For Fanon, anticolonial violence was not only necessitated by the structuring of colonialism – in its exclusion of the colonised from politics – but would come to play a transformative role in the process of decolonisation. 'At the level of individuals,' Fanon writes, 'violence is a cleansing force' because it 'frees the native from his inferiority complex and from despair and inaction . . . and restores his self-respect' (Fanon 1967: 74). In 'All Wi Doin is Defendin', Johnson connects the violence of the oppressed to the oppression that engenders it, and defends the right of the oppressed to respond to violence: 'all oppression / can do is bring / passion to de heights of eruption, / and songs of fire we will sing' (Johnson 1975: 26). But Johnson is much less sanguine about the harmful effects of violence than Fanon, and much more concerned with its potential to be redirected among the oppressed and to generate new forms of injustice and oppression. In 'Five Nights of Bleeding', for example, we see 'rebellion rushing doun the wrong road' as 'the bitterness erupts like a hot-blast', and 'it's war amongst the rebels'. Desperately the poem's repeated refrain intones 'madness . . . madness . . . war' (1975: 17, 15).

Many of the poems explore the interaction between inner and outer forces through a multi-layered system of metaphors that connect communal culture (and especially music), subjectivity, and the collective history of slavery and racism through the deep bass beat of reggae. As 'muzik of blood / black reared / pain rooted / heart geared', the pumping bass is both the music that encodes the memories of oppression and resistance that sustain community, and the pulse of the heart that sustains each individual life and rises to passion in defending that life and its social conditions of possibility. As Johnson writes elsewhere, reggae is 'an essentially experiential music . . . in the sense that the music is true to the historical experience of the people, that the music reflects the historical experience' (Johnson 1976: 398). Similarly, 'Reggae Sounds' describes a 'bass history' that is a 'moving' and 'hurting black story' (Johnson 1975: 56). Here the phrase 'bass history' plays on the musical term (bass) and its homophone 'base', suggesting that reggae is both a history from below and a history of the emotions and experiences considered 'base' by traditional poetics. 'Doun de Road' identifies the social forces that define the limits of contemporary experience:

> yes, the violence of the oppressor runnin wild;
> them pickin up the yout them fe suss;
> powell prophesying a black, a black, a black conquest;
> and the National Front is on the rampage. (Johnson 1975: 22)

But the present comes from somewhere, and the poem laments 'that history should take such a rough route / causing us this bitterness and pain on the way' (Johnson 1975: 22). In the long prose poem 'John De Crow', that history is identified with colonialism and capitalism: 'from out of the mouth of Europe came plunder . . . carrying suffering south', the expression of 'the greed of men and the need for capital's growth' (1975: 41).

In 'Bass Culture', reggae music becomes the blood or dynamic force of collective experience, its rhythm modulated by the pressures and constrictions placed upon it: 'all tensed up / in the bubble and the bounce / an the leap and the weight drop', it is 'culture pulsing', it is 'de cultural wave [of] of a dread people' which is 'burstin outta slave shakkle' (1975: 57, 58). Johnson's metaphorical web of blood, rhythm and pulse figures subjectivity as dynamic and reactive, fluid but viscose: it is enlivened by an inner pulse or dynamism, but it is sticky and carries a kind of plastic memory of its earlier experiences. Its rhythm therefore emerges in the interaction between inner and outer, between social world, collective experience and subjective agency. Thus *Dread Beat and Blood* is fundamentally concerned with the different possible forms that the suppressed dynamism of 'life' might take. Damned up or suppressed within a social world that refuses justice and recognition, this dynamism is intensified, generating a 'latent powa' that may grow and grow to uncontainable proportions, 'hotta dan de hites of fire / livin heat doun volcano core' (1975: 58). Like the swelling magma deep in the earth's crust, the heat and pressure build to an explosive force, where

> spirits riled
> an rise and rail thunda-wise
>
> . . .
>
> in a form resembling madness
> like violence is the show;
> burstin outta slave shakkle,
> look ya! Boun fe harm the wicked. (Johnson 1975: 58)

But such an explosion by definition can often not be controlled, as the poem 'Dread Beat and Blood' explores:

> rocks rolling over hearts leaping wild,
> rage rising out of the heat of the hurt;
> and a fist curled in anger reaches a her,
> then the flash of a blade from another to a him,
> leaps out for a dig of a flesh of a piece of skin.
> and blood, bitterness, exploding fire, wailing blood, and bleeding.
>   (Johnson 1975: 55)

Here the pressure of oppression leads to 'fratricide . . . with brother killing brother', a violence directed not at oppression but within the community (1975: 22).

However, the volume also sees other 'forms' that this welling force might take: 'dig doun to the root of pain' exhorts the voice of 'Reggae Sounds', and 'shape it into violence for the people' (1975: 56). That is, violence might be 'shaped' and directed towards social goals that refor-mulate the conditions that engender violence. And in 'Bass Culture' the poem's voice invokes the combination of 'destruction all around' and 'love', 'soh life tek the form whey shiff from calm / an hold the way of a deadly storm' (1975: 58). In being able to 'shiff' (shift) between 'calm' and 'deadly storm', the reactive force of suppressed rage is directed ('hold the way') in its expression, so that instead of being locked into a cycle of violence, it may be orientated towards a different possible future:

When the wall mus smash,
And the beat will shiff
As the culture allta
When oppression scatta. (Johnson 1975: 59)

This orientation to another possible future structures the two parts of 'Two Sides of Silence', which begins in a situation where 'To us, / . . . silence has no meaning', but looks to another time 'where sweet clothed sounds / can rebound round / . . . through a mellow, / purer, silent space' (1975: 36, 37).

Some of Linton Kwesi Johnson's best known poems were written after *Dread Beat and Blood*, including 'Sonny's Lettah', 'It Dread inna Inglan', 'New Craas Massakah' and 'Di Great Insohreckshan', which renames what were officially called the 'Brixton riots' in 1981 and records a different oral history of the events and their meaning. But it was *Dread Beat and Blood* that established Johnson as a poet and a performer, and in his role as a public intellectual, a role he has pursued through his political activism with the Race Today Collective, his jour-nalism and through his articulation of 'sowshalism', a vernacular social-ism connected to community struggles and self-organisation (Johnson 2006: 73). The volume articulated the pain and suffering of a generation of young black British people, and provided a site for thinking through both the damage done by violence and its potential to create different possible futures. Though still critical of the racism in contemporary Britain, and especially the assault on communities and civil liberties con-ducted in the name of the 'war on terror', in a recent interview Johnson points out that '[t]hrough our rebellion, we helped change Britain' (Johnson and DiNovella 2007: 33). In another interview, Johnson has to remind his interviewer that 'We are Europeans and we are part of Europe.' 'In the same way that one can speak about African-Americans,' Johnson explains, 'one can talk about black Europeans, because we are part of Europe.' And in a riposte to Powell's call for the repatriation of non-white British people, he adds, 'Europe will never be white again. Never' (Johnson and Caesar 1996: 79–7).

Enemies Within: Tony Harrison's V

If Linton Kwesi Johnson's poetry responded to the construction of black communities as an alien presence within the national territory, the discourse of the 'enemy within' was not restricted to the descendants of former colonial subjects. In this context, it is worth briefly considering another influential but less famous speech by Enoch Powell, 'The Enemy Within' delivered in 1970, just a year before Britain concluded its withdrawal from 'East of Suez'. In an extraordinarily inflated rhetoric of impending social and civilisational collapse, the speech conjures a vast, diffuse and yet somehow closely co-ordinated 'enemy', whose threat is on a par with Nazism or nuclear war, and whose 'forces . . . aim at the actual destruction of our nation and society as we know them or can imagine them' (Powell 1991: 245, 246). Although its 'most perfect' and 'most dangerous' manifestation is said to be the 'West Indian, African, and Asian population' now living in Britain, it turns out that this 'enemy' is largely comprised of a rather unmenacing collection of protesting students, liberal intellectuals, Irish civil rights marchers and campaigners against South African apartheid (1991: 245, 248, 247). Collectively, this 'enemy' is to be understood as a powerful 'minority' that seeks to inveigle, disarm and dominate a peaceful and well-meaning 'majority', the 'we' for whom Powell claims to speak (1991: 246). While Powell's 'Rivers of Blood' speech had already articulated an English ethno-nationalism that could legitimise racism through the language of culture, what is so revealing about this less well remembered speech is that it demonstrates how this culturally based othering could be extended beyond non-'English' populations to the 'English' themselves (see Mercer 1991: 435–6). Once the 'enemy' status of visibly different communities had been established, it became potentially transferable to anyone judged disloyal to the 'nation'.

Although Powell's speech has now been largely forgotten, his conception of 'the enemy within' came to play a central role in the energetic cultural mobilisation of Thatcherism. In pursuing a series of conflicts – with black communities and the inner city poor in Brixton, Toxteth and elsewhere; with nationalist communities in the six counties of the north of Ireland; with Scottish rate-payers over the Poll Tax; with the unemployed over access to welfare benefits; with Labour councils attempting to maintain jobs and services; and with the British trade union movement in a series of politically driven industrial disputes – Margaret Thatcher enlisted precisely this vision of an apocalyptic internal threat. Famously, in a speech to the powerful 1922 Committee during the pivotal Miners' Strike of 1984–5, Thatcher transposed the nationalist rhetoric of the Falklands/Malvinas War to the political conflict with working-class communities *within* the nation. While in 'the time of the [Falklands/Malvinas] conflict they had had to fight the enemy without', she warned the Tory grandees, now the nation must fight '*the enemy within*', an enemy that would be 'much more difficult to fight', but which 'was just as dangerous to liberty' (Thatcher 1984; emphasis added). Just as Powell framed colonial migrants as 'non-labour', as a parasitic drain on the resources of the nation, so Thatcher was able to extend this definition to whole sections of the British working class, black and white.

That the trope of the 'enemy within' achieved such traction through the 1970s and 1980s cannot simply be attributed to the rhetorical skill or Machiavellian cunning of Powell or of the Conservative Party's speechwriters. Its appeal must also tell us something about deep-seated patterns of ideological inheritance in the post-imperial nation, and about the stresses and tensions involved in the lived experience of the disparity between local and global under the impact of neoliberal crisis. Written during the Miners' Strike in 1985, Tony Harrison's long poem *V* offers a thoughtful meditation on the emotional damage wreaked by neoliberal globalisation. Echoing Thomas Gray's 'Elegy in a Country Churchyard' (1751), Harrison's poem invites us both to expand and particularise our sense of the nation by surveying the gravestones of its less famous denizens. But this scenario is complicated by the graffiti scrawled upon them, which leads the 'I' of the poem into a confrontation with one of the vandals, an unemployed skinhead who is finally revealed to be his own 'alter ego' (Harrison 1987: 248). The poem's title comes from the shortening for 'versus' used in listing football fixtures, while the poem also plays on its homophone, 'verses'. This 'v' comes to annotate a series of conflicts that reach far beyond the soccer pitch, to include 'all the versuses of life, from LEEDS v. DERBY', through 'Black/White', 'man v. wife', 'Communist v. Fascist', 'Left v. Right', 'Hindu/Sikh', 'soul/body', 'heart v. mind', 'East/West'. But most immediately, this 'v' is embodied in the conflict between the government-run 'Coal Board' and the 'NUM', the National Union of Mineworkers (Harrison 1987: 238). The persona's discovery of his own complicity in the anger and aggression of the skinhead, and his realisation that both seek to write themselves into the social fabric from which they feel excluded, challenges easy condemnations of violence directed from the social centre to its margins. This realisation changes the terms of the conflict, from one between external entities to a conflict within: 'Half versus half, the enemies within / the heart that can't be whole till they unite' (1987: 244).

The poem's concern is with the damaging multiplication of conflict generated by polarisation, which the poem connects to the yawning gap between what is local and immediate and graspable, and the unseen national and transnational contexts within which political and economic decisions increasingly take place. The miners struck in opposition to the government closure of the coal industry in Britain, a closure that did not reflect the dwindling of a natural resource (Britain still has significant coal reserves), but manifested a political decision on the part of Margaret Thatcher's administration. Within its larger neoliberal agenda, the Conservative government looked to undermine nationalised industries and strengthen transnational corporations by breaking the most cohesive trade union in Britain, the NUM. No longer tied to any national territory, transnational corporations are able to impose lower wages and extract greater profits by threatening to move production or resource extraction to a lower wage economy. The defeat of the National Union of Mineworkers cowed the British trade union movement and encouraged the adoption of a Thatcherite neoliberal progamme by the Labour Party under Tony Blair. It also devastated former mining communities, destroying their cohesion and sapping the sense of purpose and dignity that work in the mines had given.

V frames its consideration of the damaging impact of Thatcherism's social polarisation within the disparity between the immediate and the absent. As the voice of the poem watches the animated logo of the nightly television news, a globe that grows in size from 'a taw [marble]' to 'ping pong [ball], tennis [ball]' and then 'football', it reflects on the impossibility of being able to map global complexity ('This world, with far too many people in'). The animation ends to reveal 'shots of the Gulf War', the bloody and underreported conflict between Iraq and Iran in which the United States and Britain supported Saddam Hussein's Iraq. The poem suggests a connection through homology between this conflict and those closer to home – between 'police v. pickets at a coke-plant gate' and between communities in the north of Ireland – but in his anger and confusion it utterly escapes the skinhead vandalizing the graves (Harrison 1987: 248). Instead his aggression is directed at that which appears visibly alien within his own daily experience, namely the non-white population of Leeds, and especially Muslims. Racism scaffolds his collapsing sense of self, which has been cut adrift from the self-respect engendered by work and denied the relative freedom of action allowed by a regular income. But the 'I' of the poem cannot simply condemn the skinhead, because he recognises that same structure of feeling – although without the aggressive racism – in his own father. In the immediate viewpoint of father and skinhead, the social changes that sapped the certainty of their lives and the influx of South Asian migrants into Leeds coincide, and so become linked by association:

> A pensioner in turban taps his stick
> along the pavement past the corner shop,
> that sells samosas now not beer on tick,
> to the Kashmir Muslim Club that was the Co-op. (Harrison 1987: 246)

The poem's persona remembers his father's world and sense of self shrinking with advancing age, 'squeezed by the unfamiliar' and by his 'fear / of foreign food and faces' (Harrison 1987: 246). But although recalled with pathos, this shrinkage of self presages a perspective that is dangerous and indeed potentially deadly, all the more so because it is generated from empirical experience, and so can be construed as self-evident and considered 'common sense'.

In Memoriam: Kazuo Ishiguro's *The Remains of the Day*

While Linton Kwesi Johnson's poetry could envisage different possible futures by engaging with the contemporary experience of historically engendered legacies of violence, as Harrison's poem suggests much of the cultural allure of Thatcherism lay in its ability to circumvent this fractured present by looking to an idealised and abstracted vision of the past. As Patrick Wright observed in *On Living in an Old Country*, a major study of British culture first published in 1985, 'when history is widely experienced as a process of degeneration and decline [and] [t]he future promises nothing except further decline' then 'nostalgia . . . for "roots" in an imperial, pre-industrial, and often pre-democratic past' becomes a powerful means of self-affirmation – especially when combined with 'those everyday memories of childhood which are stirred by [such] contemporary invocations of this better past' (Wright 2009: 66). In Britain in the 1980s this combination of personal and public memory was increasingly hung on a conception of 'National Heritage', embodied in the stately homes or aristocratic houses lovingly restored by the National Trust and other bodies, as well as public monuments associated with the monarchy, and even particular landscapes said to be evocative of another, older England now gone (Cannadine 2003: 238–9). This is of course not 'the' past as it 'once really was', a notion that Walter Benjamin has reminded us cannot be available in its pristine or absolute form since it never existed in such a form, but was always as contested and plural a present as this one (Benjamin 2003). Rather, it is a highly selective conception of the past that crucially 'involves the extraction of history – of the idea of historical significance and potential – from a denigrated everyday life and its restaging or display in certain sanctioned sites, events, images, and conceptions'. Thus '[a]bstracted and redeployed', Wright notes, 'history seems to be purged of political tension; it becomes a unifying spectacle, the settling of all disputes' (Wright 2009: 65). Transformed into 'History' with a capital 'H' it 'is stressed to the same measure as active historicity – the possibility of any historical development in the present . . . is denied to a consequently devalued and meaningless present-day experience' (2009: 65–6). As such, '"the past" is revalued and reconstructed as an irreplaceable heritage', which Wright describes as 'the backwards glance taken from the edge of a vividly imagined abyss' that 'accompanies a sense that history is foreclosed' (2009: 66).

As Paul Gilroy argues, this formulation of remembering is a powerful means of forgetting empire, whereby a certain memory of World War II, constructed as the plucky island nation standing alone against the continental power of Nazism, overwrites the geopolitical confrontation between the alliance of the British and French Empires, the Soviet Union and the United States on the one hand, and on the other the insurgent imperialist forces of Germany, Italy and Japan (Gilroy 2005: 87–9). And as Wright demonstrates, the 'past' so constructed functions as an insular and mythical 'Deep England', a conception of the nation removed from both empire and the migration that followed it: 'To be a subject of Deep England,' Wright observes, 'is above all to have *been there* – one must have had the essential experience . . . One must have grown up in the midst of ancestral continuities and have experienced that kindling of consciousness which the national landscape and cultural tradition prepare for the dawning national spirit' (Wright 2009: 81). In line with the culturalism of Powell, 'the movement into racism is real enough', although as Wright argues the 'particularistic experience' of national nostalgia and 'National Heritage' is not automatically 'identical with imperialist experience', even though the imaginary of empire lurks behind it 'and asserts its ruling image' over other modes of interpretation (2009: 82).

Kazuo Ishiguro's novel *The Remains of the Day*, first published in

1989 and the winner of the Booker Prize that year, is fundamentally concerned with this construction of a mythic or 'Deep England'. As Ishiguro observes,

> [A]t the moment, particularly in Britain, there is an enormous nostalgia industry going on with coffee table books, television programs, and even some tour agencies who are trying to capture this kind of old England. The mythical landscape of this sort of England, to a large degree, is harmless nostalgia for a time that didn't exist. The other side of this, however, is that it is used as a political tool – much as the American Western myth is used . . . [T]he political right . . . say England was this beautiful place before the trade unions tried to make it more egalitarian or before the immigrants started to come or before the promiscuous age of the '60s came and ruined everything. (Ishiguro, Herzinger and Vorda 1991: 139)

In *The Remains of the Day*, Ishiguro creates a kind of analogue for this process of mythic reconstruction. The novel is told entirely in the first person by its narrator, Stevens, over a few days in July 1956. The butler at what was formerly a grand stately home, Stevens takes a trip by motorcar to visit the former housekeeper, a Mrs Benn who Stevens consistently refers to by her maiden name, Miss Kenton. Stevens' narration is almost entirely concerned with the past, and especially with the years before World War II when he was the butler for Lord Darlington, an aristocratic Nazi-sympathiser. Stevens appears at first to be quite naturally recalling his earlier life prompted by his forthcoming motor trip, but quickly the novel reveals that his need to tell and retell the past is obsessive and all-consuming. The novel's interest lies in its extraordinary ability to involve us in the drama of Stevens' memory. Constantly reconstructing the past in light of the anxieties of the present, Stevens demonstrates that memory is not a neutral or objective record of the past, but a subjective and selective process that patterns and colours memory in relationship to the needs of the present – even, and perhaps especially, when those needs are unconscious or not fully understood.

Stevens' narration roams obsessively over his field of memory, avoiding what is difficult or painful and displacing unacknowledged anxieties into elaborate descriptions of trivial details or over-engineered interpretations of incidental events and bogus points of principle. Thus Stevens never once mentions his mother, a lack that suggests a desperately damaged and restricted emotional life, while his refusal to face up to Mrs Benn's marriage – and hence to his profound regret about not acknowledging his feelings for her – is continually registered in his referring to her as 'Miss Kenton'. The past is massaged and adjusted to return a picture that will justify – or failing that, at least make bearable – the experience of the present. However, as contemporary experience is itself continually changing, often in ways that are disconcerting or incompatible with the glass of memory, the past has to be relentlessly remade over and over again. Yet by reading his narration *symptomatically*, rather than literally, it is possible to glimpse beyond the projected and displaced image that Stevens moulds from the plasticity of memory. That is, if we focus on the warps and inconsistencies in the texture of Stevens' unreliable narration, and on the disparities between his narration and the fictional world of England in 1956 through which he moves, the memorial topoi and patterns of revision that his narration iterates themselves become interpretable – as *symptoms* of anxieties and obsessions that Stevens' consciousness cannot fully acknowledge or confront. Such a symptomatic reading inverts the usual calibration of significance in realist narration: in *The Remains of the Day* what the narrator considers significant or revealing is usually not so, while what goes unmentioned or is quickly dismissed as of no consequence often provides the most penetrating insights into Stevens' disconsolate condition.

In its obsessive reinscription of the past in the present of 1956, Stevens' narration traces a topography of anxiety that is imbued with post-imperial melancholy. As the Suez Crisis looms – the book begins in July 1956, coinciding with President Nasser's nationalisation of the Suez Canal – an American, Mr Farraday, now owns Darlington Hall, and the great house becomes a figure for the nation. An empty shell thrown up by an earlier stage of economic globalisation in the process of being superseded, its ostentatious show of tradition and power can now be comfortably inhabited by the new hegemon, the United States, although only in so far as it meets a certain self-affirming image that for a period flatters its new occupier. But Stevens' unhappy consciousness is not simply a function of decline, but was damaged and distorted from its origin at the highpoint of the British Empire. Revealing here are the three stories that Stevens tells about his father on the evening of day one, and his recollection of his father's death on the morning of day two. In recalling what is ostensibly a workaday anecdote to confirm his father's embodiment of the dignity appropriate to a 'great' butler, Stevens reveals almost incidentally the devastating loss of his brother, Leonard, in the Second Anglo-Boer War. Even though his father had to act as valet to the general whose blundering had directly led to the young soldier's death, 'so well did my father hide his feelings, and so professionally did he carry out his duties' that he comes to define for Stevens the notion of 'dignity' according to which he lives his own life. What is so striking in his narration of the incident is the way that it mirrors his father's emotional suppression, failing to register any personal memory of his dead brother or any anger or sadness about his loss. In a pathetically misguided inversion, his family's devastation at the hands of imperial class society is elevated to become the principle of 'dignity', which according to Stevens 'has to do crucially with a butler's ability not to abandon the professional being he inhabits' (Ishiguro 1993: 42). Moving from a spare economy to a spurious erudition, Stevens' narration reveals how the emotional skeleton of both father and narrator has been disastrously crippled by an imperial masculinity that suppresses the world of interpersonal emotional connection, through which a self-reflective and self-directing subjectivity might emerge in its relationships with others.

Deprived of the emotional infrastructure that comes from the hurt and triumphs of interpersonal engagement, Stevens must cling all the more tightly to a precast structuring of subjectivity, a kind of psychological exoskeleton that takes its impression from what appears within its social world to be the most complete, self-composed and invulnerable masculine self – the aristocrat, Lord Darlington. This is, as Hannah Arendt has pointed out, a structuring of subjectivity at one remove from fascism. Darlington echoes a string of British aristocrats who sympathised with Hitler and saw an alliance with Germany as the best way of saving the Empire and preserving peace in Europe, including Lord Rothermere, the owner of the influential British newspaper *The Daily Mail*, Lord Lothian, onetime Under-Secretary for India, Sir Oswald Mosley, leader of the British Union of Fascists, the Duke of Windsor, formerly King Edward VIII, and perhaps most closely Lord Londonderry, Churchill's cousin and Air Minister in the early 1930s (Arendt 1973: 323–4; Kershaw 2004: 31–64). Stevens laboriously constructs a sense of himself from the wreckage by tying his own life to the larger movements of history through his identification with Darlington, whose amateurish interventions in foreign affairs are interpreted as historical work of epochal importance. Darlington becomes one of those 'gentleman who were, so to speak, furthering the progress of humanity' and contributing 'to the future well-being of the empire', and 'dignity' thus becomes a function of 'years of service' in which a butler 'has applied his talents to serving a great gentleman – and through the latter, to serving humanity' (Ishiguro 1993: 117).

Stevens' narration, of course, presents a hagiographic portrait of Darlington, although in constantly shifting ground it betrays a postwar awareness of Darlington's public identification as a Nazi sympathiser, which leads Stevens repeatedly to deny his connection to his former master in the present of 1956 in a bitterly ironic echo of Peter's denial of Jesus of Nazareth. But one incident in particular suggests the destructive consequences for Stevens' own consciousness and emotional life of this identification with Darlington. Stevens recalls a conversation before the war with Miss Kenton concerning an order given by Darlington a year earlier to dismiss two Jewish maids. Miss Kenton had at the time identified the order as anti-Semitic and morally repugnant and had threatened to resign, but much to her own shame had ultimately kept her silence and position, standing by while the Jewish girls were dismissed. In his retelling of the dismissal Stevens claims that 'my every instinct opposed the idea', but in retelling their conversation about the incident a year later he cannot elide Miss Kenton's stunned amazement when he then makes this claim (1993: 148). 'As I recall,' Miss Kenton objects, 'you thought it was only proper that Ruth and Sara be sent packing,' adding that Stevens was 'positively cheerful about it' (1993: 153). In his postwar account, Stevens supplies an elaborate justification for his original compliance with the order, citing the need for them both to subordinate their judgement to the superior understanding of their master – a justification that may or may not accurately reflect his state of mind at the time. But the smooth justification he provides of his initial decision cannot be extended to the later conversation with Miss Kenton, where she articulates an alternative principle of intersubjective solidarity that might have strengthened their own capacity for judgement and action in opposition to reliance on authority: 'Do you realize, Mr Stevens, how much it would have meant to me if you had thought to share your feelings last year?' (1993: 153). Despite the impossibility of now knowing Stevens' state of mind at either moment, what the text does reveal is his inability to share deliberation with Miss Kenton. At one level it marks a change in their relationship that will ultimately give rise to her marriage to Mr Benn and the end of any possibility of their emotional intimacy; at another, it marks the further atrophy of Stevens' inner life, and the collapse of any potential for building a sense of himself in community with others – a subjectivity in community that could be morally and politically independent of the master to whom he has subordinated his will and his emotional response in the name of 'dignity'.

Arendt's account of the imperialist character and its relationship to the subjectivity of fascism is helpful in elaborating the 'metaphorical' or parable-like reading of Stevens' condition that Ishiguro maintains against realist or postmodernist interpretations of his novel, and through which he hopes to do more than just 'provide British lessons for

British people' (Ishiguro, Herzinger and Vorda 1991: 140).[3] Ishiguro's butler – and he observes to his American interviewers that '[w]e're [all] like butlers' – in a sense resembles the imperial bureaucrat that Arendt identifies as a key form of the imperialist character in *The Origins of Totalitarianism* (Ishiguro, Herzinger and Vorda 1991: 152). 'At the basis of bureaucracy,' Arendt writes, 'lies th[e] superstition of a possible and magic identification of man with the forces of history,' an identification that rejects the relative permanence of community and the 'inherent stability' of moral or juridical law in favour of 'handling each situation separately' by arbitrary and ever-changing 'decree' (Arendt 1973: 216). It is through such an identification with the 'forces of history' that Stevens builds his exoskeleton, although at one remove – by 'serv[ing] the great gentleman of our times in whose hands civilization had been entrusted' (Ishiguro 1993: 116). And it is the resultant instability that motivates his rule of memory by arbitrary decree, always rewritable and renegotiable, always flexible and open to the shifting demands of the present. But Stevens lacks the Olympian hauteur of the Imperial civil servant, and in that respect resembles more the failure of thought that Arendt saw in Adolf Eichmann, one of the central bureaucratic organisers of the Holocaust.

Without exonerating Eichmann from guilt, Arendt nonetheless argues in *Eichmann in Jerusalem* that 'Eichmann was not Iago and not Macbeth', the titanic literary figures whose ruthless calculation was self-consciously directed to the pursuit of power. For Arendt, these characters are fully cognisant of the human destruction necessary for the achievement of absolute power, and therefore are remarkable, and even in a sense courageous, in daring to transgress all human morality and law. In contrast, Arendt sees in Eichmann no such awareness, and so no such daring in transgressing the bonds of ethical responsibility and human law, but only what she called controversially 'the banality of evil'. For Arendt, Eichmann's 'extraordinary diligence in looking out for his personal advancement' combined with a chilling 'lack of imagination' – the inability to envisage in the minutest degree the human and moral significance of his actions – to 'predispos[e] him to become one of the greatest criminals of [the Nazi] period' (Arendt 1994: 287–8). Stevens, of course, is not Eichmann – or not quite. But his identification with the forces of history leads him to abnegate his responsibility even to envisage the consequences of that identification: '[T]here is little choice,' Stevens concludes at the novel's end, 'than to leave our fate ultimately in the hands of those great gentleman' (Ishiguro 1993: 244).

Arendt's formulation of the relationship between the imperial and fascist character helps respond to Ishiguro's call not to tie his novel to only one set of circumstances – as teaching only 'British lessons for British people' – but to extend its capacity to function as 'parable' also to 'the Western myth' of American popular culture (Ishiguro, Herzinger and Vorda 1991: 140). In this reading, the alternative to Stevens' 'British' emotional reticence and class deference would not simply be an aggressive individualism that glories in its lack of emotional reticence and its self-affirming transgression of social convention – i.e. the familiar expansive 'individualism' that largely dominates corporate American popular culture. For when self-assertion and the cultivation of emotion become *arbitrary* – that is, when they are unrelated to inter-subjective exposure and negotiation – then such an 'individualism' lays down the groove for a conformism that begins to resemble these earlier structurings of experience, albeit in new and unexpected ways.

Through Whose Eyes? Leila Aboulela's *Minaret*

In 'My Son the Fanatic', a short story that first appeared in *The New Yorker* in 1992, the year after the end of the Persian Gulf War, Hanif Kureishi considers a new figure in British fiction, the Islamic 'fanatic'. But Kureishi's intricate story is as much about the perception of the 'fanatic' in the West as it is about a straightforward realist representation of the figure, and so it enables a broader historical questioning of the relationship between object and perceiver. The story neatly captures Britain's complex positioning in this global hall of mirrors by locating the 'Western' view in Parvez, the Pakistani-born taxi-driver who begins to spy on his teenage son Ali, the 'fanatic' of the story's title who was born and raised in Britain. Parvez believes at first that his son is taking drugs, only to learn to his horror that he has become an observant Muslim. Attempts at discussing Ali's embrace of religion reveal the long-established but unspoken estrangement between father and son, and culminate in Parvez's physical attack on the boy, who responds without retaliation but with the question that ends the story: 'So who's the fanatic now?' (Kureishi 1997: 131).

This final question, and the assault that engendered it, points the reader back to a symptomatic reading of the story that resembles the approach invited by Ishiguro's *The Remains of the Day*. Although narrated in the third person, the story is told through Parvez's eyes, and so employs what critics term an unreliable focaliser (rather than an unreliable narrator), whose viewpoint we need to scrutinise and question.[4] While Parvez is unable to acknowledge it, the recounting of events from his viewpoint allows the reader to glimpse his neglect of the family and especially his wife, Ali's mother, his rigid imposition of a spiritless conception of 'success' on his son, and his almost absolute removal from his son's emotional life, including the damaging effects of the racism Ali has grown up with. Parvez's blindness to these factors means, of course, that he fails to see how they have powerfully shaped Ali's sense of himself and his place in the world. Indeed, if the text allows us to read Ali's embrace of Islam as an expression of his attempt to assert an alternative set of values based on self-respect, family responsibility and adherence to some kind of palpable moral frame-work, it is striking that the path he has chosen almost exactly inverts those aspects of his father's behaviour that have caused him such pain: Parvez's emotional adultery with Bettina, a local prostitute; his heavy drinking; his removal from family life and parental responsibility; and his imposition on his son of his own 'dreams of doing well in England' following his unhappy childhood experience of religion in Lahore. The story neither endorses nor condemns Ali's choice – although Kureishi is an outspokenly secular figure who elsewhere celebrates the potential of Western secularism and especially the space it allows for the expression of sexuality, and the personal and social freedom of women (Kureishi 2005). Indeed, as Sheila Ghose argues in a finely calibrated reading of Kureishi's figuring of the Muslim 'fundamentalist', his later novel *The Black Album* ends up 'recycl[ing] and reiterat[ing]' the very 'monolithic idea of the religious "fanatic"' that has become a staple of mainstream media stereotyping (MacPhee and Poddar 2007: 132). Yet in contrast, Ghose argues that 'My Son the Fanatic' 'resists Ali's reification', and works instead 'to question a presumed Western reader and thereby . . . perform a kind of self-interrogation' (MacPhee and Poddar 2007: 136, 134).

In foregrounding the question of the historical construction (or phe-nomenology) of perception, Kureishi's short story provides a useful starting point for reading Leila Aboulela's second novel, *Minaret*. Although *Minaret* was first published over a decade after 'My Son the Fanatic' in 2005, Aboulela reveals that she first began to write in 1992 when living in Aberdeen in Scotland, far from Sudan where she had grown up: 'People around me did not know much about Sudan or about Islam, the two things that made up my identity,' she records, while 'the anti-Arab and anti-Islam atmosphere in the media following the first Gulf War' focused her sense of misperception and 'made me want to write' (Aboulela and Barya 2009). Aboulela and Kureishi are, of course, very different writers. While Kureishi avows himself a secularist,

Aboulela's first novel, *The Translator* (1999), has been described as 'the first *halal* novel written in English', or the first anglophone novel that is consciously consistent with Islamic teachings (Faqir 2004: 170).[5] As Anita Sethi notes, 'Aboulela offers a very different portrayal of Muslim women in London from that in Monica Ali's *Brick Lane*,' since '[r]ather than yearning to embrace Western culture, Aboulela's women seek solace in their growing religious identity' (Aboulela and Sethi 2005). This is indeed the case in *The Translator*, which invites its readers to identify with the sense of desolation and the emotional struggle of its protagonist Sammar, a young Sudanese widow living in Aberdeen who is the single internal focaliser of the novel, and whose consciousness filters and interprets events. But while *The Translator* asks us to read Sammar's viewpoint literally, *Minaret* sets up a quite different reading position for interpreting the perspective and history of Najwa, whose subjective point of view is made more explicit as the novel's first-person narrator. I want to argue here that the failure to account for this more critical and distanced relationship leads both supporters and detractors of *Minaret* to miss its more troubled exploration of subjectivity, and indeed to simplify its implicit narrative arc.

As Wail Hassan observes, like Tayeb Salih 'Aboulela is preoccupied with migration between North and South, [with] cultural percep-tions and stereotypes, and [with] the possibilities of building bridges between former colonizer and colonized' (Hassan 2008: 298). Both *The Translator* and *Minaret* centre on female protagonists who experience a collapse in their sense of themselves on being transposed from the global South to the global North: from Khartoum to Aberdeen in the case of Sammar, and from Khartoum to London in the case of Najwa. In the case of *The Translator*, the material and social gap between North and South is articulated by Sammar on returning to Khartoum, where the unpredictability and physical disrepair of the city contrasts with the certainty and security of the public world of Scotland: 'The road they walked across was pitted with potholes, strewn with rubble ... [t]he playthings of children who lived on the streets' (Aboulela 1999: 145). But while the instability of the public world in Sudan contrasts with the regulated predictability of Scotland, it is offset by her memory of a dif-ferent way of living that is summoned when she discusses her childhood in Sudan with her Scottish colleague Rae, with whom she is falling in love:

She said, 'At night we used to sleep outdoors. We used to pull our beds out at sunset, so that the sheets would be cool later. Every night I saw bats in the clouds and the grey blur of a bird . . . In the distant past, Muslim doctors advised nervous people to look up at the sky. Forget the tight earth. Imagine that the sky, all of it, belonged to them alone . . . But the sky was free, without any price, no one I knew spoke of it, no one competed for it. Instead, one by one those who could afford to began to sleep indoors in cool, air-conditioned rooms, away from the mosquitoes and flies, away from the *azan* [Islamic call to prayer] at dawn. Now when they build houses . . . they don't build them with places for people to sleep outdoors. It is a thing of the past, something I remember from my past.' (Aboulela 1999: 44–5)

Rae, a non-believer but a sympathetic academic who studies Arabic politics, interprets Sammar's memory for her as the diagnosis of Western modernity as the real 'enemy' of the Islamic world, an enemy 'already . . . inside' the Muslims of the global South, and 'what makes them no longer confident of their vision of the world' (1999: 45). Western modernity strips experience of its meaning, beauty and rootedness in the past, cashing it in for material affluence and the security of the immediate physical environment – at least for those who can afford it. Within this framework, Rae argues that 'Islam gives dignity to those who otherwise would not have dignity in their lives' (1999: 199). The authority of Rae's analysis within the novel is confirmed by the snatches of interviews with Muslim fighters that Sammar is employed to translate; but the novelistic authority of Sammar's conception of faith is established when Rae not only reciprocates her love, but comes to accept the 'dignity' offered by Islam for himself (1999: 156, 199).

Wail Hassan argues that Sammar's story 'completes the project' of Salih's classic postcolonial text, *Season of Migration to the North*, by inverting its outcome. Where Salih's narrative is one of 'failure' that 'reflects the disappointments of the 1960s and 1970s', Aboulela's novel provides a 'narrativ[e] of redemption and fulfillment through Islam', and 'so materializes the slogan of the Islamist movement that emerged in the mid-1970s: "Islam is the solution"' (Hassan 2008: 300). But this interpretation can only be extended to *Minaret* if Najwa's narration is read literally, and not symptomatically. Najwa, like Sammar, has moved from Sudan to Britain; but where Sammar had come with a husband, child and career, and perhaps most importantly a past life in Sudan she can remember and grow nostalgic for, Najwa arrives as a refugee whose family is broken and dispersed. Her father is hanged as a member of the corrupt postcolonial government now overthrown; her twin brother Omar is imprisoned in Britain for selling drugs and knifing a policeman; and her mother dies painfully in exile from an illness. Exiled from the sheltered, Westernised lifestyle of the Sudanese ruling elite, Najwa can discover little of value or meaning in looking back at her former life in Khartoum, which if anything resembles her new life in London. Left alone, and unneeded even by her imprisoned twin, she is bereft of a life she can mourn – a past whose passing she can regret, or whose remembrance might now give her hope or orientation. 'There are all kinds of pain, degrees of falling,' Najwa reflects painfully, remembering the news of her father's execution. 'When Baba was hanged, the earth we were standing on split open and we tumbled down and that tumbling had no end,' she recounts, observing that '[w]e became unfamiliar to each other simply because we had not seen each other fall before' (Aboulela 2006: 61).

To an extent, the narrator of *Minaret* resembles that of *The Remains of the Day*, for as Najwa assumes a new life as a devout Muslim and servant to a wealthy Egyptian-Sudanese family in the present of 2003, she looks back obsessively to her youth in Khartoum in 1984 and 1985 and to the early years of her exile in 1989 and 1990. But where Stevens returns to the past in order to retell his actions and decisions in the most favorable light possible, Najwa rakes over her past in order to convict it all the more of its vacuous and blinkered character, and confirm its complicity in the fall that subsequently consumes her family. 'Years later,' she records, 'I looked back for signs of tension,' recalling that 'I don't think I spoke to [my father] much,' and that 'I know he didn't think a lot about me . . . because I was a girl and Mama's responsibility' (2006: 16, 78). Alongside this sense of interpersonal disconnection, a key motif in her memories of Sudan is her removal from the lives of the great mass of the Sudanese population, as signalled by her Western food, music, pastimes and dress, by her afternoons spent at the American Club in Khartoum and by shopping trips to London. What memories she can discover of the people and culture beyond the elite bubble she had inhabited are glimpses of the routines of devotion undertaken by the family servants or the poorer students she first encounters at Khartoum University, and which in retrospect take on the glow of an aberrated and borrowed identification. What animates that devotion and what its routines entail is foreign to her, and cannot come to memory because it was never shared or understood. Even the memories of her intuitive respect for the girls wearing *hijab* (modest dress including a headscarf) seem manufactured – 'They never irritated me,' she recalls, only to question herself, 'did they?' (2006: 134).

Just as Stevens' excessive detailing of memory undermines his account of the self that has emerged from it, so Najwa's disconsolate scrutiny of her threadbare memories calls us to question the consciousness that now attempts to reconstruct the course of its formation or *bildung*. And because that consciousness seeks to rebuild itself through a particular version of religious devotion and through a new life as a servant and observer of other people's families, the novel invites us to question that outlook and the interpretation of the world it offers. A key moment in the traumatic past from which that consciousness has emerged combines a desperate moment of crisis in Najwa's life with news of Saddam Hussein's invasion of Kuwait – and by implication the decades of military intervention in the Middle East by the United States and Britain that are to follow. Alone and vulnerable, Najwa gives in to the sexual advances of her boyfriend Anwar, an exiled student radical who had once denounced her father, leaving her desolate and all the more desperate for a return to the security of a past that is not just absent but was never there. As the news of military action turns out to be of the invasion of Kuwait, and not the fall of the regime in Khartoum which might have allowed her return to Sudan, she stares disconsolately at the solidity and predictability of London that is denied to the denizens of the unstable postcolonial regimes bequeathed by European colonialism and American hegemony:

> I . . . thought that whatever happened in the world, London remained the same, constant: continuous underground trains, the newsagents selling Cadbury's chocolates, the hurried footsteps of people leaving work. That was why we were here: governments fell and coups were staged and that was why we were here. For the first time in my life, I disliked London and envied the English, so unperturbed and grounded, never displaced, never confused. For the first time, I was conscious of my shitty-colored skin next to their placid paleness. (Aboulela 2006: 174)

While in *The Translator* Sammar also registers the painful dislocation between North and South as we have seen, it is offset by an experience of Sudan that sustains the memory of an alternative to Western modernity, a memory that she can identify with the Islam within which she has lived and grown up. But for Najwa there is no space of memory outside of Western modernity, no past that can be invoked to orientate her negotiation of the 'empty space . . . called freedom' which is her experience of that modernity (2006: 175). And so she manufactures a version of religious devotion from the remembered glimpses of ritual whose context she did not understand, and from the '[b]its and pieces' of religious teaching on Arabic television which 'make [her] feel solid' (2006: 98).

The novel clearly marks its narrating consciousness as damaged and its perception as disastrously skewed, although in being shown the conditions that have given rise to Najwa's sense of self we are asked to view it sympathetically. What Najwa conceives as love for the religiously observant young man Tamer proves insubstantial, and she begins to realise that what she 'adored [was] that glow and scent of Paradise' she saw in his youthful certainty and unbrokenness, an innocent righteousness that allows her to conjure the memory of 'a young Omar' who in fact never existed (2006: 256, 68). Her resolution in the face of Tamer's mother, Doctora Zeinab, quickly dissolves, and the drastic disproportion of the comparison she makes between Doctora Zeinab and Tamer and her own mother and Omar indicates that her judgement is badly flawed (2006: 264–5). 'What happened stunted me,' she acknowledges (2006: 71). Throughout the present of the novel there is a gap evident between Najwa's conception of her religious devotion and the outlook of other Muslim women. While Najwa shrinks from arguing or discussing ideas, and looks to ritual to 'forget everything around me', the young, British-born Muslim women she meets 'have individuality and an outspokenness I didn't have when I was their age', and 'strike [her] as very British, very much at home in London', with '[s]ome wear[ing]' hijab, [while] some don't' (2006: 79, 77). Their ease in negotiating between their faith and their secular lives and their ability to express their own ideas 'puzzle[s]' Najwa, although she 'admire[s] them' (2006: 77). Expressing a similar admiration for Doctora Zeinab – 'What would life be if I were like her; professional, capable and mobile, not bogged down' – her own half-acknowledged despair breaks through, as she reveals 'I have always been wary of sleeping pills as I can't trust myself with them' (2006: 205). She sees how her friend Shahinaz's life 'moves forward, pulses, and springs', while of her own she remarks 'I circle back, I regress; the past doesn't let go' (2006: 216).

Najwa's own articulation of religious devotion, then – encapsulated in a self-abnegating desire not only to be withdrawn from the social life around her through her role as a servant, but to be the 'family's concubine, like something out of *The Arabian Nights*' – is clearly not endorsed by the text. Najwa knows she cannot share this desire with Shahinaz, an indication not only of its distance from secular feminism, but also from the diverse community of Muslim women who inhabit the fictional world of the novel. In the context of Najwa's attempt to suppress the guilt and loss that now frames her life, this desire is readable as the distorted and desperate longing of a damaged life that pursues not the restoration of an 'authentic' Islam, but builds instead a melancholy and frangible schema of religious devotion from the wreckage of the postcolonial world. Even the language she uses to describe her fantasy draws on the history of Orientalist thought that she has inherited through her elite upbringing: as Wail Hassan points out, *The Arabian Nights* is itself an Orientalist rendering of the Arabic *Book of the Thousand and One Nights* (Hassan 2008: 313 n13).

My argument here is that read symptomatically, *Minaret* provides a much more insightful understanding of the globalised predicament of post-imperial Britain than literal readings by either its supporters or detractors may suggest. However divergent their evaluation, such literal readings see Najwa undertaking a narrative of redemption which tends to cast British culture straightforwardly either as multi-cultural home or alien civilisation. Mike Phillips, for example, reads the novel as tracing an arc of redemption, in which 'Najwa journeys from pride and confusion to humility and peace' (Phillips 2005). This endpoint envisages the construction of a stable subjectivity, at home with its place in London and within the nation. Wail Hassan also pursues a literal reading of Najwa, but sees her narrative of redemption as an expression of a 'fundamentalism' that is inimical to Western secular and democratic values (Hassan 2008: 317). Thus, the novel is again seen to narrate Najwa's journey to a fixed and stable subjectivity, but it is a subjectivity that is alien to the freedoms of London and the West, and that craves submission to the authority of religion and patriarchy. While both readings share the same trajectory of subjectivity, the first locates it within an easy multi-culturalism, while the second locates it within the imaginary of Samuel Huntingdon's 'clash of civilizations', which claims that 'Arabs . . . and Westerners are not part of any broader cultural entity' but inhabit separate and opposed 'civilizations' (Huntingdon 1993: 24). But just as the novel undermines such a trajectory of subjectivity, it also undermines both of these conceptions of Britain and Najwa's relation to it. The novel's London is not an untroubled multi-cultural home: Najwa is harassed on a bus, and she knows that there 'are . . . places in London that aren't safe, where our very presence irks people' (2006: 111). But neither is it an alien civilisation that denies participation or resists understanding or negotiation: Muslim women can build their own lives as participants in the broader society – Najwa's friend Shahinez is accepted onto a degree course as well as bringing up her children. And of course Najwa's background is thoroughly Westernised: her version of Islam is not a retreat into a hermetically sealed 'civilisation' locked in the past, but is itself a contemporary fabrication, that carries the warps and contortions of her own damaged life. The narrative does not figure London either as a secure and insular retreat from the South or as a discrete and alien monolith opposed to it, but imagines it as a point where North and South intersect, although this relationship remains uneven and asymmetrical, and fraught with difficulty and tension.

Aboulela's discussion of the novel's title is revealing here: as she explains, 'The title of the novel *Minaret* was actually chosen by the publisher and my original titles were *Regression* or *Innocent Again*' (Aboulela et al. 2007). Where the title *Minaret* appears to endorse the power of orientation that Najwa sees in the structure of the Regent's Park mosque – 'We never get lost because we see the minaret of the mosque and head home towards it' – both of the other titles suggest a more diffident, self-critical and disorientated stance: most obviously *Regression*, but also *Innocence Again*, which connotes the wistfulness of a return to an arrested moment of development that perhaps was never there (2006: 208). I would therefore dissent from Wail Hassan's literal assessment of *Minaret* as a 'fiction of authenticity' and an expression of 'fundamentalism' in novelistic form, and instead read the novel symptomatically as a much more complicated and open fiction than this judgement allows (Hassan 2008: 316, 317). In doing so I respect, but also acknowledge my distance from, Aboulela's own account of her first two novels:

[B]y acknowledging the postcolonial discourse through the characters of Anwar and Rae, I acknowledge that it exists and I am not completely opposed to it, I do admire it, but it does not paint the whole picture or tell the whole story. To me faith is more than that and if modern day, secular discourse does not have the language to explain what I want to explain, then I have to make up this language or chart this new space. (Aboulela et al. 2007)

In the case of *Minaret*, Aboulela expresses her view that 'yes, Najwa will overcome the guilt . . . it will be the *Hajj* [pilgrimage to Mecca] that will be the final stage in her process of completely getting over the past and becoming a new person' (Aboulela et al. 2007). This is an aspiration that manifests the author's hope for her protagonist, but it is not an event that occurs in the novel, which ends instead in a reverie of guilt and sadness, with the *Hajj* just a future plan yet to be undertaken. It is an aspiration that I can respect, but does not bind my interpretation. And perhaps the novel's capacity both to challenge hegemonic interpretation and retain its interpretative openness suggests a valuable vocation for literature in our postcolonial and post-imperial predicament. For unlike the much celebrated postmodernist valorisation of indeterminacy, which always risks confirming the viewpoint of 'what is', *Minaret* requires respect for aspirations towards other possible worlds – and yet without disallowing the plurality of critical interpretation.

Histories of the Present: Ian McEwan's *Saturday* and Andrea Levy's *Small Island*

In bringing this study to a close, I would like to look at two different fictional responses to the history we have considered here, namely Ian McEwan's *Saturday* published in 2005, and Andrea Levy's *Small Island*, published a year earlier. In each case, the question I want to pose is how this history can be lived and made meaningful in the present, and how it might or might not illuminate different possible futures.

Ian McEwan's *Saturday* is set on 15 February 2003, the day of anti-war demonstrations in London and across the world, in which millions of people, including a million in London, protested against the impending invasion of Iraq. This is a past that is so recent it can be mistaken for the 'contemporary', although the two years of hindsight that the novel enjoys plays a pivotal role in its functioning. Taking place on a single day in a single city, London, and focalised through the perspective of its protagonist, the consultant neurosurgeon Henry Perowne, the novel seems to invite comparison with Joyce's *Ulysses* and Woolf's *Mrs Dalloway*, although it lacks the ability of these novels to triangulate narration, memory and subjectivity. Rather than exploring how the limits of subjectivity are shaped through interaction with a larger world whose histories cannot be visible or fully present to the self, the novel sets up a standoff between an obscure and epistemologically treacherous external world and the solipsism of the atomised and isolated subject, locked in its own purely private and integral experience. In this empiricist scenario, the novel's protagonist, the neurosurgeon Perowne, becomes an epistemological hero, because his medical training constrains him from acceding to subjective prejudice, and keeps his steady gaze focused on the painstaking work of empirical observation.

This empiricist vision is established in the opening episode, where Perowne refuses to over-interpret a struggling plane flying over London, which immediately brings to mind the media images of 9/11. The clarity of Perowne's consciousness depends on its awareness of the dangerous intrusion of subjective limitation, its unsentimental understanding that an 'excess of the subjective' involves 'the ordering of the world in line with your own needs', and 'an inability to contemplate your own unimportance' (McEwan 2005: 16–17). This sceptical and apparently 'unsubjective' eye is contrasted to the self-importance and solipsism of the marchers gathering for the demonstration, whose slogan 'Not in My Name' appears to Perowne not as a statement of the illegal and undemocratic nature of the political decision for war, but an admission of 'the cloying self-regard' of the marchers (2005: 71). Looked at dispassionately, according to Perowne, events are confusing and uncertain, and the observer must face 'a future no one can read' (2005: 147). But rather than accepting what in the novel is presented as an indisputable truth – the equal uncertainty of all futures – the protesters are caught up within their own self-indulgent schemes, 'visionary projects for peaceable realms, all conflicts resolved, happiness for everyone, forever' (2005: 176). But the sceptical and empirically minded Perowne refuses to be seduced by such visions, so that the novel can translate his empiricism into what is conceived as political wisdom: 'Beware the utopianists, zealous men certain of the path to the ideal social order. Here they are again, totalitarians in a different form' (2005: 286). 'No more big ideas,' Perowne concludes, distilling Anglo-American postmodern pragmatism into an easily swallowed pick-me-up: 'The world must improve, if at all, by tiny steps' (2005: 74). Yet if Perowne must distance himself from the anti-war protesters, we are to understand that it is not a subjective decision, an expression of the hardness of his heart; indeed, he 'might have been with them, in spirit at least' if he had chosen, as they, to indulge his own sentiment (2005: 72). Fortuitously, his treatment of an exiled Iraqi intellectual had brought to his attention empirical data that apparently escaped the millions demonstrating around the globe; now 'acquainted with the sickly details' of 'the massacres in Kurdish Iraq, [and] in the Shi'ite south', Perowne judges that '[i]t's likely most of [the demonstrators] barely registered' these atrocities, yet suddenly 'now find they care with a passion for Iraqi lives' (2005: 72–3).

As this passage demonstrates, the novel's empiricism – like all empiricisms – is a partial and constructed perspective, although taking its own perceived 'scepticism' as magical proof against epistemological error, it lacks a developed self-awareness of that fact. Indeed, not only were Saddam Hussein's crimes against humanity widely publicised by the anti-war movement, but anti-war arguments drew attention to the West's support for Saddam in the Iran-Iraq War, including Western complicity in enabling the production of the chemical weapons used against the Kurds in the notorious Anfal campaign of 1988, as well as their refusal to cut support once it was revealed (Khalidi 2009: 155–6; McDowall 2000: 357–60; Yildiz 2007: 31–3). For many, this tacit support threw into question the motives of Britain and the US, suggesting a different kind of scepticism from Perowne's, one that develops and extrapolates from the accumulation of experience to construct (albeit conditional) frames of evaluation and judgement. Perowne's perspective, in contrast, is literally atomistic; he rejects the involvement of anything not immediately present, and locates all causality within the empirical present, in a combination of 'luck' and DNA, the 'invisible kinks and folds of character, written in code, at the level of molecules' (2005: 282, 281). In contemplating warnings about the catastrophic consequences of the invasion, Perowne directs his scepticism towards all scenarios equally, since all futures are claimed to be equally and indifferently unknowable, and the past offers no guide for the future (except selectively, by revealing the marchers' supposed hypocrisy). 'It's a future no one can read,' Perowne sagely intones (2005: 147). Yet this blanket scepticism does not suspend judgement, but simply enables the status quo. It is the demonstrators who are undermined, being seen as fellow travellers of totalitarianism, while the 'War on Terror' is merely 'being clumsily handled, particularly by the Americans' (2005: 80).

However, as was manifestly clear by 2005 when the novel was published, the protesters *had* been able to read these futures more accurately than was presented by government publicity campaigns. In fact, the novel's blanket scepticism distorts in its own particular way, excluding the possible analytical frameworks that emerge through historical experience – in this case, of the ongoing history of Western support for compliant dictatorial regimes and its self-interested military interventions – by equalising all positions and rendering them all equally uncertain. If perception is reduced to a discrete now in which all futures are equally unlikely, then certainty can be found only in fortuitous moments of clear observation, as in Perowne's diagnosis of the criminal Baxter who threatens Perowne and his family. Judgement becomes exclusively a matter of the particular qualities and skills of the judging individual or perceiving 'I', rather than a question of the comparative validity of different interpretative frameworks. And here the ostensibly democratic and rational claims of Perowne's scepticism break down, for if right judgement depends on the qualities of particular individuals, then it must only be those individuals who should 'exercise authority and shape events' (2005: 288). Perowne's fantasy of a 'race of extraterrestrial grown-ups . . . needed to set right the general disorder, then put everyone to bed for an early night' is clearly playful (2005: 122). But the novel's outcome casts Perowne in just such a paternalistic role, for he 'knows how the system works' and feels justified in manipulating it to his desired end (2005: 288).

The novel's strident empiricism, equalising scepticism and paternalism of course all have a historical precedent in the Victorian age, and it is not surprising that its twin heroes are Matthew Arnold and Charles Darwin. But it is Arnold's 'confused alarms' upon 'a darkling plain', rather than Darwin's powerful inductive reasoning, that really sets the terms for the novel's pragmatism (McEwan 2005: 291). Like Arnold's 'Dover Beach', which is included at the end of the novel, the novel can lament 'the turbid ebb and flow / Of human misery' because it is safely ensconced in an England that is not threatened with invasion, and written from a point of view for which a continuation of the status quo would not be uncomfortable in the least. For those treated well by existing arrangements, 'tiny steps' ('if at all') are much more desirable than any 'big ideas', and a sceptical attitude to change provides an alibi for rejecting 'social justice' and for keeping undisturbed the global distribution of 'bad luck' (2005: 74, 282).

Although set around World War II, Andrea Levy's *Small Island* is in this respect a much more contemporary novel. There are plenty of big ideas here, but set within social experience they are tested, reconfigured, replaced or reinvented. So Queenie Buxton, a farm girl from the North of England, visits the British Empire Exhibition at Wembley in 1924: but instead of being impressed by the superiority of British civilisation and the primitiveness of her colonial subjects, for her these large-scale organising frameworks begin to fray when she is confronted by the unexpected politeness of a 'big nigger man' in the African pavilion (Levy 2004: 5). More painfully, Hortense, a light-skinned Jamaican migrant whose damaged upbringing has encouraged her to buy into the colonial ideology of the 'civilising mission' and the 'mother country', learns through the bitter experience of racism in London that the universal claims of liberal imperialism are a fraud. But as her husband Gilbert most clearly articulates, this disheartening experience does not lead him to give up on demands for equality and solidarity. On witnessing the segregation practised on US army bases during his war service in the British Royal Air Force, Gilbert connects the racism of Nazi Germany to that of the Allied military, yet resolves to make the fight against Nazism his own in order to challenge colonial racism: 'I was ready to fight the master race theory. For my father was a Jew and my brother is a black man.' Explaining his reasoning to his cousin Elwood, who prefers to work for social change in Jamaica rather than going to fight in the war, Gilbert declares that 'If this war is not won then you can be certain nothing here will ever change' (2004: 110).

Just as Fanon saw how the discursive formations of empire become reinterpretable and reconfigurable within changing patterns of social experience, so Levy's novel demonstrates through the migrations and shifting predicaments of its narrative arc how the larger frameworks of meaning through which the characters live are renegotiated, albeit painfully and at considerable cost. This constant repositioning of frames is announced in the novel's title, as the 'small island' shifts from being one of the Lesser Antilles when compared to Jamaica, to Jamaica when compared to Britain and ultimately to Britain when compared to North America. But this reinterpretability extends to the novel's retrospective construction of the Windrush moment, which is rendered now not pristinely but through the decades of racist politics and immigration legislation that was to follow the violence of Nottingham and Notting Hill. The migrant experience recorded so disjunctively by Lamming and Selvon itself becomes a part of the material of British literary tradition, though now expanded to include the aspirations and actions of women, both white and black. But this history has not thereby been rendered 'safe' or inert for the present. In the boarding house run by Queenie, Levy rewrites the story recounted by Enoch Powell in his 'Rivers of Blood' speech, of the white war widow who refuses to rent rooms to non-whites, and finds herself undermined by bureaucratic council staff and savage immigrants alike (Powell 1991: 378). Or rather, the novel imagines another history that might have given rise not to this scenario, but to a different possible future. Where, in Powell's speech, the landlady's refusal of non-white tenants testifies to her steadfast sense of national identity, in *Small Island* Queenie – believing herself to be a war widow – is happy to take their rent. Queenie is not untouched by the racism of colonial culture, and her desire for the handsome Jamaican airman Michael Roberts is clearly marked with exoticism (Levy 2004: 240). But in bearing a mixed race baby, she turns to Hortense and Gilbert to adopt the child, confiding that 'I trust you . . . I know you. You are good people' (2004: 430).

Understood as offering an alternative history of the present to that conjured by Powell, the novel's ending is not idealised. As Hortense and Gilbert leave the boarding house with the baby, there is an element of optimism in their newfound mutual respect, and in their dedication to building a life together in Britain. But the fact that mother and adoptive parents agree that a mixed race child will fare so badly with white parents that adoption is a viable solution presents an ominous picture of the racism of postwar Britain. Interestingly, the novel's earlier setting lends it a more critical edge on the present than the more optimistic endings of many other recent novels that consider multi-cultural British society, such as Zadie Smith's *White Teeth* (2000) and Monica Ali's *Brick Lane* (2003).[6] Through *Small Island's* narrative arc, Hortense and Gilbert may have come to establish a sense of themselves as able to face the challenges ahead, but we know full well that the history that is to come will involve struggles they cannot yet imagine. In rewriting this past moment, the novel confirms its still living significance for our own present.

Notes

1. That is, I am suggesting that just as Benjamin reads James Ensor's paintings as anticipations of the emergence of Nazism some two decades later, so Selvon's novel can be read as an anticipation of Powellism.
2. Johnson released an album with The Roots also entitled *Dread Beat and Blood* in 1978 that includes six poems from the volume, and further poems from it appear on later albums by Johnson recorded with The Dub Band.
3. For a fuller presentation of my argument here, see MacPhee 2011b.
4. For a discussion of focalisation, see Rimmon-Kenan 2002.
5. Aboulela's literary influences are, however, eclectic. Alongside the pivotal secular Sudanese writer Tayeb Salih, Aboulela lists as important literary influences Jean Rhys, Anita Desai, Doris Lessing, Ahdaf Soueif and Buchi Emecheta (Aboulela and Barya 2007).
6. I am indebted to Susan Alice Fischer for suggesting this comparison, although its articulation here is my own.

Bibliography

Abbas, Tahir (ed.) (2005), *Muslim Britain: Communities under Pressure*, London: Zed Press.

Aboulela, Leila (1999), *The Translator*, New York: Black Cat/Grove.

—(2006), *Minaret*, London: Bloomsbury.

Aboulela, Leila et al. (2007), *Interview with Leila Aboulela* <http://www. abdn.ac.uk/sll/complit/leila.shtml> (accessed 25 April 2010).

Aboulela, Leila and Mildred Kiconco Barya (2009), 'A Certain Beauty and a Certain Happiness', *Pambazuka News* 435 (27 May) <http://www.pambazuka.org/en/category/African_Writers/56579> (accessed 25 April 2010).

Aboulela, Leila and Anita Sethi (2005), 'Keep the Faith', *The Guardian* (5 June), <http://books.guardian.co.uk/departments/generalfiction/story/0,,14 99352,00.html> (accessed 12 October 2006).

Abu-Lughod, Janet (1989), *Before European Hegemony: The World System A.D. 1250–1350*, New York: Oxford University Press.

Ahmad, Aijaz (1992), *In Theory: Classes, Nations, Literatures*, London: Verso.

Anand, Mulk Raj (1983), 'The Sources of Protest in My Novels', *The Literary Criterion* 18: 4, 1–12.

—(1995), *Conversations in Bloomsbury*, Delhi: Oxford University Press.

Anderson, Benedict (1983), *Imagined Communities: Reflections on the Origin and Spread of Nationalism*, London: Verso.

Anderson, David (2005), *Histories of the Hanged: Britain's Dirty War in Kenya and the End of Empire*, London: Weidenfeld and Nicholson.

Anderson, Perry (1992), *English Questions*, London: Verso.

Anon. (1958), 'The Habit of Violence', *Universities and Left Review* 5: 4–5.

Appadurai, Arjun (1996), *Modernity at Large: Cultural Dimensions of Globalization*, Minneapolis: Minnesota University Press.

—(ed.) (2005), *Globalization*, Durham, NC: Duke University Press.

Arden, John (1994), *Plays I*, London: Methuen.

Arden, John and Georg Gaston (1991), 'An Interview with John Arden', *Contemporary Literature* 32.2 (Summer): 147–70.

Arendt, Hannah (1973), *The Origins of Totalitarianism*, San Diego: Harcourt Brace.

—(1994), *Eichmann in Jerusalem: A Report on the Banality of Evil*, Harmondsworth: Penguin.

Arrighi, Giovanni (1994), *The Long Twentieth Century*, London: Verso.

—(2007), *Adam Smith in Beijing: Lineages of the Twentieth-First Century*, London: Verso.

Assies, Willem (2003), 'David versus Goliath in Cochabamba: Water Rights, Neoliberalism, and the Revival of Social Protest in Bolivia', *Latin American Perspectives* 30.3 (May): 14–36.

Auden, Wystan Hugh (2007), *Selected Poems*, New York: Vintage.

Balibar, Etienne (1991), 'Is there a "Neo-Racism"?', in Etienne Balibar and Immanuel Wallerstein, *Race, Nation, Class: Ambiguous Identities*, London: Verso, pp. 17–28.

Baucom, Ian (1999), *Out of Place: Englishness, Empire, and the Locations of Identity*, Princeton: Princeton University Press.

Benjamin, Walter (1977), *The Origin of German Tragic Drama*, trans. John Osborne, London: Verso.

—(1996), 'The Task of the Translator', in Marcus Bullok and Michael Jennings (eds), *Walter Benjamin: Selected Writings 1913–1926*, vol. 1, Cambridge, MA: Belknap/Harvard University Press, pp. 253–63.

—(1999), 'Experience and Poverty', in Michael Jennings, Howard Eiland and Gary Smith (eds), *Walter Benjamin: Selected Writings 1927–1934*, 4 vols, Cambridge, MA: Belknap/Harvard University Press, vol. 2, pp. 731–36.

—(2003), 'On the Concept of History', in Howard Eiland and Michael W. Jennings (eds), *Walter Benjamin: Selected Writings 1938–1940*, 4 vols, Cambridge, MA: Belknap/Harvard University Press, vol. 4, pp. 389–400.

Bernstein, J.M. (1991), 'Introduction', in T.W. Adorno, *The Culture Industry*, London: Routledge, pp. 1–27.

Bhabha, Homi (2004), *The Location of Culture*, London: Routledge.

Bloch, Ernst (1977), 'Nonsynchronism and the Obligation to its Dialectics', *New German Critique* 11 (Spring): 22–38.

Boehmer, Elleke (2002), *Empire, the National, and the Postcolonial 1890–1920*, Oxford: Oxford University Press.

Bourne, Jenny (2007), 'The Beatification of Enoch Powell', *Institute for Race Relations News* (21 November), <http://www.irr.org.uk/2007/november/ha000019.html> (accessed 18 May 2008).

Brecht, Bertolt (1964), *Brecht on Theatre: The Development of an Aesthetic*, trans. John Willett, New York: Hill and Wang.

Brendon, Piers (2007), *The Decline and Fall of the British Empire 1781–1997*, London: Vintage.

Brennan, Timothy (2006), *Wars of Position: The Cultural Politics of Left and Right*, New York: Columbia University Press.

Burkert, Walter (2004), *Babylon, Memphis, Persepolis: Eastern Contexts of Greek Culture*, Cambridge, MA: Harvard University Press.

Cain, P.J. and A.G. Hopkins (1993), *British Imperialism: Crisis and Deconstruction 1914–1990*, London: Longman.

—(2002), *British Imperialism 1688–2000*, Harlow: Longman.

Cannadine, David (2003), *In Churchill's Shadow: Confronting the Past in Modern Britain*, Oxford: Oxford University Press.

Caygill, Howard (1998), *Walter Benjamin: The Color of Experience*, London: Routledge.

Césaire, Aimé (2000), *Discourse on Colonialism*, New York: Monthly Review Press.

Chambers, Iain (1994), *Migrancy, Identity, Culture*, London: Routledge.

Chatterji, Partha (1998), 'Beyond the Nation? Or Within?', *Social Text* 56 (Autumn), 57–69.

Chen, Kuan-Hsing and David Morley (eds) (1996), *Stuart Hall: Critical Dialogues in Cultural Studies*, London: Routledge.

Childs, Peter (ed.) (1999), *Post-Colonial Theory and English Literature: A Reader*, Edinburgh: Edinburgh University Press.

Churchill, Winston S. (1974), *Winston S. Churchill: His Complete Speeches 1897–1963*, ed. R.R. James, vol. 7, New York: Chelsea House.

Colley, Linda (1992), *Britons: Forging the Nation 1707–1837*, New Haven: Yale University Press.

Connor, Steven (1996), *The English Novel in History 1950–1995*, London: Routledge.

Dawson, Ashley (2007), *Mongrel Nation: Diasporic Culture and the Making of Postcolonial Britain*, Ann Arbor: University of Michigan Press.

Dirlik, Arif (1997), 'The Postcolonial Aura: Third World Criticism in the Age of Global Capitalism', in Anne McClintock, Aamir Mufti and Ella Shohat (eds), *Dangerous Liaisons: Gender, Nation, and Postcolonial Perspectives*, Minneapolis: Minnesota University Press, pp. 501–28.

Dworkin, Dennis (1997), *Cultural Marxism in Postwar Britain*, Durham, NC: Duke University Press.

Eagleton, Terry (1983), *Literary Theory: An Introduction*, Oxford: Blackwell.

Eliot. T.S. (1962), *Notes Towards the Definition of Culture*, London: Faber and Faber.

—(1975), *Selected Prose of T.S. Eliot*, New York: Harcourt.

Elkins, Caroline (2005), *Britain's Gulag: The Brutal End of Empire in Kenya*, London: Jonathan Cape.

English, James (ed.) (2006), *A Concise Companion to Contemporary British Fiction*, Oxford: Blackwell.

Ernst, John (1998), *Forging a Fateful Alliance: Michigan State University and the Vietnam War*, East Lansing: Michigan State University Press.

Esty, Jed (2004), *A Shrinking Island: Modernism and National Culture in England*, Princeton: Princeton University Press.

Evans, Eric J. (2004), *Thatcher and Thatcherism*, London: Routledge.

Fanon, Frantz (1967), *The Wretched of the Earth*, trans. Constance Farrington, Harmondsworth: Penguin.

—(2008), *Black Skin, White Masks*, trans. Richard Philcox, New York: Grove Press.

Faqir, Fadia (2004), 'Lost in Translation', *Index on Censorship* 33.2: 160–70.

Fisk, Robert (2010), 'Blair should take responsibility for Iraq. But he won't. He can't', *The Independent* (3 September) <http://www.independent.co.uk/opinion/commentators/fisk/robert-fisk-blair-should-take-responsibility-for-iraq-but-he-wont-he-cant-2069231.html> (accessed 3 September 2010).

Gikandi, Simon (1996), *Maps of Englishness: Writing Identity in the Culture of Colonialism*, New York: Columbia University Press.

Gilroy, Paul (1991), *'There Ain't No Black in the Union Jack': The Cultural Politics of Race and Nation*, Chicago: University of Chicago Press.

—(1993), *The Black Atlantic: Modernity and Double Consciousness*, Cambridge, MA: Harvard University Press.

—(2005), *Postcolonial Melancholia*, New York: Columbia University Press.

Grandin, Greg (2007), *Empire's Workshop: Latin America, the United States, and the Rise of the New Imperialism*, New York: Holt.

Greene, Graham (2004), *The Quiet American*, London: Vintage.

Hall, Catherine (ed.) (2000), *Cultures of Empire: Colonizers in Britain and the Empire in the Nineteenth and Twentieth Centuries*, New York: Routledge.

Hall, Stuart (1960), 'Serjeant Musgrave's Dance', *New Left Review* 1 (January/February): 50–1.

—(1995), 'Negotiating Caribbean Identities', *New Left Review* 209 (January/February): 3–14.

—(2000), 'Old and New Identities, Old and New Ethnicities', in Les Back and John Solomos (eds), *Theories of Race and Racism*, London: Routledge, pp. 144–53.

—(2002), 'Calypso Kings', *The Guardian* (28 June), <http://www.guardian.co.uk/culture/2002/jun/28/nottinghillcarnival2002.nottinghillcarnival> (accessed 2 January 2008).

Hall, Stuart, C. Critcher, T. Jefferson, J. Clarke and B. Roberts (1978), *Policing the Crisis: Mugging, the State, and Law and Order*, London: Palgrave Macmillan.

Harrison, Tony (1987), *Selected Poems*, Harmondsworth: Penguin.

Harvey, David (2007), *A Brief History of Neoliberalism*, New York: Oxford University Press.

Hassan, Wail (2008), 'Leila Aboulela and the Ideology of Muslim Immigrant Fiction', *Novel: A Forum on Fiction* 41.2/3 (Spring/Summer): 298–318.

Head, Dominic (2008), *The State of the Novel: Britain and Beyond*, Chichester: Wiley-Blackwell.

Heffer, Simon (2008), 'Powell, (John) Enoch (1912–1998)', *Oxford Dictionary of National Biography*, Oxford: Oxford University Press, <http://www.oxforddnb.com.navigator-wcupa.passhe.edu/view/article/69398> (accessed 28 May 2009).

Hegel, G.W.F. (1977), *The Phenomenology of Spirit*, trans. A.V. Miller, Oxford: Oxford University Press.

Hewison, Robert (1981), *In Anger: Culture in the Cold War 1945–60*, London: Weidenfeld and Nicolson.

Hinds, Lynn Boyd and Theodore Windt (1991), *The Cold War as Rhetoric: The Beginnings 1945–1950*, New York: Praeger.

Horsman, Reginald (1981), *Race and Manifest Destiny: The Origins of Anglo-Saxonism*, Cambridge, MA: Harvard University Press.

Huntingdon, Samuel P. (1993), 'The Clash of Civilizations?' *Foreign Affairs* 72.3 (Summer): 22–49.

Ishiguro, Kazuo (1993), *The Remains of the Day*, New York: Vintage International.

Ishiguro, Kazuo, Kim Herzinger and Allan Vorda (1991), 'An Interview with Kazuo Ishiguro', *Mississippi Review* 20.1/2: 131–54.

James, C.L.R. (1992), *The C.L.R. James Reader*, ed. Anna Grimshaw, Oxford: Blackwell.

Jameson, Fredric (1990), 'Modernism and Imperialism', in Terry Eagleton, Fredric Jameson and Edward Said, *Nationalism, Colonialism, and Literature*, Minneapolis: University of Minnesota Press, pp. 43–68.

—(1998), 'Notes on Globalization as a Philosophical Issue', in Fredric Jameson and Masao Miyoshi (eds), *The Cultures of Globalization*, Durham, NC: Duke University Press, pp. 54–80.

Johnson, David and Prem Poddar (eds) (2005), *A Historical Companion to Postcolonial Thought in English*, New York: Columbia University Press.

Johnson, Linton Kwesi (1975), *Dread Beat and Blood*, London: Bogle-L'Ouverture.

—(1976), 'Jamaican Rebel Music', *Race and Class* 17.4: 397–412.

—(2006), *Mi Revalueshanary Fren*, Keene, NY: Ausable Press.

Johnson, Linton Kwesi and Burt Caesar (1996), 'Interview: Linton Kwesi Johnson Talks to Burt Caesar', *Critical Quarterly* 38.4: 64–77.

Johnson, Linton Kwesi and Elizabeth DiNovella (2007), 'Linton Kwesi Johnson', *The Progressive* 71.2 (February): 33–6.

Jones, Clive (2004), *Britain and the Yemen Civil War 1962–1965*, Brighton: Sussex Academic Press.

Joyce, James (1986), *Ulysses*, New York: Vintage.

Kaplan, Martha and John Kelly (2004), '"My Ambition is Much Higher than Independence": US Power, the UN World, the Nation-State, and their

Critics', in Prasenjit Duara (ed.), *Decolonization: Perspectives from Then and Now*, London: Routledge, pp. 131–51.

Kavanagh, Dennis (1987), *Thatcherism and British Politics: The End of Consensus*, Oxford: Oxford University Press.

Kershaw, Ian (2004), *Making Friends with Hitler: Lord Londonderry, The Nazis, and the Road to War*, Harmondsworth: Penguin.

Khalidi, Rashid (2005), *Resurrecting Empire: Western Footprints and America's Perilous Path in the Middle East*, Boston: Beacon Press.

—(2009), *Sowing Crisis: The Cold War and American Dominance in the Middle East*, Boston: Beacon Press.

Kipling, Rudyard (1987), *Kim*, Harmondsworth: Penguin.

Kohl, Benjamin (2002), 'Stabilizing Neoliberalism in Bolivia: Popular Participation and Privatization', *Political Geography* 21: 449–472.

Kolko, Gabriel (1994), *Anatomy of a War: Vietnam, the United States, and the Modern Historical Experience*, New York: New Press.

Kundnani, Arun (2007), *The End of Tolerance: Racism in Twenty-First Century Britain*, London: Pluto Press.

—(2009), *Spooked: How Not to Prevent Violent Extremism*, London: Institute of Race Relations.

Kureishi, Hanif (1997), *Love in a Blue Time*, London: Faber and Faber.

—(2005), 'The carnival of culture', *The Guardian* (4 August), <http://www.guardian.co.uk/religion/Story/0,2763,1542252,00.html> (accessed 6 August 2005).

Lamming, George (1992), *The Pleasures of Exile*, Ann Arbor: Michigan University Press.

Larkin, Philip (1983), *Required Writing: Miscellaneous Pieces 1955–1982*, New York: Farrar, Strauss and Giroux.

—(2003), *Collected Poems*, New York: Farrar, Strauss and Giroux.

Lazarus, Neil (1999), *Nationalism and Cultural Practice in the Postcolonial World*, Cambridge: Cambridge University Press.

—(ed.) (2004), *The Cambridge Companion to Postcolonial Studies*, Cambridge: Cambridge University Press.

Levy, Andrea (2004), *Small Island*, New York: Picador.

Loomba, Ania (1999), 'Turning Point: Fundamentals and English Studies', *Textual Practice* 13.2: 221–5.

Loomba, Ania, Suvir Kaul, Matti Bunzl, Antoinette Burton and Jed Esty (eds) (2005), *Postcolonial Studies and Beyond*, Durham, NC: Duke University Press.

McCarthy, Thomas (2009), *Race, Empire, and the Idea of Human Development*, Cambridge: Cambridge University Press.

McDowall, David (2000), *A Modern History of the Kurds*, London: I. B. Taurus.

McEwan, Ian (2005), *Saturday*, New York: Anchor Books.

McKibben, Ross (2006), 'Sleazy, Humiliated, Despised', *London Review of Books* 28. 12 (7 September): 3–6.

McLeod, John (2004), *Postcolonial London: Rewriting the Metropolis*, London: Routledge.

MacPhee, Graham (1996), 'Value, Tradition and the Place of the Present: The Disputed Canon in the United States,' *Angelaki* 2.2 (Summer): 65–73.

—(2002), *The Architecture of the Visible*, London: Continuum.

—(2003), 'Technology, Time, and the Return of Abstract Painting', in Jonathan Harris (ed.), *Critical Perspectives on Contemporary Painting*, Liverpool: Liverpool University Press/Tate Gallery, pp. 109–37.

—(2011a), 'Introduction: Culture and Political Community', *College Literature* 38.1: xi–xxiv.

—(2011b), 'Escape from Responsibility: Ideology and Storytelling in Arendt's *The Origins of Totalitarianism* and Ishiguro's *The Remains of the Day*', *College Literature* 38.1: 176–201.

MacPhee, Graham and Prem Poddar (eds) (2007), *Empire and After: Englishness in Postcolonial Perspective*, Oxford: Berghahn.

Malick, Javed (1995), *Towards a Theatre of the Oppressed: The Dramaturgy of John Arden*, Ann Arbor: University of Michigan Press.

Marx, John (2005), *The Modernist Novel and the Decline of Empire*, Cambridge: Cambridge University Press.

Mazower, Mark (2009), *No Enchanted Place: The End of Empire and the Ideological Origins of the United Nations*, Princeton: Princeton University Press.

Mercer, Kobena (1991), '"1968": Periodizing Politics and Identity', in Lawrence Grossberg, Cary Nelson and Paula Treichler (eds), *Cultural Studies*, New York: Routledge, pp. 424–38.

Metcalf, Thomas (1995), *Ideologies of the Raj*, Cambridge: Cambridge University Press.

Moore-Gilbert, Bart (1997), *Postcolonial Theory: Contexts, Practices, Politics*, London: Verso.

Morris, Mervyn (1983), 'People Speech: Some Dub Poets', *Race Today* 14.5: 150–7.

Nasta, Susheila (ed.) (1988), *Critical Perspectives on Sam Selvon*, Washington, DC: Three Continents.

—(2002), *Home Truths: Fictions of the South Asian Diaspora in Britain*, Basingstoke: Palgrave.

North, Michael (1999), *Reading 1922: A Return to the Scene of the Modern*, Oxford: Oxford University Press.

Orde, Anne (1996), *The Eclipse of Great Britain: The United States and British Imperial Decline 1895–1956*, New York: St Martin's Press.

Orwell, George (1952), *Homage to Catalonia*, New York: Harcourt Brace Jovanovich.

—(2002), *Essays*, New York: Everyman.

Osborne, John (1958), *The Entertainer*, New York: Criterion.

Ovendale, Ritchie (1996), *Britain, the United States, and the Transfer of*

Power in the Middle East, 1945–1962, London: Leicester University Press.

Parry, Benita (1987), 'Problems in Current Theories of Colonial Discourse', *Oxford Literary Review* 9.1: 27–58.

Paul, Kathleen (1997), *Whitewashing Britain: Race and Citizenship in the Postwar Era*, Ithaca: Cornell University Press.

Paulin, Tom (1997), 'Into the Heart of Englishness', in Stephen Regan (ed.), *Philip Larkin: Contemporary Critical Essays*, Basingstoke: Macmillan, pp. 160–77.

Peden, G.C. (2007), *Arms, Economics, and British Strategy: From Dreadnoughts to Hydrogen Bombs*, Cambridge: Cambridge University Press.

Phillips, Mike (2005), 'Faith healing', *The Guardian* (11 June), <http://books.guardian.co.uk/reviews/generalfiction/0,6121,1503752,00.html> (accessed 6 June 2007).

Porter, Bernard (2006), *Empire and Superempire: Britain, America and the World*, New Haven: Yale University Press.

Powell, Enoch (1967), *Exchange Rates and Liquidity*, London: Institute of Economic Affairs.

—(1991), *Reflections of a Statesman: The Writings and Speeches of Enoch Powell*, London: Bellew.

Powell, Enoch and Angus Maude (1970), *Biography of a Nation: A Short History of Britain*, London: John Baker.

Prashad, Vijay (2007), *The Darker Nations: A People's History of the Third World*, New York: New Press.

Premnath, Gautam (2000), 'Remembering Fanon, Decolonizing Diaspora', in Laura Chrisman and Benita Parry (eds), *Postcolonial Theory and Criticism*, Cambridge: D.S. Brewer.

Procter, James (2000), *Writing Black Britain 1948–1998: An Inter-disciplinary Anthology*, Manchester: Manchester University Press.

Ramazani, Jahan (2009), *A Transnational Poetics*, Chicago: Chicago University Press.

Rimmon-Kenan, Shlomith (2002), *Narrative Fiction: Contemporary Poetics*, London: Routledge.

Rose, Gillian (1996), *Mourning Becomes the Law: Philosophy and Representation*, Cambridge: Cambridge University Press.

—(1998), 'Walter Benjamin – Out of the Sources of Modern Judaism', in Laura Marcus and Lynda Nead (eds), *The Actuality of Walter Benjamin*, London: Lawrence and Wishart, pp. 85–117.

Roy, Arundhati (2004), *Tide? Or Ivory Snow? Public Power in the Age of Empire*, <http://www.democracynow.org/static/Arundhati_Trans.shtml> (accessed 17 August 2004).

Rushdie, Salman (1991), *Imaginary Homelands: Essays and Criticism 1981–1991*, New York: Granta/Penguin.

Ryan, Ray (2002), *Ireland and Scotland: Literature and Culture, State and Nation 1966–2000*, Oxford: Clarendon/Oxford University Press.

Said, Edward (1993), *Culture and Imperialism*, New York: Knopf.

—(2001), 'The Clash of Ignorance', *The Nation* 273.12 (22 Oct.): 11–14.

Sands, Philippe (2005), *Lawless World: America and the Making and Breaking of Global Rules*, London: Allen Lane.

Sassen, Saskia (2000), 'Spatialities and Temporalities of the Global: Elements for a Theorization', *Public Culture* 12.1: 215–32.

Saunders, Frances Stonor (1999), *The Cultural Cold War*, New York: New Press.

Selvon, Sam (1985), *The Lonely Londoners*, London: Longman.

—(1989), *Foreday Morning: Selected Prose 1946–1986*, ed. Kenneth Ramchand and Susheila Nasta, London: Longman.

Schoen, Douglas (1977), *Enoch Powell and the Powellites*, New York: St Martin's Press.

Springhall, John (2001), *Decolonization since 1945: The Collapse of European Overseas Empires*, London: Palgrave.

Sivanandan, Ambalavaner (2008), *Catching History on the Wing: Race, Culture, and Globalization*, London: Pluto.

Stein, Mark (2004), *Black British Literature: Novels of Transformation*, Columbus: Ohio State University Press.

Tew, Philip (2007), *The Contemporary British Novel*, 2nd edn, London: Continuum.

Thatcher, Margaret (1978), 'TV Interview for Granada's *World in Action* ("Rather Swamped")', *Margaret Thatcher Foundation*, Speeches, Interviews and Other Statements (27 January), <http://www.margaretthatcher.org/document/103485> (accessed 5 November 2009).

—(1984), 'Speech to the 1922 Committee ("The Enemy Within")', *Margaret Thatcher Foundation*, Speeches, Interviews and Other Statements (19 July), <http://www.margaretthatcher.org/document/105563> (accessed 5 November 2009).

Tillotson, H.M. (1995), *With the Prince of Wales's Own: The Story of a Yorkshire Regiment 1958–1994*, Norwich: Russell.

Travis, Alan (2002), 'After Forty-Four Years Secret Papers Reveal Truth about Five Nights of Violence in Notting Hill', *The Guardian* (24 August), <http://www.guardian.co.uk/uk/2002/aug/24/artsandhumanities.nottinghillcarnival2002> (accessed 20 August 2009).

Utley, T.E. (1968), *Enoch Powell: The Man and His Thinking*, London: Kimber.

Vallely, Paul (1999), 'Bradford rises above the ashes', *The Independent* (14 January), <http://www.independent.co.uk/arts-entertainment/bradford-rises-above-the-ashes-1046906.html> (accessed 6 June 2009).

Viswanathan, Gauri (1989), *Masks of Conquest: Literary Studies and British Rule in India*, New York: Columbia University Press.

—(1991), 'Raymond Williams and British Colonialism', *Yale Journal of Criticism* 4. 2: 47–66.

Waters, Chris (1997), '"Dark Strangers" in Our Midst: Discourses of Race and Nation in Britain, 1947–1963', *The Journal of British Studies* 36.2 (April): 207–38.

Westad, Odd Arne (2007), *The Global Cold War*, Cambridge: Cambridge University Press.

Wicke, Jennifer (1988), *Advertising Fictions: Literature, Advertisement, and Social Reading*, New York: Columbia University Press.

Williams, Raymond (1957), 'Working Class Culture', *Universities and Left Review* 1.2 (Summer): 29–32.

—(1971), *George Orwell*, New York: Columbia University Press.

—(1973), *The Country and the City*, New York: Oxford University Press.

—(1989), *Resources of Hope: Culture, Democracy, Socialism*, London: Verso.

Winder, Robert (2004), *Bloody Foreigners: The Story of Immigration to Britain*, London: Abacus.

Woolf, Virginia (1981), *Mrs Dalloway*, San Diego: Harcourt.

Wright, Patrick (2007), *Iron Curtain: From Stage to Cold War*, Oxford: Oxford University Press.

—(2009), *On Living in an Old Country*, Oxford: Oxford University Press.

Yildiz, Kerim (2007), *The Kurds in Iraq: Past, Present, and Future*, London: Pluto Press.

Young, Robert (2001), *Postcolonialism: An Historical Introduction*, Oxford: Blackwell.

Zephaniah, Benjamin (1996), *Propa Propaganda*, Tarset: Bloodaxe.

Further Reading

Anderson, Perry (1992), *English Questions*, London: Verso.
Collects a series of important essays by Anderson on the cultural politics of Britain, including 'Components of the National Culture'.

Appadurai, Arjun (1996), *Modernity at Large: Cultural Dimensions of Globalization*, Minneapolis: Minnesota University Press.
A widely read text from one of the most influential figures in contemporary globalisation theory.

Arrighi, Giovanni (1994), *The Long Twentieth Century*, London: Verso.
An important study of the transition from British to US hegemony from the perspective of world systems theory.

Bhabha, Homi (2004), *The Location of Culture*, London: Routledge.
A collection of many of the central essays by a widely read and influential figure in postcolonial studies.

Chen, Kuan-Hsing and David Morley (eds) (1996), *Stuart Hall: Critical Dialogues in Cultural Studies*, London: Routledge.
A collection of a range of essays by Stuart Hall and by other scholars discussing his work. Includes Hall's essay 'New Ethnicities'.

Dawson, Ashley (2007), *Mongrel Nation: Diasporic Culture and the Making of Postcolonial Britain*, Ann Arbor: University of Michigan Press.
A highly readable and critically astute analysis of key figures and movements in diasporic culture in Britain.

Esty, Jed (2004), *A Shrinking Island: Modernism and National Culture in England*, Princeton: Princeton University Press.
A valuable cultural analysis of the legacy of late modernism for postwar British culture and national identity.

Gilroy, Paul (2005), *Postcolonial Melancholia*, New York: Columbia University Press.
A keenly argued intervention in contemporary British cultural politics by a major scholar in the field.

Kundnani, Arun (2007), *The End of Tolerance: Racism in Twenty-First Century Britain*, London: Pluto Press.
A critical account of the mutating structures of racism in contemporary Britain.

Lazarus, Neil (ed.) (2004), *The Cambridge Companion to Postcolonial Studies*, Cambridge: Cambridge University Press.
Rigorous but accessible collection of essays that helps to chart the emergence of postcolonial studies as a field, and critically considers many of its central assumptions and theoretical ideas.

Loomba, Ania, Suvir Kaul, Matti Bunzl, Antoinette Burton and Jed Esty (eds) (2005), *Postcolonial Studies and Beyond*, Durham, NC: Duke University Press.
Wide-ranging collection of essays that consider the contemporary relevance of postcolonial studies as an analytical framework.

McLeod, John (2004), *Postcolonial London: Rewriting the Metropolis*, London: Routledge.
Literary study of London as a postcolonial metropolis that ranges across the postwar period to the present.

MacPhee, Graham and Prem Poddar (eds) (2007), *Empire and After: Englishness in Postcolonial Perspective*, Oxford: Berghahn.
Recent collection of essays that focus on the relationship between Englishness and British national identity in the context of the history of empire and its contemporary legacies.

Marx, John (2005), *The Modernist Novel and the Decline of Empire*, Cambridge: Cambridge University Press.
Innovative account of the relationship between the late modernist novel and the end of empire.

Moore-Gilbert, Bart (1997), *Postcolonial Theory: Contexts, Practices, Politics*, London: Verso.
A clear and even-handed historical analysis of the work of three of the most prominent postcolonial critics, Said, Spivak and Bhabha.

Nasta, Susheila (2002), *Home Truths: Fictions of the South Asian Diaspora in Britain*, Basingstoke: Palgrave.
An expansive critical history of major writers from the South Asian diaspora in Britain, including Selvon, Naipaul and Rushdie.

Procter, James (2000), *Writing Black Britain 1948–1998: An Interdisciplinary Anthology*, Manchester: Manchester University Press.
A very useful anthology of black British writing over the second half of the twentieth century.

Ryan, Ray (2002), *Ireland and Scotland: Literature and Culture, State and Nation 1966–2000*, Oxford: Clarendon/Oxford University Press.
A careful reading of selected Scottish and Irish writers that reflects on the cultural dynamics of national identity in the space opened up by a receding post-imperial British identity.

Sivanandan, Ambalavaner (2008), *Catching History on the Wing: Race, Culture, and Globalization*, London: Pluto.
A collection of many of Sivanandan's key essays and political analyses, including 'The Hokum of New Times'.

Stein, Mark (2004), *Black British Literature: Novels of Transformation*, Columbus: Ohio State University Press.
A defence of the literary category of black British literature, which prioritises the significance of the *bildungsroman* as a current and still evolving form.

Young, Robert (2001), *Postcolonialism: An Historical Introduction*, Oxford: Blackwell.
An influential critical history of postcolonial studies.

Index